"This is profound book on a deep subject by an erudite and reflective group. It is hard to think of a better group of people to tackle the subject. And it is a very contemporary subject looking at the world today."

Professor David Tuckett U.C.L., *Fellow British Psychoanalytic Society*

"The central role of forgiveness in psychic life is attested in this book with various authors' inspiring chapters, ranging from deep reflections on clinical matters, to literature, religion, and music, and a chapter on the Holocaust, this book is full of illuminating insights."

Rosine Perelberg *is a Distinguished Fellow and Past President of the British Psychoanalytical Society*

Psychoanalytic Approaches to Forgiveness and Mental Health

Psychoanalytic Approaches to Forgiveness and Mental Health considers the role of forgiveness in mental life, concerning both forgiving and being forgiven.

Each chapter addresses concepts including the superego, repetition compulsion, enactment, and notions such as sacrifice, penance, justification, absolution, and contrition. The contributors consider both their professional and clinical experience and their ethical, cultural, or philosophical background when considering aspects of forgiveness and its impact on clinical practice. The book is an attempt to open the subject of forgiveness, not to reach ethical conclusions nor to formulate pious psychological behavioural axioms. It also considers the weight of feeling unforgiven and of holding the lifelong resentment or vengeful wishes of the unforgiving.

Psychoanalytic Approaches to Forgiveness and Mental Health will be key reading for psychoanalysts and psychotherapists in practice and in training and for other professionals interested in the role of forgiveness in mental life. It will also be of interest to academics and students of psychoanalytic studies, philosophy and spirituality.

Ronald Britton is a training and supervising analyst with the British Psychoanalytical Society. He first trained as a doctor, and then as a child psychiatrist; he was chair of the Department of Children and Parents at the Tavistock Clinic, where he was involved in treatment of deprived children and their parents. This experience was influential to his psychoanalytic thinking where he maintains the importance of 'childhood' as a formative experience.

Aleksandra Novakovic is a training and supervising analyst of the British Psychoanalytic Association and a group analyst. She was a consultant clinical psychologist, joint head of the Inpatient & Community Psychology Service, and she worked with patients with severe mental health problems and facilitated staff groups for mental health teams. She worked at Tavistock Relationships and supervised on the Reflective Practice Course at IGA.

Psychoanalytic Approaches to Forgiveness and Mental Health

Edited by
Ronald Britton and
Aleksandra Novakovic

Routledge
Taylor & Francis Group

LONDON AND NEW YORK

Designed cover image: Getty | Nastasic

First published 2024
by Routledge
4 Park Square, Milton Park, Abingdon, Oxon OX14 4RN

and by Routledge
605 Third Avenue, New York, NY 10158

Routledge is an imprint of the Taylor & Francis Group, an informa business

© 2024 selection and editorial matter, Ronald Britton and Aleksandra Novakovic; individual chapters, the contributors

British Library Cataloguing in Publication Data
A catalogue record for this book is available from the British Library

Library of Congress Cataloging-in-Publication Data
A catalog record has been requested for this book

ISBN: 9781032427942 (hbk)
ISBN: 9781032427911 (pbk)
ISBN: 9781003364313 (ebk)

DOI: 10.4324/9781003364313

Typeset in Times New Roman
by Taylor & Francis Books

To my wife Martha with love, whose capacity to forgive I rely on daily – Ron

With love to my granddaughters Elena and Sofia – Aleksandra

Contents

Acknowledgements

We would like to thank the contributors to this book and express our deep gratitude for their patience and for their inspiring contributions. We would like to thank Susannah Frearson and Saloni Singhania, our Routledge editors for their unswerving support for this book and we are very grateful to Margery Gretton and Martha Papadakis for their invaluable help in editing our chapters. We would like to thank our patients and colleagues who have, perhaps unknowingly, contributed ideas and experiences. We particularly want to acknowledge Chris Mawson posthumously for his chapter, and his partner Donna Savory for her readiness to let us keep for publication the chapter he had sent to us. We would like to thank the editors of the *International Journal of Psychoanalysis* for allowing us to reprint John Steiner's paper and the editors of the *Journal of Couple and Family Psychoanalysis* to reprint Francis Grier's paper. We would both like to express our gratitude to Routledge for allowing us to use material from our previously published work by Routledge. We found it very rewarding that our belief in this project materialised in the form of this book and our collaboration provided us with support to take the initial conception towards a realisation.

About the Editors and Contributors

Ronald Britton, FRCPsych, Distinguished Fellow at the British Psychoanalytic Society, retired from practice in 2022. He was awarded the IPA Outstanding Scientific Achievements Award (2013) and the Sigourney Award for Psychoanalytic Achievements (USA) (2014). He conducted supervision seminars in Germany and New York for ten years. He is author of *The Missing Link, Parental Sexuality in the Oedipus Complex* (1988); *Belief and Imagination* (1998); *Sex, Death and the Superego* (2003); *Between Mind and Brain* (2015); and "Klein & Bion" a chapter in the *Textbook of Psychoanalysis*, of the American Psychiatric Association (2011).

Aleksandra Novakovic is a training analyst of the British Psychoanalytic Association and a group analyst. She was a consultant clinical psychologist and joint head of the Inpatient & Community Psychology Service, she worked with patients with severe mental health problems and facilitated staff groups for mental health teams. She was a consultant visiting lecturer at Tavistock Relationships and supervisor on the Diploma Course in Reflective Practice in Organisations at the IGA, London. She edited *Couple Dynamics* (Karnac, 2015) and co-edited a book on group analytic organisational consultancy with David Vincent (Routledge, 2019).

Hiroshi Amino is a psychoanalyst, Fellow of the British Psychoanalytical Society, consultant medical psychotherapist, and member of the Royal College of Psychiatrists. Having had basic training in psychoanalytic psychotherapy and psychiatry in Japan, he moved to the UK to have further psychoanalytic psychotherapy training at the Tavistock Clinic. After his qualification as psychoanalytic psychotherapist from the British Psychoanalytic Council, he undertook psychoanalytic training in the British Psychoanalytical Society. He has been working both in Adult Service at the Tavistock Clinic and in his private practice. He has recently taken the role of service manager of Adult Service at the Tavistock Clinic.

Francis Grier is editor-in-chief of the *International Journal of Psychoanalysis*, a training analyst of the British Psychoanalytical Society, and a couple psychotherapist. He works in private practice in London. He has written and edited papers, chapters and two books on couple psychotherapy, including *Oedipus and the Couple* (2005, Karnac), and papers for the IJP on two Verdi operas (*Rigoletto* and *La Traviata*), on a gendered approach to Beethoven, on musicality in the consulting room, and on the music of the drives and perversions. Before training psychoanalytically, he was a professional musician. In 2012 he was awarded a British Composer Award.

Karl Figlio came to psychoanalysis from natural sciences and the history and philosophy of science, which is reflected in his book, *Psychoanalysis, Science and Masculinity* (London/Chichester/Philadelphia: Whurr, Wiley, Brunner Routledge). He taught the history of science and medicine at Cambridge and was founding director of the Centre for Psychoanalytic Studies (now the Department of Psychosocial and Psychoanalytic Studies) at the University of Essex. He is a clinical associate at the British Psychoanalytical Society; a senior member of the Psychoanalytic Psychotherapy Association, BPF; professor emeritus at the Department of Psychosocial and Psychoanalytic Studies, University of Essex; and in private practice. His book, *Remembering as Reparation: Psychoanalysis and Historical Memory*, was published by Palgrave in 2017.

Claudia Frank is a psychoanalyst in private practice in Stuttgart, training analyst for the DPV/IPA. She was previously in the Department for Psychoanalysis, and Psychosomatics at Tübingen University. She is author of *Melanie Klein in Berlin* and papers on Antigone; Giacometti; and Morandi; she was co-editor of *Jahrbuch der Psychoanalyse* between 2002–2013; and she has done important research on Klein's early psychoanalytic child cases in Berlin.

David Millar read chemistry at the University of Newcastle-upon-Tyne, theology at St Catharine's College, Cambridge, and was Vicar of West Dean, Sussex. Leaving the church in 1975, he read psychology at Birkbeck College London and trained as a clinical psychologist at the University of Leeds. He is a lifetime honorary senior clinician at the Tavistock and Portman NHS Foundation Trust, where he was a consultant clinical psychologist and head of the Tavistock multidisciplinary adult psychoanalytic psychotherapy training. He is a fellow, training and supervising analyst and one-time chair of education of the British Psychoanalytical Society.

Chris Mawson was a training and supervising analyst of the British Psychoanalytic Society. He trained at the Tavistock Clinic in psychoanalytic psychotherapy with children and adolescents. He had a special interest in the work of Wilfred Bion and is the editor of *The Complete Works of W.R. Bion* (2014, Karnac). Other publications include: "The use of play technique in understanding disturbed behaviour in school" (1986,

Psychoanalytic Psychotherapy), *Bion Today* (editor, 2010, Routledge), "Interpretation as Freud's specific action, and Bion's container-contained" (2017, *International Journal of Psychoanalysis*), *Three Papers of W.R. Bion* (editor, 2018, Routledge), and *Psychoanalysis and Anxiety: From Knowing to Being* (2019, Routledge).

Ignês Sodré was born in Brazil, where she qualified as a clinical psychologist before coming to London to train at the British Institute of Psychoanalysis. She is a distinguished fellow and a training and supervising analyst of the British Psychoanalytical Society. She has taught extensively in London and abroad, published many papers on theoretical and clinical psychoanalysis and on literature, and two books: *Imagining Characters: Six Conversations about Women Writers* (1995), which she co-authored with A.S. Byatt, and *Imaginary Existences: A Psychoanalytical Exploration of Phantasy, Fiction, Dreams and Daydreams* (2015).

John Steiner is an internationally highly regarded training analyst of the British Psychoanalytical Society, who was formerly a psychiatrist at the Maudsley Hospital and a psychotherapist at the Tavistock Clinic. He was given The Sigourney Award for Outstanding Achievement in Psychoanalysis. He has retired from clinical practice but continues to supervise and write. He is the author of a number of influential papers and several books: *Psychic Retreats* (1993), *Seeing and Being Seen* (2011), and *Illusion, Disillusion and Irony in Psychoanalysis* (2020). He has also edited and written introductions to: *The Oedipus Complex Today* (1989), *Psychoanalysis, Literature and War*, by Hanna Segal (1997), *Rosenfeld in Retrospect* (2008), and *Melanie Klein's 1936 Lectures on Technique* (2017).

Gerhard Wilke studied anthropology at King's College, Cambridge, and trained as a group analyst at the Institute of Group Analysis in London. He taught on the MA Course in Group Analysis at the Institute of Group Analysis and is a training analyst on the German group analytic training at GRAS. Gerhard is an honorary fellow of the Royal College of General Practice and the IAGP. His books include: *How to be a Good Enough GP* (Oxford, 2001). *The Art of Group Analysis in Organisations* (London, 2014). *Breaking Free of Bonkers, How to Lead in Today's Crazy World of Organisations* (London, 2018).

Introduction

The experience of anyone practising psychotherapy or psychoanalysis is that mental health is seriously affected by feeling unforgiven or being unable to forgive if the people involved are close and important figures in their life. In everyday life in marriage, work, or love, forgiveness is part of the daily traffic of our relationships, if we find that relatively easy we are fortunate. For some, it is fraught in general and for others the particular issues concerned may be very large or emotionally disturbing. To forgive is natural, but like many things that are natural, such as childbirth, it can be difficult and it can go wrong.

What the practice of analysis demonstrates is that feeling forgiven and being unforgiving is crucial in mental life. Yet little seems to have been written in the analytic literature specifically on forgiveness and how it relates to familiar psychoanalytic concepts such as guilt, reparation, mourning, obsessional-compulsive disorder, or depression.

This is a book of essays on the subject of forgiveness by a number of experienced psychoanalysts and group therapists. They have not been asked to do it collectively but individually and it does not seek a consensus. It has been written by the authors based on their own clinical experience not on any religious or other doctrines. We all of us have a hinterland of some sort from our antecedents, whether religious or secular, political, philosophical, in which beliefs about justice, forgiveness, and retribution play a part.

There is a good deal of common ground nevertheless, arising from training and experience, which emerges in these essays and there are recurrent themes: such as the significance of the early experience of the life of mothers and babies, the triangular nature of family lifem and the intergenerational nature of our mental lives with ghostly presences and re-enactments.

The book is an attempt to open up the subject of forgiveness, not to reach ethical conclusions nor to formulate pious psychological behavioural axioms, so there is no conclusions section at the end of the book. We think what is more relevant is what readers make of it in relation to their own lives. The more we know of the mental preoccupations of the past through anthropology, excavation, exploration and literature, the more evident it is that some issues have been conspicuous from the outset of our species, amongst these are being forgiving and feeling forgiven.

Chapter 1

The lost good object regained: coexisting parts of self and the generosity of forgiveness

Aleksandra Novakovic

Introduction

Hurtful interactions happen and some injuries occur in relationships with parents, children, partners, family, friends, etc. When these injuries are acknowledged, the person who feels injured can be forgiving and the person who was hurtful can feel forgiven. Conversely, one encounters grievance, an inability to forgive and the experience of feeling unforgiven.

Thinking about forgiveness, I pose two questions:

- What are the "hurts" that occur and reoccur in the process of growing up and growing old that can be difficult to come to terms with and to forgive?
- What is it that "allows" a person to forgive and what are the processes involved in forgiveness?

From the earliest infancy to old age individuals are confronted with having to manage the experience of frustration and injuries in relationships with their significant others. The first part of this chapter, "What is difficult to forgive?", presents situations and experiences in everyday affairs and relationships that could be difficult to forgive.[1]

The second part of this chapter, "Dynamics of forgiveness", explores some features and processes of forgiveness that are interconnected and linked to the depressive position. To consider aspects of forgiveness, literary passages and vignettes from clinical work are presented and discussed.[2]

Part I: What is so difficult to forgive?

There are injuries that inevitably arise in relationships. In work with patients and in life in general, I have found that the hurts and consequent grievances that can be difficult to work through and forgive coalesce into three domains: early infantile experience, oedipal conflicts in childhood and reverberations of these in later life, such as the conflicts in the adult couple relationship, and fears, envy and hatred around loss, ageing and death. In summary:

DOI: 10.4324/9781003364313-1

- Early infantile experience
- Oedipal conflicts
- Threat of loss and death

These three domains are not presented in the above, perhaps logical, order as the quotation from Proust's work, discussed in "Oedipal conflicts" at the end of Part I, is also considered in a different context at the beginning of Part II. Therefore, I will first present some feelings around loss and death, then I will reflect on hurtful experiences in infancy and, lastly, on the experience of anguish in the oedipal situation.

The aim here is not to provide a comprehensive account of anxieties, defences and dynamics in these domains but to focus on a particular hurtful experience, situation or interaction that can be forgiven or not.

Loss and death

All people are confronted with anxieties about dying and death. Jacques (1988 [1965]) describes the unconscious links between the experience of life and thoughts of death. His view is that the intensity of persecutory anxieties about loss and death depend on the balance between a person's ability to acknowledge the loss and to mourn and accept it, and the feelings of frustration, hatred, persecution and guilt aroused by the loss.

I shall be discussing some anxieties and defences that emerged in a staff group with a palliative care team working with elderly patients, which was facilitated fortnightly over three months. It was not possible to offer longer-term work but it was agreed with the manager that this short input would help them to think about whether the staff group might contribute to team-work in the future. Coincidentally, our "time-limited" work together was also an important aspect of the day-to-day work of this team.

Palliative care staff group

In our preliminary meeting, the team appeared to be interested in the pro-spect of the group work, yet, at the same time, keen to return to their care work as soon as possible. They quickly decided they wanted to go ahead with the staff group, demonstrating how, in a short space of time, they could make decisions. It would seem as if the limited time their patients had left to live compelled them to be very efficient and they came across as busy, competent and brisk.

At the first group, members of the team gathered in a quick, enthusiastic and somewhat expectant manner. Monica, the manager, made a joke, asking whether we should have a prayer. Everybody laughed. Tina, one of the team's doctors, presented her patient, a 79-year-old woman, who was refusing to be examined by her or treated by anyone else from the team. Sonia, a team nurse, said that it seemed pointless to insist on helping someone when they declined help. They explained that there was a professional dilemma: How much responsibility could be taken? Should they insist? They all agreed that it was difficult when a patient refused their help and concluded that it was helpful if they all experienced the same difficulty, as it brought them closer together.

When patients refused their help, the meaning of their work was brought into question, reinforcing their doubts about what help they were able to give and how they could help when their patients died. In discussing feelings about being rejected by a patient, their individual experiences became something that happened to everybody in the team.

They discussed how they did not work in a rigid way. For example, they could not "cut off" a patient in the middle of a telephone conversation and, as a result, patients could delay them. Their profession was not one in which they could interrupt work with a patient at a moment's notice. Monica said that she herself was not a "watch" person and pulled up her sleeve to show that she was not wearing a wristwatch.

The staff experienced their patients on the telephone as being on a lifeline that they could not sever by ending the conversation at a given time, as it felt unmanageable, even cruel, to define boundaries and set limits. The emphasis on their absolute availability reflected a collective pressure to provide ideal care. They were caught up in denial of watches and time and in defending against their own guilt, resentment and feelings of hopelessness that "things cannot be put right".

As I came into the room, I found the group enjoying themselves, laughing and appearing to be somewhat excited. Maksim, the lead doctor, put his bleeper down on his shoe and the others enquired what that meant. He said it was a new style and they all laughed. Maksim said that he was actually very surprised to receive a Christmas gift from the team, in which he was called a sex maniac, or something of the kind. Everybody laughed heartily. I suggested that perhaps a party had started for me because this was our penultimate meeting. Marko, a junior doctor, seriously suggested that it might be better if they had a party when somebody joined the team. They all agreed that it could feel a bit strange to have a party when somebody was leaving. Monica critically considered how there was always a farewell party when somebody left: one would almost think people were pleased that someone was leaving. I said that perhaps they had certain ways of dealing with separation.

Manic defences, with exciting and quick interactions, were more prominent than usual and were, I thought, also related to the ending of our work.
Feelings about my impending departure were mixed. There was relief, even
some triumph, as they prepared to celebrate with a party. Then, they became
suddenly concerned about having farewell parties and proposed a "welcoming a new person" party instead. I believe this was indicative of their
apprehension about feeling relieved when a terminally ill patient died.

> In the last group, the separation and ending were denied. At times, the
> group seemed oblivious to my presence: they did not discuss the ending
> of the group, though it was remarked upon in a matter-of-fact way. They
> thanked me quickly and somewhat dismissively. At some point in the
> group, I felt isolated, forgotten and buried with the past. The present did
> not exist: it was either the already-gone-past or it was the future that I
> would not share with them.

After the group, I walked away in a pessimistic mood, questioning the
meaning of staff group work. Then, gradually, I had a sense of a loss. I was left
feeling sad that I would not be seeing this team again, that the patients were
dying and that the staff stayed on to care for them. It is very likely that staff
evoked in me feelings that their dying patients evoked in them about their survival, having a future and a life yet to come, and I felt guilty about being able to
leave and live. But there was something more disturbing, a kind of vacuum – it
was *the future that I would not have* with this team.

Now, I think that they could probably not forgive me for *going into my life*
and that this mirrored their anxieties about how unforgiving their patients
might be. The capacity to feel forgiven for surviving depends on the subject's
belief that the internal parental figures are forgiving and give their "blessing"
to the subject to go on living and to have a good and abundant life in a
future that will not be shared.

Early infantile experience

There are moments when any infant is bound to feel hurt and uncontained
with its distress and one can speculate that birth is one of those
situations:

Infant Sorrow
My mother groan'd! my father wept.
Into the dangerous world I leapt:
Helpless, naked, piping loud;
Like a fiend hid in a cloud.
Struggling in my fathers hands:
Striving against my swaddling bands:

Bound and weary I thought best
To sulk upon my mothers breast.
> (Blake, 1967, p. 151)

Blake describes a moment of anguish at birth, the mother's pain and the father's sorrow. In his poem, the process of being born is presented as a fundamentally new and overwhelming experience. Although firmly held and "bound", the infant is profoundly "helpless". Now "naked", outside its mother's body, the infant "sulks" at this momentous change.

Psychoanalysts consider the experience of birth from a particular vertex, reflecting on how the trauma of birth or a difficult delivery might impact on the relationship between mother and baby and manifest in later life. Klein (1993 [1957]) thought the prenatal state implied an experience of security and unity and suggested that there is a universal yearning for this state, which can stem from anxiety aroused in birth but also from idealisation. I believe that, regardless of the experience of birth and tendency for idealisation, the longing for primal unity remains in some form and on some level and that it can never be completely worked through or "forgiven", only sublimated.

Forgiveness is something first experienced with the mother, when she contains the infant's anger, resentment or "sulking" and lets it "know", through her loving gaze, her voice and her touch, that it is good and lovable. A belief in the possibility of being forgiven is one of the quintessential features of a relationship with God in Christianity. The hope of salvation through God's absolution is an attribute of His true love and goodness. For an infant, this is a blissful experience at the mother's breast of her love and goodness, which has survived the storm of its rage

"Seeing" moves Blake deeply. In his poem, "On Another's Sorrow" (1994), he asks if we can "see" another person's woe and grief and "not seek for kind relief?" (p. 71). Gipps (2022) emphasises a loving gaze:

> The humanity of the other is, in my opinion, ultimately only disclosed by a loving, trusting, gaze: I'm thinking here too of Jesus on forgiveness: "not 7 but 77 times should you forgive your brother". In the loving gaze of the forgiving other we come to know our own humanity, and through this "loop of grace" – where we're brought to experience the other's love, trust in our lovability, and thereby make ourselves even more visible – we finally come to trust ourselves as lovable. And we can then feel humane despite our failings ... The point I want to make is: there is I think a natural confluence of psychoanalysis and the Christian faith here.

Popovic (1940) states that "Lovingly to think, feel, live and know ..." is the Christian Orthodox way and, for the New Testament man, the principal creative force is love.

> Its [Love's] categorical imperative is: love in order to know. True knowledge of all things depends on love: it is conceived in love, grows in love, and reaches perfection in love. I love, thus I know. Knowledge is emanation of love.[3]
>
> (p. 222)

When this imperative is applied to a mother and baby relationship, the meaning would be that it is only through her love that the mother knows (gets to know) her infant.

Balzac (1991 [1842]) describes a mother's love in unconditional terms suggestive of a divine goodness and sacrifice: "This smile proved to this young parricide that the heart of a mother is an abyss at the bottom of which there is always a forgiveness" (p. 226).[4] He captures the essence of a supremely good, idealised mother, and her profound, inexhaustible love and absolute forgiveness. As Segal (1998) points out, there is always a kernel of idealisation in the experience of the goodness of internal and external figures and some features of idealisation play a role in adult emotional life and are forever present.

The child's experience that it can be murderously angry with its mother whilst, at the same time, in another chamber of its heart, trusting that she loves it, that she "sees" its distress and will "seek relief", is vital. It is from such experience that the capacity to forgive develops. However, it is inevitable that some frustrations and hurts are unwittingly or knowingly caused by parents and other significant figures. Klein (1993 [1937]) points out that if the grievances towards our parents can be worked through and if we "have forgiven them the frustrations we had to bear, then we can be at peace with ourselves and are able to love others in the true sense of the word" (p. 343).

Oedipal conflict

I will now consider the anguish and loss of belief in the goodness of parental objects, as illustrated in segments from Proust's (2002 [1919]) "In the Shadow of Young Girls in Flower" (*In Search of Lost Time*, Vol. 2). These passages show vividly the possible intensity of suffering in the oedipal triangle. As in any reflection on a work of art, my interpretation is but one of many.

In this passage, Proust captures the protagonist's distress following his separation from his parents, who remained together whilst he was sent on a holiday with his grandmother to a seaside resort in Balbec. When he and his beloved grandmother checked into the Grand Hotel, he felt disconcerted and critical of his new surroundings. By the time he found himself alone in an unfamiliar hotel room, he was in a state of turmoil:

> I would have liked at least to lie down for a moment on the bed: but that would have done me no good, since I would have been incapable of

granting any rest to that bundle of sensations that the waking body, even the material body, is for each of us, and also because the unknown objects which surrounded it, by forcing it to keep its perceptions in a permanent state of defensive alertness ... In that room of mine at Balbec, "mine" in name only, there was no space for me: it was crammed with things which did not know me, which glared my distrust of them back at me, noting my existence only to the extent of letting me know they resented me for disturbing theirs.

(p. 245)

The protagonist was unable to control "that bundle of sensations". Tormented by his own phantasies, he projected them into the room and invested parts of himself into the "unknown objects" that "surrounded" him. The scattered "sensations" then combined in the "clock" and the "curtains".

Without let-up, in some unfamiliar tongue, the clock, which at home I would have never heard for more than a few seconds a week, on surfacing from a long reverie, went on making comments about me, which must have sounded offensive to the tall violet curtains, for they stood there without a word in a listening posture, looking like the sort of people who will shrug their shoulders to show they are irked by the mere sight of someone.

(p. 245)

The father/clock was in dialogue with the mother/curtains and he could not grasp the "unfamiliar tongue" of his parents' sexuality. The curtains, with disdain, or perhaps just aloof, pointed out the intruder in "their" room to the clock. Then, with a "shrug" of her "shoulders", the curtains casually gestured to the clock that this newcomer was not worth noticing. He was inconsequential because, at that moment, he was positioned outside the parental relationship, or rather, his parents' relationship was *outside* him. He had a glimpse of his parents as a couple who had a life of their own and he had a shockingly painful realisation that they were separate from him.

The hurt he felt pierced his heart, evoking rage and hatred that made him feel very persecuted:

Deprived of my universe, evicted from my room, with my very tenancy of my body jeopardized by the enemies about me, infiltrated to the bone by fever, I was alone and wished I could die.

(p. 246)

Being "evicted" was equal to exclusion from life itself. He was horrified, the anxieties "infiltrated" his core and his existence was "jeopardized". His parents turned into terrifying figures and he only wished to "die" and be delivered from this torment.

Part II: Dynamic of forgiveness

I discuss here the three aspects of forgiveness that are intrinsically linked to the depressive position. Although these features are presented under separate headings, they are interdependent, not discrete entities and processes. I do not claim that this list is exhaustive:

- Finding the lost good object
- Coexisting different parts of self
- Generosity

Finding the lost good object

The capacity to find the lost good object is not synonymous with forgiveness but it is essential in forgiveness. Two situations when a good object is recovered will be described, one from Proust's novel, when the protagonist recovers his belief in the existence of good objects, and the other from a patient group.

The lost good object regained: continuation from Proust's "In the Shadow of Young Girls in Flower"

In the passages cited above, the protagonist had a devastating realisation that the parental couple's relationship did not include him and that he was not in a space *with* them or *between* them. This was agonising. He projected murderous feelings into his parents and became extremely disturbed when they transformed into "enemies" who wanted to destroy him. Then, there was a dramatic turn of events:

> It was then that my grandmother entered the room and, as my shrivelled heart expanded, broad vistas of hope opened to me.
>
> (p. 246)

The "shrivelled heart" is a metaphor for the loss of good internal objects, a withered internal presence, or, rather, an absence of goodness and love.

> I fell into my grandmother's arms and pressed my lips to her face as though that were how to take refuge in the greatness of heart she offered to me. Whenever my mouth was on her cheeks or her forehead, I drew from them something so nourishing, so beneficent, that I had all the immobility, gravity, and placid gluttony of an infant on the breast.
>
> (p. 247)

When he saw his grandmother, his "heart expanded" as hope in life and trust in goodness prevailed. He found "refuge" in her generosity as she freely "offered" him her heart. Whilst being in the grip of an intensely persecutory experience, something happened that allowed him to recover his good lost object. What enabled him to feel contained was not only the external reality, his grandmother's loving presence and *her* goodness, but *his* internal reality, *his capacity to regain his good objects*. This ability to find the lost good internal object, which expands and opens the heart, is a fundamental experience in the process of forgiving.

The lost good object regained: group with elderly patients on an acute psychiatric ward

This group is a weekly in-patient therapy group on an acute psychiatric ward for elderly patients, which I co-facilitated with two nurses. The patients were in their 70s and 80s. Here, I present a moment when the experience of a good object or goodness was recaptured in this, perhaps, unlikely setting:

Betty said she was very upset with Yanos who pushed her at lunchtime and grabbed the first table, the best table. He denied this and they started arguing. Helen said that Betty was certainly pushed on purpose. Yanos insisted that he was holding the door and that it was the door that hit her. He then remembered that, when he was small, somebody hit him over the head with a brick slate and he protected his head with his fists. The slate broke and he was scolded, since if he had not put his hands over his head, the slate would not have broken.

I said he remembers this injustice and I wondered if he now also felt unjustly treated. He said yes and, without expressing much feeling, continued to think about his mother, who left him with his grandmother and rarely saw him. Helen said how difficult it had been for him. Someone mentioned the rings that Yanos previously spoke about. These rings appeared to be gold but were not. They were made of something bad. Yanos said that he feels like those rings, concluding that he was not good and that they all were not good; just like the rings, they were bad quality and everybody agreed.

Betty said she could not stand herself because she was like Dr Jekyll and Mr Hyde. She could be so good and so bad. She could change so much and she did not know why she changed like that. Geraldine said she was worried it was too difficult for her family and she cried. She felt guilty about not being able to do things for herself; her arm was broken and she felt so utterly helpless. I said how being in hospital reminds them that they cannot manage on their own and that they need to have things done for them.

A lively discussion ensued with angry undertones about bad GPs, bad medication and treatment. Betty commented how she is sometimes worried, when she goes out for a weekend, whether she will find her bed taken up. There was debate about hospital food and how bad it was.

Betty said how she does not find any meaning in the group and on the ward. Actually, she feels as bad as ever.

Peter said he would like to go back to his home country to die there. Betty had to go out of the room. Then, he reflected, perhaps, he would like, also, to laugh once again, as he laughed before, when he was young with his full belly. Yes, he would like to be able to laugh again and how he had not laughed like that for a long, long time. He loves music and, when he hears certain music, he feels alive and feels something going through his legs. He remembered how he used to dance and how he loved that. As he spoke about the music and dancing, everybody listened carefully.

Louise, the nurse, said that music is life, which they enjoy, and they all laughed, imagining how Peter must have danced. Matilda, another nurse, said music is the food of love and Peter was very pleased. Meanwhile, Betty came back. Peter said he was born just after the First World War. His mother sang to him very much when he was a baby. She sang songs of peace and freedom. Geraldine thought about the difficulties of war and how different those times were. They remembered how everybody stuck together, how people supported each other, how people were close and there was sadness in thinking how, nowadays, everything was different.

There was an experience of scarcity; there were not enough good things to go around which, perhaps, also resonated with the time they felt they had ahead, and their terror about the loss of capacities and inevitable death. Yet, I want to stress that anxieties, related to the feelings of loss and fears of death, the experience of impoverishment and subsequent greed, are not age-related and can pervade at any point in life. The patients consciously and unconsciously attacked their carers for a number of reasons and this contributed to their persecutory guilt and dread that their needs were intolerable, fears that they would be punished and expelled and that there was so little space for them to be kept in mind, in the ward and in the group.

Peter spoke about a need to feel full again, to fill the emptiness, and he mentioned the unmentionable – that he wanted to go home to die. But it then emerged that he would not be alone and empty, he would be full, connected with his good past, his land, his parents and all his loves, his good internal objects. Death, love, sexuality and birth were interconnected. He was conceived during the war, with love and war intertwined. Finally, with the triumph of love over war, he was born in freedom and peace and loved at his mother's breast. Whilst Peter was recounting this, there was a moment of shared experience of something gratifying and worthy that was followed by a sad acknowledgement of something good that had been lost. What was even briefly experienced as good, but truly lost and now in the bygone past, was paradoxically brought back to life in a tender moment of remembrance, which evoked a sorrow and that painful feeling of "never more".

Coexisting different parts of self

How is it possible that different feelings and states of mind can coexist, such as the pain of being injured by one's love and, at the same time, the sense of tormenting the loved one? I believe that Shakespeare's Sonnet below captures such a state of mind.

Sonnet 120

That you were once unkind, befriends me now,
And for that sorrow, which I then did feel
Needs must I under my transgression bow,
Unless my nerves were brass or hammered steel.
For if you were by my unkindness shaken,
As I by yours, y' have pass'd a hell of time,
And I, a tyrant, have no leisure taken
To weigh how once I suffer'd in your crime.
O, that our night of woe might have remember'd
My deepest sense, how hard true sorrow hits,
And soon to you, as you to me, then tendered
The humble salve which wounded bosoms fits!
But that your trespass now becomes a fee;
Mine ransoms yours, and yours must ransom me.
(Shakespeare, 1999, p. 120)

In this sonnet, the subject is aware of the pain that he both inflicted and suffered and, at the same time, he feels love for his beloved and recalls how he felt loved. He makes a plea for their mutual suffering and wounding to cancel each other out, hoping this will fairly balance in the scales of justice.

Shakespeare puts this in a relational context where both parties transgress, which is a complex and realistic depiction of the relationship between two people. The subject is suffering, remembering the "night of woe" and "how hard true sorrow hits", whilst at the same time he knows about the "tyrant" part of self that "trespasses". The debt is cancelled, if the mutual trespass becomes a fee that ransoms and liberates both.

However, there is no apology here, no repentance, only acknowledgement that one was hurtful as well as hurt. Although there is a certain crudeness in the bargain that is offered, as an appeal for cancellation of the mutual debt, there is nevertheless a conceptual shift that expands the field of what is known and the subject is aware of the pain that *both* he and his love suffered. This conveys the subject's capacity to hold in mind the concurrent divergent experiences: the simultaneously injured and injuring parts of self and the other.

Coexistence of different "parts" of self within a "whole"

My interpretation of Bion's (1991[1975]) trilogy, *A Memoir of the Future*, is that he makes use of a group of characters to express complex relationships between different parts of the personality. In this work, different "characters", such as "Bion", "Myself", "Twenty Years", "Mind", "Body", "Girl", "Boy", etc. relate with each other. I think he is drawing attention to a constellation of different internal objects and the relationship between these objects, which can be understood as a "group in the mind".

The coexistence of different internal objects and different relations between these objects is a phenomenon that also manifests in dreams and can be referred to as a "dream group". Resnik (1995) makes use of Matte-Blanco's concept of "multiple dimensions" to provide a structure for understanding dreams and otherwise chaotic and incomprehensible phenomena, like the coexistence of part and whole-object relations and the potential, in dreams, for thoughts or feelings to occupy simultaneously both the whole ego and only a part of the ego. Resnik points out that:

> When we dream, we become multiple personalities, experiencing our adventures in time and space simultaneously through each of the protagonists.
>
> (Resnik, 1995, p. 10)

To signify a dynamic process and a plurality in forgiveness, an analogy is drawn between the "dream group" and the "group in the mind". The dynamic experience of forgiving can be conceptualised as a coexistence of different parts of self and relations between these "parts" within a "whole".

There is a certain dissonance in the process of forgiveness. For instance, the subject feels the pain, hate and urge to avenge the inflicted hurt but, at the same time, has other feelings, memories or thoughts about the injuring other, which are incongruent with the suffering caused by the injury and with the aroused hostility. If the subject does not resort to projection, there ensues a struggle to withstand the diverse and contradictory feelings, akin to vacillating without the grounding that more synchronised and integrated feelings provide. It is in the process of forgiveness that the diverse, conflicting feelings combine, integrate and evolve into a new, broader and more realistic experience of self and the other.

The dynamic of forgiveness can also be conceptualised as a shift from a paranoid to a depressive state of mind. For example, an injury by a loved person can evoke a feeling of being suspended and "pulled" in different directions. There is a dialectic internal tension caused by experiencing the incompatible, concurrent feelings both about oneself and the injuring other, with some feelings being characteristic of a more paranoid frame of mind and others of a depressive position. That is a state of disquiet, a state of enduring a painful and disturbing ambivalence.

What allows a transformation of ambivalence, in which the disparate and conflicting feelings about the internal and external objects can be brought closer and integrated? Some highlight the predominance of loving feelings, others highlight the significance of understanding the cause and effect of how the injury happened. Jacques, as cited earlier, and psychoanalysts in general, emphasise the necessity of acknowledging, mourning and accepting loss, in this instance the loss caused by the injury inflicted by another person. Bion (1988 [1962]) stresses "learning from experience", postulating that, if x knows y, this "does not convey a sense of finality, that is to say, a meaning that x is in possession of a piece of knowledge called y but rather that x is in the state of getting to know y and y is in a state of getting to be known by x" (p. 47).

Working through the ambivalence and finding the lost good object requires learning from the experience in the process of getting to know one-self and the other, and in getting to be known by the other, in mourning the loss, the hurt or the feeling that one was damaged in some way by the injury and the predominance of loving feelings. When the ambivalent split feelings about self and the other are brought closer and juxtaposed, different coex-isting elements, phantasies and relations between self and the other can bind into a new "whole".

The point I am making is that one essential feature of forgiveness is the ability to concurrently hold in the mind the disparate, conflicting "good" and "bad" parts of self and the other. If, in the process of forgiveness, these coexisting parts and relations between them can be contained, they can transform into a new, evolving "whole" or whole new objects. The whole new objects, nevertheless, hold a potential for splitting, but there is also a possibility of integrating the new aspects into a new, richer and more encompassing "whole" or into the whole new objects.

The dreams discussed in the next section contain these elusive, paradoxical and different, coexisting relations and parts of self.

Amalda

I will now discuss two dreams from the last year of Amalda's analysis. These dreams show a shift in her capacity to forgive, a capacity not yet con-solidated but, nonetheless, coexisting with her various recriminations in an ongoing struggle. She could identify with different internal objects and rela-tions between them, ranging from the persecuting phantasies of what others are doing to her, and what she is doing to others, to a more integrated, whole-object way of relating.

First dream
    She was in an old house in an attic. There were a lot of mice and rats around and it was very dirty. She heard a doorbell and realised that the Rat Protection Society was coming. All the rats and mice ran out of

sight but one remained, lying dead on the floor, and she pushed it under a sofa with her foot in order to hide it from the Rat Protection Society. She went downstairs and opened the door and there was a group of people dressed in bright colours and baseball hats. The next thing she remembers is that she was holding a cat in her arms, whilst on the edge of a wall, and the cat suddenly fell out of her hands. She was worried about the cat but then saw that it had landed safely on the ground when it calmly walked away.

The Rat Protection Society is such an evocative representation of the pathological organisation, the mafia gang, and the hold that they have over their victim, as described by Rosenfeld (1987). But these figures did not convey ferocity and ruthlessness. Amalda thought that the group, with the men in baseball hats, looked ridiculous. Despite their colourful clothes, they were unimpressive, mundane and a parody of a gang. She experienced the Rat Protection Society quite differently from the same gang in a dream she had had some years before, when she was mesmerised by their power and violence.

The destructive, cruel internal objects represented by the rats and mice were still active in the "attic" of the "old house" of her mind and the Rat Protection Society stood for the impulse to defend these manic and destructive figures. Simultaneously, she wanted to free herself from this nasty infestation of having been harshly chastised in her childhood and these cruel figures no longer had such a hold over her. The cat provided protection and could help her to be free from the damaging impulses and influences, yet she held it in a precarious place and in a precarious manner, so it fell.

Amalda's conflict with coexisting and split parts of herself manifested in her concurrently forging a Rat Protection Society and providing an antidote, the cat. There were also conflicting feelings about the cat: she had an urge to get rid of it and she dropped it, yet simultaneously she wanted to protect the cat and she rescued it.

Second dream

A dustbin was on fire under a tree. Somehow, with the help of a woman, she and the woman went around and contained the fire. There were some very fine edges around the fire that looked like ashes and, in the dream, she thought this could be used to nourish the ground and help things to grow.

The "ashes" were the remnants from the "fire" caused by the destructive "mice" and "rats" but these inner figures were also burning in the "dustbin" of her mind. Furthermore, the contents of the dustbin did not only expose the "bad" things within her but, concurrently, the time she threw away, the good experiences and memories discarded and binned like, for example, her affection and appreciation of her mother's support, her dropped projects and her deposed hopes about being more alive, creative and loving.

In this dream, Amalda expressed a belief that all these mingled remnants and parts of her that underwent the "fire" of analysis could be used to "nourish the ground and help things grow". There were feelings of remorse and guilt about the waste and destructiveness, a need to restore and give back something nourishing to the "ground" of analysis that held her and helped her "to grow", and she dreamt this dream, remembered it and brought it to analysis.

The dustbin represented both the damage she felt she endured and inflicted, as well as the good things she had lost. Likewise, there was a fire of destruction and violence but also a fire that illuminated and transformed the rubbish into the ashes for development. "Dustbin" and "fire" represented various elements and processes between them that were brought together in the "ashes", that is, they were united into a new "whole" or into the whole new object.

She was tentatively accepting both the "bad" and "good" things within her combined in the "ashes". Depending on what state of mind she was in, she could still feel persecuted by some internal and external figures but there was also a process of integration and forgiveness, and she could recapture the lost and newly discovered "goodness" of some internal and external figures.

For the first time, before her last summer break, she said that she would miss me, acknowledging her affection, and she was able at times to have a more integrated experience of her objects and relationships, and a deeper and broader range of experiences of herself and others.

The Smile
There is a Smile of Love
And there is a Smile of Deceit
And there is a Smile of Smiles
In which these two Smiles meet ...
(Blake, 2016, p. 298)

This is a first stanza of a longer poem. In the context of discussing coexisting and divergent experiences, I see this stanza as depicting the integration of concurrent streams: feeling of love despite feelings of hate for the injury, or treachery of deceit. "Smile of Deceit" is a smile that hides the true passions of the soul. The full truth is concealed from the other and, perhaps, from oneself too – there is a reality that cannot be expressed or known about.

The "Smiles of Smiles" is the most sublime of smiles because of its sincerity and because this is where love and hate meet. It is a smile that flows from two springs, where the flow of love encompasses the current of hate and love prevails in the transformation and containment of the tensions between the opposites. How feelings of love and hate are experienced or denied, introjected or projected, integrated or split, is of crucial significance in early development and later life.

"Smile of Smiles" is Blake's depiction of a transcendent union in "which these two Smiles meet". This is an integration of a split between love and hate that is not an amalgamation, nor is it a separate existence, but a confluent stream. It is a "meeting" of different parts of self within the larger whole, an integration that holds an inherent possibility to change the course into a paranoid-schizoid domain and back to a depressive state of mind. These positions are two dynamically interdependent constellations of love versus hate, trust versus fear, forgiveness versus grievance, and reflect fundamental aspects of existence.

Generosity

In this section, I consider the generosity of forgiveness in relation to envy and reparation.

Generosity of forgiveness and envy

In Dostoyevsky's (2008 [1869]) novel *The Idiot* the interaction between two protagonists captures an experience of envy in one and an understanding of the generosity of forgiveness in the other.

Prince Myshkin, or the idiot as some refer to him, is a young man in his late 20s considered to be a childlike, naïve man. At times people saw him as being hopelessly stupid, and at other times, as an embodiment of goodness and truthfulness, even wisdom. Ippolit is an 18-year-old student in the final stage of consumption. It is thought that he will die in a matter of weeks, if not days. He is a clever and troubled young man with bouts of contempt for the individual and society.

All in Myshkin's circle move to a resort in Pavlovsk for their summer holidays. One evening during a large merrymaking gathering with a lot of champagne Ippolit says that he wants to read what he wrote the previous night. After some indecision, he reads "My necessary explanation: Après moi le deluge". The account was very long, and he presents various relations, situations and ideas. Many become impatient with the length of the reading. When he finishes, some express discontent and others engage in other topics. Ippolit dashes to the veranda, takes out a small pistol and presses it to his forehead. The pistol does not fire. After a brief commotion, they find that the firing cap had not been put on and he faints.

A few days later, Ippolit and Myshkin meet by chance. Ippolit notices that Myshkin looks happy and he wants to say something scathing but holds back. Ippolit becomes very critical of his work and says that it was written in turmoil. Myshkin is sorry that Ippolit has renounced what he wrote, as it was honest and there were some funny passages in it. When Ippolit hears about "funny passages", he frowns and closely observes Myshkin's face to discern whether he is pretending. Relieved and believing in Myshkin's sincerity, he replies that one must die. The conversation continues briefly before they part and, at the end, Ippolit suddenly asks:

> "Well, all right, well, tell me yourself then, what would be the best way for me to die in your opinion? . . . So as to be most . . . virtuous, I mean? Well, go on!"
> "Pass by us and forgive us our happiness!" said the prince in a low voice.
> "Ha-ha-ha! Just as I thought!"
>
> (p. 552)

Ippolit is excruciatingly aware that others have a life ahead of them and this provokes his anger, resentment and envy. Myshkin understands him and says that he needs to forgive others for their happiness – a happiness that could also arise precisely because of the vicinity of his death. The containment and transformation of Ippolit's envy would entail being in touch with complex feelings around his impending death and with the mourning of his profound loss.

Myshkin understands the restorative influence that the generosity of forgiving would have on Ippolit. He asks him to forgive others for their happiness, meaning to "let" others "have" their lives, although it hurts him immeasurably to know that he will *never* have such happiness. If Ippolit could allow others to have what is denied to him, in this act of generosity and feeling that he *can give* and that *he gives*, he would find his good lost objects and regain his goodness.

Generosity of forgiveness and reparation

Generosity is expressed in the desire to give something beneficent and nourishing to the other and in the ability to take this in with trust, enjoyment and gratitude. The capacity to forgive and come to terms with hurts and disappointments is another feature of generosity. It is the injury caused by the other, such as feeling betrayed or cruelly treated, that can be mourned and forgiven, or not. Kernberg (1995) succinctly describes this in a couple relationship:

> To be able to attack one's partner sadistically yet witness the survival of his or her love; to be able to experience in oneself the transition from relentless rage and devaluation to guilt, mourning, and repair – these are invaluable experiences for the couple.
>
> (p. 93)

The nature and domain of the injury are also significant. A person may have a particular sensitivity, a valency, for a particular kind of injury and some hurts hurt some people more than others. Also, the response of the person who inflicted the injury is relevant. For example, the offender may feel genuine remorse and a need to make amends.

In forgiving, the debt is cancelled, and this is a point that Shakespeare makes in the sonnet on love discussed earlier. Generosity in letting go of a debt or grievance is based on the trust that there are good things in the subject, in the other and in the relationship that have survived the injury. Rhodes (2022) points out that forgiveness is a move from a position of an omnipotence of the unforgiving injured self to an acknowledgement of imperfection and potential goodness within oneself and the other. It is an understanding that the other is not perfectly good nor perfectly bad and, likewise neither, is oneself.

Reparation, as Klein uses the concept, refers to the reparation of damage that the subject has inflicted on the other, in phantasy or in reality, and it derives from a depressive guilt and concern for the other. The process of reparation in forgiveness is fundamentally different because it does not stem from a depressive guilt but from the generosity of mercy and compassion.

Intra-psychically, the subject is putting right the injury inflicted by another person by *repairing the damage to oneself* caused by the other and by *repairing the damaging "other"* within oneself. The subject is "allowing" the experience of being injured by another to be repaired and this requires both mourning the hurt and loss caused by the injury and the generosity, mercy and compassion for the other, be it an internal or external figure.

There is a link between mourning and generosity. Both require letting go of what one "has". In the process of mourning, this would be feeling the pain of "letting" the loss "happen" and "giving up" the lost object, the loss of someone or something significant. The generosity would require "letting go" of an injury, debt or grievance. Furthermore, generosity manifests in the capacity to "give away" to another something that is good and worthy such as recognising a good aspect of the injuring other. Forgiveness requires both the capacity for mourning and generosity

One may add that generosity is in forgiving, not in forgetting, since injustices, hurts and fears reside "somewhere" in the heart, dormant or aroused, depending on whether one is in the paranoid-schizoid or depressive position. However, "If the meaning of the past is changed by forgiveness, its influence on the future is also changed" (Westcott, 2017).

The gratitude and love in *giving* and *taking* something nourishing is but one feature of generosity in relationships. The reparative process of *finding* the lost goodness and *giving it back* to the other is a different kind of *giving* – it is a generosity of forgiving.

Conclusion

In all phases of life, individuals are confronted with frustrations and injuries in relationships with significant others. I have found that the wounds that can be difficult to forgive coalesce into three domains: early infantile experience, oedipal conflicts and anxieties about loss and death. Forgiving entails finding the lost good object, mourning the hurt in the encounter with the other, capacity for generosity and reconciliation of some conflicting parts of self that leads to the recognition of the fallibility of the other and of our flawed, split and vulnerable self.

Notes

1 The focus here is on everyday affairs and relationships in different phases of life with significant others. It is beyond the scope of this chapter to address the unforgivable acts on the individual and social levels.
2 In this chapter I use material from As My Shrivelled Heart Expanded: The Dynamics Of Love, Hate, and Generosity in the Couple. In Novakovic, A. & Reid. M. (Eds.), Couple Stories: Application of Psychoanalytic Ideas in Thinking about Couple Interaction. London: Routledge, and The Group as a Whole, the Individual in the Group, and the Group in the Individual. In Novakovic, A. & Vincent, D. (Eds.), Group Analysis Working with Staff, Teams and Organisations. Abingdon: Routledge.
3 "Љубављу мислити, осећати, живети, знати … Њен категоричан императив гласи: љуби, да би познао. Истинско знање у свему звиси од љубави: оно се зачиње у љубави, расте љубављу, достиже савршенство помоћу љубави. Ја љубим, значи: ја знам. Знање је еманација љубави" (Popovic, 1940, p. 222).
4 "Ce sourire prouvait à cette jeune parricide que le coeur d'une mère est une abîme au fond duquel se trouve toujours un pardon" (Balzac, 1991 [1842], p. 226).

References

Balzac, H. (1991 [1842]). *La Femme de trente ans*. France: Librarie Générale Française.

Bion, W.R. (1988 [1962]). *Learning from Experience*. London: Maresfield Library.

Bion, W.R. (1991 [1975]). *A Memoir of the Future*. London: Karnac.

Blake, W. (1967). Infant Sorrow. In: *Songs of Innocence and of Experience*. Oxford: Oxford University Press.

Blake, W. (1994). On Another's Sorrow. In: *The Songs of Innocence. The Selected Poems of William Blake*. Ware: Wordsworth Editions.

Blake, W. (2016). The Smile. In: Esiri, A., (Ed.), *A Poem for Every Night in the Year*. London: Macmillan Children's Books.

Dostoyevsky, F. (2008 [1869]). *The Idiot*. Oxford: Oxford World's Classics.

Gipps, R. (2022). Personal communication.

Jacques, E. (1988 [1965]). Death and the Mid-Life Crisis. In: Bott Spillius, E. (Ed.), *Melanie Klein Today: Developments in Theory and Practice: Volume 2: Mainly Practice* (226–248). London: Routledge.

Kernberg, O. (1995). Aggression, Love, and the Couple. In: *Love Relations: Normality and Pathology* (81–96). New Haven and London: Yale University Press.

Klein, M. (1993 [1937]). Love, Guilt and Reparation. In: *Love, Guilt and Reparation and Other Works* 1921–1945 (306–343). London: Karnac.

Klein, M. (1993 [1957]). Envy and Gratitude. In: *Envy and Gratitude and Other Works 1946–1967* (176–235). London: Karnac.

Novakovic, A. (2018). "As My Shrivelled Heart Expanded": The Dynamics Of Love, Hate, and Generosity in the Couple. In: Novakovic, A. & Reid. M. (Eds.), *Couple Stories: Application of Psychoanalytic Ideas in Thinking about Couple Interaction.* London: Routledge.

Novakovic, A. (2019). The Group As a Whole, the Individual in the Group, and the Group in the Individual. In: Novakovic, A. & Vincent, D. (Eds.), *Group Analysis Working With Staff, Teams and Organisations.* Abingdon: Routledge.

Popovic, J. (1940) *Филозофија Љубави и сазнања. У: Достојевски о Европи и Словенству* (211–236). Београд: Нови Дани.

Proust, M (2002 [1919]). *In the Shadow of Young Girls in Flower.* London: Alan Lane & Penguin Press.

Resnik, S. (1995). Introduction. In: *Mental Space* (1–11). London: Karnac.

Rhodes, J. (2022). Personal communication.

Rosenfeld, H.A. (1987). A Psychoanalytic Approach to the Treatment of Psychosis. In: *Impasse And Interpretation* (3–27). London: Routledge.

Segal, H. (1998). *Phantasy. In: Introduction to the Work of Melanie Klein* (11–23). London: Karnac.

Shakespeare, W. (1999). 120. In: *Shakespeare's Sonnets* (120). London: Penguin.

Westcott, B. (2017). *Essence of Group Analysis.* Unpublished paper.

Chapter 2

Forgiving as malice relented: the depressive position in action

Chris Mawson

The roots of forgiving

It is Shakespeare in his play *Cymbeline* who makes clear that forgiveness can simply take the form of relinquishing malice against the offender: can

> Kneel not to me.
> The pow'r that I have on you is to spare you;
> The malice towards you, to forgive you. Live,
> And deal with others better.
> (Shakespeare, *Cymbeline*, Act 5, Scene 5)

Forgiving – forgiefan, forgifen, forgeaf, forꝥiaf, forgif – are the earliest recorded instances of the term that became the verb 'to forgive' appear in Old English texts in which the '*-giefen'/'-gifan'/'-geaf*' and '*-gif*' component signifies something beyond giving *to* another. Around 900 CE it appears that *forgiefan* was sometimes a synonym for giving, as in bestowing. Before being taken up in a Latinate form to give '*pardonner*', to grant a pardon, the term seems to have undergone a bifurcation through being associated with the similar sounding 'forego'. From this route we get forgiving not as a 'giving to', but a 'giving up' – as ceasing to harbour wrath or rancour, and the choosing of a path away from direct actions springing from the impulsion of an extreme, indignant state of being. *Wrath* is a term dating from the Old English of the same period (950 CE), and it relates to primordial states of deep godlike indignation, vehement anger, intense exasperation, and boiling resentment. Lucretius, in his 1st.-century epic philosophical verse *De rerum natura* (On the nature of things), included wrathful states when he wrote of the need for truth-seeking words 'that set the bounds to lust and terror'.

In the ancient Laws of Cnut (Canute), from around the same period, there is in the Old English[1] a reference to how, in situations of great eagerness to act on powerful feelings and impulses, a person 'should consider what to do *and what to forego*'.

DOI: 10.4324/9781003364313-2

The *rancour* of unforgiving states of mind, also indicated in the early ety-mology, signified the deep-rooted bitter, ill feeling that was known to persist if inner forgiveness fails to be an option. It is close in meaning to Shake-speare's use of the word 'envenoming' when he wrote of the unkind divisions of envy. The idea appears again in *Othello* in relation to jealousy and envy with the line: 'The thought whereof/doth, like a poisonous mineral, gnaw my inwards'.

Coleridge, writing in a vein entirely consistent with this line of thought, expressed in plain words how wrath and malice against one who is loved rankles the unforgiving heart:

Alas! they had been friends in youth;
But whispering tongues can poison truth;
And constancy lives in realms above;
And life is thorny; and youth is vain;
And to be wroth with one we love
Doth work like madness in the brain.
               (Coleridge, 'Christabel', 1797)

Ceasing to harbour wrath means no longer giving the feelings such a ran-corous lodging, affecting both self and object, and this intrapsychic situation will be discussed later in relation to the depressive position as described by Klein, and its particular type of container/contained relationship as con-sidered by Bion, following which the particular quality of forgiving achieved by the character Cordelia in the dénouement of King Lear will be considered in the light of the ideas developed in the chapter to that point.

Forgiving as relenting malice articulates a set of meanings that acknowl-edges our harshness as human beings, a signification that unlike 'granting pardon' puts emphasis on our cruel and vengeful impulses, the gratification of which has becomes relented or renounced if we are to go beyond the talion world of 'an eye for an eye', and in which everyone is entitled to claim their actual pound of flesh.

The words of Shakespeare from *Cymbeline* from the beginning of the chapter will immediately be recognised as resonant. Forgiving is here clearly harnessed to sparing from one's own power to inflict hurt. It foregoes power in the vertical dimension of hierarchy and entitlement, and it nods strongly towards promoting the value of ethics particular to lateral human relationships:

Kneel not to me.
The pow'r that I have on you is to spare you;
The malice towards you, to forgive you. Live,
And deal with others better.

The conclusion of the verse, 'Live, and deal with others better', after a mention of power and malice, foregoing abjection from the other, is as concise a description of forgiving in the depressive position as we could hope to find. It is also in accord with one of the first recorded Anglo-Saxon instances of the term 'forgive', a plea for mercy uttered by a mother imploring a powerful assailant to spare her baby, to hold back from his violence. In that early example forgiving has no surrounding context of right and wrong, deserving or underserving, only the raw power to do harm. It is such a basic meaning, in a plain and earthy reminder of humankind's readiness for the unreflective immediacy of violent solutions and violent delights – a propensity for which is masked under the later, more refined Latinate connotation of granting pardon in a set of legal, theological and financial frameworks.

The later developments of the term are culturally interesting in relation to religious observance and commercial obligations, but in these transactions the later use of the term, in which the '-*gif*' is taken as corresponding to the '-*donner*' of *pardonner*, a 'giving *to*' carries more of a connotation in which the *formal act* of giving forgiveness takes the foreground, and the basic inner motive remains unannounced, enabling forgiveness to be associated strongly with religious precedent and with it, an identification with 'goodness'.

A consideration of the object relations of forgiving as *relenting* to an aggressive or malicious impulse engages us much more intimately with the earliest configurations of mental life. It is argued that pursuing this line of thought provides a more truthful account of the object-relationship in play in the uncertain tension between grievance and relenting, which can be found lying behind formal claims and shows of certain forgiveness, where the complacent ease of expression appears often to convey an organised day-dreamed phantasy role-system of faux-theological goodness and benevolence.

This less comfortable perspective brings us much closer to the internal object relations and primordial impulses aroused when we are feeling wrathful, at being wronged, insulted, or owed-to, than we find in the perspective of deciding under what conditions we might be persuaded to bestow our pardon. The latter signification, it is argued, in its narrative story-telling structures and in its emotional resonances, has the power to induce in the self-benevolent, 'feel good' connotations, and is ill-suited to help us in facing our real feelings, often malign, when we feel wronged. The real relationship, shorn of self-idealisation, normally involves a sharp and bleak type of tension in our very being, where we have to know who we are when we are shown to be unrelenting, by saying, 'No!' to forgiveness.

Depressively informed understanding

What movement of forces within the personality lie behind an authentic impulse to forgive in the sense of relenting, of mitigating or allaying the force of a harmful action or response? Posed in this way the question orients us to the object relations of the inner world, particularly those involved in grievance, resentment, wrath and anxiety – which, as mentioned earlier, are primordial aspects of the human being that hide behind the mask of our forgiveness as a benevolent pardoning. With the emphasis on a forgiving impulse as movement towards the *relenting* of a potentially cruel act, a set of signifiers is set in train that discloses the human being as both destructively and constructively inclined, with the outcome never guaranteed. In this way, the dual signification of our term is disclosive of our dual instinctual nature as human beings. Melanie Klein's concept of the depressive position is crucial in the mental shift from ruthlessness[2] to relenting. and from demanding forgiveness to seeking it. It is to this concept that I now turn.

Melanie Klein's concept of the depressive position

Our spite towards people in the outer world, when they let us down or seem to act against our interests, seems to be represented differently in the inner world according to whether our leading anxiety is bound up with perceived threats to our continued *existence*, or sometimes (under narcissism) the uninterrupted validation of our daydreamed selves, or whether, in contrast, our main source of anguish is bound up with the perceived *welfare* of the internal and externally loved figures of our lives, socially and psychically. The former anxiety, that of existential threat, predisposes us towards a paranoid orientation that drives us to ever-increasing division in our perceptions and alliances, hence the term 'paranoid-schizoid', and the former towards what Klein termed a depressive position, in which we need to take responsibility for our own aggression and hostility, and for discriminating between what Britton (personal communication) called 'a good object behaving badly' and 'a truly bad object being bad'. Judgements involving understanding and forgiving under the latter principle do, by necessity, include that the judging self is also known as both good and bad, possessing benign and malevolent impulses, for which we ourselves are responsible. Under Klein's paranoid-schizoid mentality, there is minimal need to consider sparing the other who has insulted, frustrated, or failed us. At the threshold of the depressive orientation to others, and their inner representatives, awareness of own questionable motives and intentions enters the scene, and this painful self-knowledge includes recognising our malice, and need for status and for power over others, and to suffer pain because we have caused harm to real human beings whose existence cannot easily be made not to matter. This is at the root of Heidegger's use of the concept of *Sorge*, the specific caring for existence. It is close to the particular sense in which Klein used the term depressive concern, a particular kind of anguish, stemming from our sense of bringing harm to our loved internalised figures, originally and prototypically our mother and her breast. The quality of anxiety, induced by the combination of unconscious phantasy and preconscious realistic observation in this painful relationship, she called depressive anxiety. As indicated above, it differs from the anxiety felt when the over-riding concern is with the self and its extinction by forces felt to be dangerous to its continued existence as a coherent unit, in that depressive pain makes us agonise and fret about the welfare of the other, and our real or supposed part in causing them harm. According to this model, as developed by a number of authors, when the self is enabled to develop a capacity to withstand this particular form of pain without turning away from the experience, for as long as this happens there is a thriving, commensurate with the degree of guilt and responsibility that can be tolerated, of the ego's capacities for containment, thinking, communication, and differentiation of states of being. The ruthlessness of the more primitive position, in which paranoia is the leading anxiety and violent division is the main defence against it, gives way to attempts to maintain an ongoing concern for the welfare of the object and its representatives in the outer world. The capacity for separateness also allows the development of symbols that are no longer simply concretely equated with the concrete events from which they are partly formed. Reparative and creative solutions are sought out in the depressive mentality, as long as it lasts, and this can bring some relief from the worst phantasies of ruin. With the depressive orientation, situations no longer need to be ideal, because the idealised picture becomes gradually more recognisable as the enemy of the ordinarily good.

Klein, and her students and colleagues who explored this model in their work with children and adults, as well as groups and couples, observed that what she had brought together under this term, the depressive position, was just that – a position, a configuration, and not a 'stage', which once negotiated provided a solid platform and foundation for growth of the personality that never again had to be rocked and returned to being close to its foundations.

Klein's findings in child analysis suggested a subtle and complex range of psychological functions that grew from this beginning of a move from raw ruthlessness in the inner world of infants and small children, chief amongst them, as mentioned just now, the power to form symbols distinct from concrete bodily objects. Symbols allow us to begin to relate to the people close to us as being themselves thinking beings who feel, observe, and think about *us*. It becomes possible to allow human relationships to be subjected to reparative actions, as well as foregoing further aggressive action towards those who are loved as well as hated. In other words, sparing the objects of our inner and outer worlds from our worst excesses. These possibilities are not available to the child who simply feels they are retaliating against what Britton calls 'a bad object acting true to form'. With the onset of the depressive position, we may learn to conceive of the entity discussed earlier, 'a good object behaving badly' – quite an advance, and one predisposing to forgiveness early on in life, partly because it allows for another, closely related conception, one that has the power to reduce a portion of inner guilt: that oneself might be a good self that has behaved badly.

So, although as human beings we are enclosed for much of the time in a fearful 'zero-sum game' in which our very survival is felt, unconsciously, to be continually at stake, we sometimes enter another configuration in which what matters most is the well-being and continued healthy existence of those who care for us, and towards whom we feel precarious, anxious loving gratitude. In such a depressively informed 'couple state of mind' (Morgan, 2018), we come to realise that our own destructive impulses pose the greatest danger, not those of the others. Real forgiveness makes sense with this realisation: that *we* are the danger, but this can be sought meaningfully only when the object to whom we need to make amends is perceived as a whole object, since phantasies or perceptions of damage to partial objects are dealt with adequately by disavowal and the repeated application of splitting as a defence. In other words, the depressive loss and ensuing guilt makes sense only when the self is capable of apprehending anxiety situations involving whole objects in the inner world and the outer. It was to consider the situation in which the emphasis on anxiety shifts to the welfare of the other that Melanie Klein developed her concept.

The mental pain of this realisation leads the infant to find ways of reducing the ruthlessness and violence of their primitive emotions, and when they cannot, at least to deflect the worst onto substitutes. Klein makes clear that in the new configuration, the ego's voice, as it were, says something like: my mother is disappearing, she may never return, she is suffering, she is dead. No, this can't be, for I can revive her. In contrast to a predominantly paranoid version of events in a situation of depressive guilt and anxiety it is the self that seeks forgiveness, not the recalcitrant object that should beg it from the aggrieved self. In 1936 Klein's colleague, Joan Riviere, wrote movingly of the depressive predicament:

> all one's loved ones within are dead and destroyed, all goodness is dispersed, lost, in fragments, wasted and scattered to the winds; nothing is left within but utter desolation. Love brings sorrow, and sorrow brings guilt; the intolerable tension mounts, there is no escape, one is utterly alone, there is no one to share or help. Love must die because love is dead. Besides, there would be no one to feed one, and no one whom one could feed, and no food in the world. And more, there would still be magic power in the undying persecutors who can never be exterminated – the ghosts. Death would instantaneously ensue – and one would choose to die by one's own hand before such a position could be realized.
>
> (Riviere, 1936, p. 313)

This description of extreme depressive pain seems hardly more bearable than the intense persecution and dread that Klein considered as characterising the inner climate of dread existing in the paranoid position, against which the primary defence was to attack the object, whilst simultaneously partitioning or fragmenting the ego that made such experiences possible. In that constellation hate begets harm and harm in turn begets hate, but a change made possible in the depressive position is that awareness of hate and harm, where tolerable, can mobilise efforts in two directions at once – towards sparing the object from further harm, and making reparative efforts where possible. These movements are not possible when confusion or wrath, the latter described by Klein as 'maximal primal sadism', is at its height, but they become so with the new opportunity arising at the dawning of the small infant's grasp of her mother *as a whole*, rather than her being present to awareness as a bewildering kaleidoscopic cycling of separately animated and threatening 'thing presentations'.

So, to reiterate, with the beginning of a feeling that the object is not wholly bad, and the self not wholly good or innocent, the stage is set for new possibilities, notably sparing, reparation, and its symbolisation of experience and reparation, so that the 'talion' principle embodied in 'an eye for an eye', or demanding 'a pound of flesh' from the debtor, no longer feels that it is right action.

Note that this amounts to a radical shift in the individual's *ethical stance*, because self-preservation is no longer the be-all and end-all of existence. Because of greater integration of the personality, life is no longer experienced as though it were a simple play with a central character, alone of significance, surrounded by 'extras' playing 'bit-parts'. No longer are all impulses and events felt to happen exclusively to the self, and for as long as this orientation is sustained, and the welfare of the self alone is no longer felt to be of such paramount importance, love, care and concern come to co-exist with, and not be banished by, anxiety.

Forgiveness becomes, then, a possibility both in the inner and outer worlds when the leading anxiety is depressive in its basic orientation, and in 1946 Klein developed her ideas about the infantile depressive position further, to take account not only of the forgiving impulse but, more importantly, the need felt for a *reparative form* of guilt that stems from a full recognition of both love and hate in the depressive orientation to fellow human beings. It is a form of guilt that lends itself to being constructive and realistic rather than self-abasing and masochistic, spurring the person felt to be in need of being forgiven to real attempts at repairing damage, and where this is not possible directly, seeking ways to achieve it, at least partially, by symbolic means.

This form of guilt, together with the ontological form of guilt that arises from existence itself, can be considered as authentic guilt, as contrasted with the guilt-tinged persecution that arises from severe internal criticism and punishment, and which often passes for guilt. An internally derived accusation of badness is readily confused, by the self and by others, with the ego's own assessment of its impulses and responsibility felt for the consequences in inner and outer reality. This brings us to the subject of inauthentic forgiving, which I will now consider by drawing on an existential concept of Jean-Paul Sartre.

False forgiveness and bad faith

Forgiveness appearing too swiftly after insult or harm rouses our suspicion that the one granting forgiveness may be more concerned to appear generous than actually being so. When anxiety has not been given time for 'working-through', a painful process, easy forgiveness is likely to be an imitation. The same is true of contrition. Parents who aim to transmit what they might regard as 'solid Christian virtues' might insist to their children that they straightaway forgive their brother or sister, even before finding out what has actually happened between them. There is the risk that under such conditions, children might learn to perform forgiveness rather than having an authentically forgiving experience. Heidegger's concept of *das man*, the 'generalised everydayness', is relevant here. 'To be a good father, one behaves like this', for example, or 'to be a Christian person one always forgives, just as he did'. From a psychoanalytic perspective, such *mauvaise foi* is obtained through a process known as 'imitative projective identification' – Together they give the intentionality: 'Just as I am seen as, so a I will be taken to be'.

Proust referred to '*L'habitude*' to refer to a similar habit of generalised orienting to the world, both physical and social. In the same vein, James Gooch reported an interchange with his analyst, Bion, who had asked him if he was more concerned to sound like a good father or to *be* one, an ontological question that reminds us of Sartre's illustration of his concept of *mauvaise foi* (bad faith), expressed by Sartre in the following passage:

> But what are we then if we have the constant obligation to make our-selves what we are, if our mode of being is having the obligation to be what we are? Let us consider this waiter in the cafe. His movement is quick and forward, a little too precise, a little too rapid. He comes toward the patrons with a step a little too quick. He bends forward a little too eagerly; his voice, his eyes express an interest a little too solici-tous for the order of the customer. Finally there he returns, trying to imitate in his walk the inflexible stiffness of some kind of automaton while carrying his tray with the recklessness of a tight-rope-walker by putting it in a perpetually unstable, perpetually broken equilibrium which he perpetually re-establishes by a light movement of the arm and hand. All his behaviour seems to us a game. He applies himself to chaining his movements as if they were mechanisms, the one regulating the other; his gestures and even his voice seem to be mechanisms; he gives himself the quickness and pitiless rapidity of things. He is playing,

he is amusing himself. But what is he playing? We need not watch long before we can explain it: he is playing at being a waiter in a cafe. There is nothing there to surprise us.

(Sartre, 2013 [1943], p. 82)

False forgiveness is, in this sense of Sartre's, 'waiterly'. In the inauthenticity, being seen as forgiving, and by implication, a 'good charitable person', becomes more important than experiencing the need to be forgiven. This brings us to the other existential concept touched upon earlier, also relevant to the depressive position version of forgiving – that of 'care' as a specific term in the philosophy of Heidegger.

Forgiveness and Heidegger's concept of *Sorge* (Care)

The concept of Care (*Sorge*) is a specialised term for Heidegger in *Being and Time* (2010 [1927]), and not one to be approached simply by applying what we understand by the term 'care' from other contexts, in which charity is emphasised, or by applying its everyday meaning of 'offering loving consideration'. For Heidegger it is not the 'loving self' that is at the core of the concept of Care; *Sorge* denotes the 'mattering' of the *existence* of human beings *as* fellow humans, beings whose existence as philosophising subjects, in relation to all questions of the human condition, is central, however hidden this may be beyond tangible concrete instances of care and fear. It is important to realise that for Heidegger, *Sorge* is an anguished state of being, and one not to be reduced to questions of desire, or even being loving. It is important to note that the mode of Being that Heidegger calls 'with-being' (*mitsein*) is also considered ontological, that is to say, 'of being'. Existentially speaking, relations of forgiveness and non-forgiveness take place within this mode of being-with in which the understanding and attunement to the fellow human element (Freud's *Nebenmensch*) may be more or less present, more or less nurtured.

Heidegger's concept of *Sorge* is consistent, in how it relates to psychically real forgiving, with Klein's concept of the depressive position, insofar as *without* the anxiety pertaining to the existence of the other as a fellow human being, whose existence as such (in the realm of being) matters, no forgiveness can be considered as real.

In the next, and final section, forgiving will be considered as it presents in the dénouement of *King Lear*, with a crucial moment of *anagnorisis* (a dramatic recognition) occurring between the King and his wronged daughter, Cordelia. Her forgiveness, the audience realises, has happened already within her. She does not (any longer) harbour the malice towards her father that he believes warrants the loss of her love for him, and the desire to end his life.

Cordelia and Lear: 'No cause, no cause'

Near the end of *King Lear*, the audience witnesses Cordelia renouncing in plain speech the need to punish her father or to break her bond with him. It was the simple expression of this bond of love that had been proved insufficient for his grandiosity in the opening scene of the play, and which had spurred him to reject and to disenfranchise her.

As Roy Schafer (2005, p. 389), from a psychoanalytic standpoint, and Edward Tayler (1990), from a literary and semiological point of view, have both discussed, the key communication from her, that Shafer takes to be a 'waiving of forgiveness' (as distinct from being forgiving), takes the form of a two-word phrase, 'No cause, no cause'. Tayler (ibid., p. 17) makes much in his fascinating paper of the distinction between this instance of repetition, and the mere use of repetitiousness for emphasis. He calls it an example of the 'proleptic form' of the play, as contrasted with the moving forward of its plot.

'Prolepsis' in this sense turns out to be an important concept for the ideas of this chapter, because in the 'plot' line a character can be said to have forgiven another character, as an 'event' in the storyline signalled in the narrative by (for example) a formal 'pardon' being uttered and accepted, but human contradiction and conflict is *maintained* in the resonances and clashes of the 'vertical', 'chord-like' dimension of the text as it is concurrent with prosodic features of communication (the rhythm and sound and pitch and gesture), and it is here that the real complexity, incompleteness and the sheer *hiatus* between professed attitudes and innermost states of the characters resides and makes itself known to the audience subliminally. In other words, the patterns being discussed involve communicative elements that are not primarily functioning as parts of a temporal progression of the story, but which have their effect (a) as 'preconceptions' foreshadowing aspects of the play that have not yet 'happened' in the narrative 'chain', but are 'prefigured forms' in which resonance and echo of words are more important than linear meaning,[3] and (b) as simultaneously occurring modifiers and 'commentaries' on what otherwise would pass in hearing with an unremarkable and commonplace 'everydayness'. It is the dimension that is mainly responsible for the complexity and longevity of these plays, a power beyond their story-telling.

All this is to make clear that, in King Lear, the main concealed 'proleptic form' is, as Tayler shows, the signifying pairs of terms pointing to the nothing of existence. The audience are all the time being led, unconsciously in the play, to the recognition that forgiveness, or no forgiveness, all the characters in the real undercurrent are moving in their various ways towards silence and the nothing. In Heidegger's terms, they are, behind it all, beings-toward-death, and as Tayler makes abundantly clear, this is what is at the root of Shakespeare's use of acoustic resonance in the signifiers: 'No' and 'Know', 'Known' and 'None', and 'Know a thing' and 'Nothing'. Here we have the fullest recognition of the rift between Knowing and Being.

In a moment it will be explained why this is of value in understanding the deepest stratum of Cordelia's statement: 'No cause, no cause'. Its meaning can be considered as a repudiation of the need for conventional pardoning in one dimension – the 'ontic', that is to say what can be known, agreed, managed – and at the same time, recognised as having an ontological reference. This possibility will be revisited and made clearer in the conclusion. But first, the 'No cause' scene between father and daughter will be described, following which Schafer's belief that it represents not a forgiving but a waiving of forgiveness will be questioned, and rejected in favour of an alternative conclusion, that in the fullness of the play, her forgiving is real, every bit as real as the love she had, at the beginning of the play, made plain to her father in the following terms. Saying she has been made unhappy by her father's insistence on oratory as a sign of love, she says:

I cannot heave
My heart into my mouth. I love your Majesty
According to my bond, no more nor less

The words resonate with lines from another play, *Loves' Labours' Lost*, with: 'A heavy heart bears not a nimble tongue', and 'Honest plain words best pierce the ear of grief'.

But sometimes plain speech is not heard. In a fit of temper, Lear had clearly heard *bond* as though she had merely said she loved him dutifully, and moved with alarming speed and violence immediately to disown and banish her. If only he had listened to the depth of meaning in the word 'bond' as she spoke it, its congruence with her whole manner, and had paid more attention to the superficiality of his other daughters' protestations of idealised 'love'. Nevertheless, at the dénouement of this arc there is a true recognition at last, which will now be set out.

The submissive self-serving flattery of Cordelia's 'yea-saying' sisters cannot masquerade as love indefinitely; Lear loses his remnants of integrity and loses his mind to paranoia, eventually falling into incoherent vagrancy on moorland where we meet him rainswept in a great thunderstorm with his Fool and the trusted Kent, disguised as a man named Caius.

Eventually, Cordelia meets her father, at the French camp near Dover. Before Lear wakes, Cordelia, speaks feelingly in a way that shows she has already worked through some of her most destructive feelings towards him. Had she not, she would not have spoken as she did of restoration and repair. Lear hears these surprising words as he is still fully expecting her dire revenge for his past actions:

O my dear father! Restoration hang
Thy medicine on my lips; and let this kiss
Repair those violent harms that my two sisters
Have in thy reverence made!

That Lear's truest daughter has a mind to forgive wrongs against her, and is minded towards repair more than revenge, has already been prefigured at the beginning of Act IV when she says, of her father's mental deterioration:

> All blest secrets,
> All you unpublish'd virtues of the earth,
> Spring with my tears! be aidant and remediate
> In the good man's distress! Seek, seek for him;
> Lest his ungovern'd rage dissolve the life
> That wants the means to lead it.

These words are the signs of her heartfelt urge to help him, 'Be aidant', she says, 'and remediate in the good man's distress!'

Remediate is a particularly apt word. It conjures the three signifiers (a) *to counteract* something, (b) *to provide a remedy for* something, and (c) to *take remedial action against* something. These terms can be seen to relate not only to Lear's evident parlous state, obvious from the text, but to Cordelia's own awareness of those forces within her that would otherwise join with her father's inwardly directed, self-dissolving rage. It may well be to counteract her own intimations of retributive rage that, in these lines, she summons her virtues in the service of reparation.

Though her father goes to kneel before her, Cordelia, at first unrecognised, says, 'No sir, you must not kneel', words that for us, reading this now, resonate with the lines quoted earlier from *Cymbeline*, 'Kneel not to me'. In both places, the hierarchical is renounced in favour of the lateralised *mitmensch* relationship between fellow human beings.

'I think this lady to be my child Cordelia', says Lear as his mental fog begins to clear. 'And so I am, I am', she responds.

Another double exposition, one in which it is open to us to recognise two Cordelias present at the same time, the lady (adult) and the child. Lear notices Cordelia's tears, he 'knows' that she does not love him, but this he cannot really know, whether there is 'no' love or love. Earlier he has pronounced the word 'love' as a virtual homonym for the French 'L'oeuf', again a signifier of 'Nought'. The King offers to take poison from her, because to his mind she has 'just cause' to be envenomed towards him, or even to take his life, and he will accept it.

Referring to Cordelia's sisters, Regan and Goneril, he says, 'You have some cause, they have not'. But she says simply (or not so simply), 'No cause, no cause'.

Now, Schafer's (2005, p. 389) interpretation is that Cordelia, by uttering these words, is *waiving* the question of guilt and forgiveness. In using this term, Schafer is indicating a setting-aside in a somewhat formal context, in line with the discussion earlier in the chapter on the distinction between pardoning and relenting malice. It is true that Cordelia is forsaking retribution, but is this to be interpreted as 'waiving forgiveness' or (as I would think) waiving the need for a pardon? As Tayler noted, the punning on 'No/Know' forms the major resonance of the deep structure of the play as a whole. Using it as a guiding principle, we might conclude not that Cordelia has waived anything except the formality of granting official pardon, just as at the outset of the play she had withheld a similarly 'official', on-demand valedictory paean to the King. This is a convincing arc in the drama in which we see the constancy and truth of the character of Cordelia.

We therefore have some grounds for considering that Cordelia has gone some way into the depressive position of her feelings towards her father, into her 'know–cause' relationship with him, within herself as an identity-defining object-relationship, in order to have worked through her conflict between love and vengefulness to the point where it could be contained sufficiently to allow her to retain a loving relationship to him in spite of any lingering pain and resentment. In this view, we would see her forgiveness as the uncertain but real outcome, provisional perhaps but nonetheless authentic for that fact, of having contained and worked through the storms of persecution and depression inevitable in his cruel rejection of her. Schafer is surely right when he questions whether forgiveness can ever be 'total', but this is similar to asking whether any of our motives, our mental achievements, our character, can ever be 'pure'. Dramaturgically, psychoanalytically, and existentially, nothing of the kind is feasible.

Schafer's point that forgiving and unforgiving elements of the self co-exist is a good one. In fact, what has been described as the mechanism of double exposition expresses this, as well as carrying the function of resonant multiple signification that is so characteristic of Shakespeare and Marlowe. It appears too in biblical texts of the Old Testament. In the story of Abraham and Isaac, for example, the Angel calls out to the father as he is about to sacrifice his son (in obeisance to the 'Lord' aspect of God): 'Abraham, Abraham' – the repetition can be heard in the aurally induced anticipations, stirred so readily in the oral tradition as indicating the simultaneous presence of 'two Abrahams'[4] – two fathers – one who would seek to preserve the life of his son, the other who derogates him to a position and consideration inferior to that in which he holds his God, who, in common with King Lear, demands always to be counted above every other Being in importance, even in the biblical example to the point of reinforcing self-importance through the willingness of the mortal to carry out child sacrifice.

Cordelia says 'No' to all this. She remains true to herself and suffers the consequence of denying the narcissist his extravagant praise at the beginning of the play, and at the end she remains true in her 'No cause'. This, I would maintain, is because in order to come to a properly informed judgement, according to which we choose whether to relent or to exact retribution, we have to *know ourselves*. This is what Cordelia has worked through, in herself, already – before her reunion with her father. She has come to 'Know cause' and has no need for being knelt-to and no need for Lear to attack himself for her sake. Implicit here is that those violent actions would themselves seed new adverse actions, they would create new causes. Relenting malice, then, on this basis, would in modern language have an element of 'enough already'. On this analysis, and on Tayler's reading of the play, this is forgiving. It needs no pardon, but it does require the working through of the pain of malice towards a loved object. This is all the more likely to have the ring of truth if behind it all, there is the recognition that is perhaps the most difficult to bear in Shakespeare's play, that whatever we come to in terms of doing right and being wronged, what is cause and what is the effect, what is just and what is unjust, what we deserve and what is owed, we come from nothing and we end in nothing, and everything ends in silence.

Notes

1 *Þæt he.smeage.hwæt him sy to donne & to forganne* (a1000: Laws of Cnut §85 in B. Thorpe Anc. Laws Eng. (1840) I. 424).
2 Absence of the quality of being compassionate; pitilessness; the absence of fellow-feeling and of sorrow for another; without compassion [OED].
3 The relationship between proleptic form and narrative progression corresponds to the distinction in structural linguistics between the dimensions termed 'paradigmatic/ synchronic' and 'syntagmatic/diachronic'.
4 As discussed by Judith Elkan (1989) The binding of Isaac: A psycho-analytic perspective. *European Judaism: A Journal for the New Europe*, 22, 2 (Winter 89/Spring 90): 26–35.

References

Coleridge, S. T. (1997). *The Complete Poems of Samuel Taylor Coleridge*. London: Penguin Classics.

Elkan, J. (1989). The binding of Isaac: A psycho-analytic perspective. *European Judaism: A Journal for the New Europe*, 22, 2 (Winter 89/Spring 90): 26–35.

Heidegger, M. (2010 [1927]). *Being and Time* (tr. J. Stambaugh; rev. D. J. Schmidt). Albany, NY: State University of New York Press.

Klein, M. (1946). Notes on some schizoid mechanisms. *International Journal of Psycho-Analysis*, 27: 99–110. 1952 version in *Envy and Gratitude and Other Works* (ed. M. Khan). The International Psycho-Analytical Library, Vol. 104, pp. 1–24. London: Hogarth, 1975.

Klein, M. (1952). The origins of transference. *Int. J. Psycho-Anal.*, 33: 433–438.

Lucretius (Titus Lucretius Carus). (50 BCE). *De rerum natura* (On the nature of things) (tr. W. E. Leonard). London: Forgotten Books, 2007.

Morgan, M. (2018). *A Couple State of Mind: Psychoanalysis of Couples and the Tavistock Relationships Model*. London: Routledge.

Riviere, J. (1936). On the genesis of psychical conflict in earliest infancy. *International Journal of Psycho-Analysis*, 17: 395–422.

Sartre, J.-P. (2013 [1943]). *Being and Nothingness* (tr. H. E. Barnes). Abingdon: Routledge.

Shakespeare, W. (c. 1901). *The Complete Works of William Shakespeare* (ed. R. G. White). New York: Sully and Kleinteich.

Schafer, R. (2005). *Cordelia, Lear, and Forgiveness. J. Amer. Psychoanal. Assn.*, 53, 2: 389–409.

Tayler, E. W. (1990) *King Lear and Negation*. English Literary Renaissance 20.1 (1990), pp. 17–39. London: Wiley Online Library.

Chapter 3

The developmental importance of forgiveness in psychoanalysis and Buddhism

Hiroshi Amino

Introduction

A lot of novels, plays and films touch upon the issue of forgiveness and the unforgivable, where the latter often carries an especially intense emotional impact. However, it is by no means easy to clarify what kinds of emotional processes are involved in forgiving and not forgiving.

Akhtar suggests that forgiving comes after active intent (Akhtar, 2002). He states:

> forgiveness comprises two mental operations, namely, the resolution of an unpleasant angry emotion within oneself, and a changed attitude toward an offending party.
>
> (p. 177)

Akhtar's statement implies that forgiveness is a mature and advanced emotional process in which one can experience and stay with intense and difficult feelings without resorting to impulsive actions, and at the same time one can put oneself into the shoes of a perpetrator. It is not very difficult to imagine a lot of developmental hurdles which can get in the way of achieving forgiveness.

I would like first to pay special attention to what prevents forgiveness from being accomplished emotionally. Here, I will bring in my own clinical experience to illustrate the profound difficulty of being able to forgive, especially in the case of traumatised experiences. I will then carry out a further discussion of the important functions of compassion and forgiveness as facilitating factors, referring to a Buddhist story by Ajātashatru. Finally, I will put forward my own thoughts about when and how compassion and forgiveness can be facilitating and hampering for emotional development.

Difficult pathway to forgiveness

Basic concept of development of primitive states

From the beginning of life, as human beings, we undergo the developmental task of moving from unintegration or fragmentation towards integration. This

DOI: 10.4324/9781003364313-3

is not by any means an easy pathway. We face a lot of developmental difficulties. Although there are various emotional difficulties at each point in the process of development, it can be said that there are two fundamental aspects that have mainly been paid attention to in the history of psychoanalysis. The first is how to hold oneself together enough so as not to fall apart in one's subjective experience. The excess of frustration and impingement beyond one's capacity to tolerate it – such as trauma in early childhood, and especially cumulative trauma – can have detrimental damage on the self (Khan, 1963). The other is how to deal with one's own destructiveness, coupled with the concomitant guilt (where the two obviously intermingle with each other), especially when experiencing frustration and pain. While Akhtar suggests that "the resolution of an unpleasant angry emotion within oneself" is the most important mental process in accomplishing the state of forgiveness, I would like to suggest that it is essential to work through the two main obstacles of too much impingement and deprivation and of destructiveness and guilt, which I will now focus on in some depth.

Too much impingement and deprivation from the environment

The first crucial developmental task for humans is the process of integration from unintegration or fragmentation, as a person comes to own his instinctual drives and body (Winnicott, 1949). At this stage, it is essential for a baby to be protected from any unmanageable impingement, so that he can gradually obtain the sense of a continuity of being (Winnicott, 1961). If a continual and unbearable impingement is imposed on him, he will constantly have to react to the environment, with the result that he will be unable to establish a basic sense of continuity of being, or he will become very fragile, even if he manages a partial sense of continuity. Such an impingement may relate to his mother (the primary carer), who pushes her own needs, desire, mess, and unbearable feelings down into him.

I would like to draw special attention to the idea that deprivation, for the premature self, will also feel like an impingement; it exacerbates the terror of physical annihilation and the massive demand of the instinctual drive, which becomes too much and too unbearable for the premature self. As a result, the infant is unable to connect to his own body, his physical sensations, and his drive impulses, as a part of himself – they may end up feeling like devastating and formidable external monsters out to destroy him. Even if some integration takes place, albeit very fragile, the infant may become victim to the terror of falling apart at any moment. The unbearable pain, the revival of a terror of annihilation, distress, and agony, and a sense of emptiness and nothingness – all of which have a close link with physical sensations – threaten the premature self. I would like to call this state primary anguish. Winnicott further describes a certain anxiety state where the fear of breakdown impinges on the self; this happens because the premature self has not been able to experience the breakdown that already happened in early life, so it appears later on as the threat of annihilation and falling apart (Winnicott, 1974).

Destructiveness and guilt

Even if the premature self survives under the onslaught of primary anguish, he then has other formidable emotional experiences of rage, fury, hate, hostility, destructiveness and murderousness. I shall call this the primary emotional explosion. Bion also suggests that if the mother fails to receive the baby's unbearable physical and emotional experiences, the baby might well end up hating all his emotional and physical experiences, which is not far from hating his own life (Bion, 1959).

It is Klein who emphasises the crucial developmental importance of bringing together several different aspects of oneself and of one's emotional views of others, which she names the depressive position; this state involves two massive tasks (Klein, 1935). The first is to acknowledge emotionally that the mother, who gives the infant satisfaction and warmth, also frustrates and hurts the child, which inevitably happens in daily life. The second is for the infant to own both parts of himself: the one that loves and the other that hates the mother, following frustration and anxiety. The infant is doomed to experience fear and anxiety – that he might destroy his mother due to his destructiveness that comes from unbearable frustration in his subjective experience, rage and fury. This can also cause his sense of guilt, which can trigger and facilitate the wish for reparation when tolerated.

Reparation

It is Henri Rey who not only emphasises the importance of reparation in human development but also makes a link with forgiveness (Rey, 1986). His significant clinical experiences with those patients in primitive states of mind led him to differentiate between *reparation proper* and *omnipotent reparation*. It is proper reparation that can help one stay with pain and guilt in the depressive position and function in a creative way. Paying attention to the reparative function of the penis in a primitive form, Rey suggests that when the infant faces the damaged object in his very early life, he resorts to the penis – which is significant because it becomes the replacement of the damaged object, but also because the penis gives to the damaged object its life. He argues further that the penis might well be "the first, amongst the first, universal representation of objects at the concrete level" (p. 218). Therefore, the penis plays an important function in representations and symbolism, and therefore proper reparation.

However, Rey adds:

> The more the object ... is damaged, the more omnipotent, not potent, the penis must be, and because of the space-centred level of thought, omnipotence is expressed in hugeness of erection and size ... defence is ... to deny the damaged or lost object by means of the megalomanic or manic penis.
>
> (p. 220)

This leads to a more manic and omnipotent reparation, where the patient's damaged object must be brought to a perfectly undamaged state in order to deny his own destructiveness; this in turn increases the sense of terror because of the denial of internal facts. Thus, the manic and omnipotence reparation creates a vicious circle.

Grievance and entitlement

When a person faces their own destructive impulses and concomitant fear of violence on their objects, the level of guilt might become too unbearable – a state which must be protected against at any cost. In my analytic experiences, I have seen those patients who are often drawn into the arena of grievance towards objects which inevitably cause frustration and pain. Steiner suggests:

> Once established, this type of retreat is very difficult to relinquish partly because the grievance provides a focus and purpose for the patient and partly because of other sources of gratification such as those related to triumph and to masochism. In some cases, the patient appears to "feed" or "nurse" the grievance and gets gratification by "keeping old wounds open".
>
> (Steiner, 1993, p. 76)

Grievance can give one stability, direction, and gratification, while it can also be used to protect oneself from fear of breakdown and unbearable emotional experiences. It can feel as if grievance gives one an ultimate source of survival. To get stuck with grievance means there is no possibility of reparation, which results in a developmental halt.

My clinical experiences have demonstrated that grievance is at times escalated into a sense of entitlement. Several patients of mine claim that they are entitled to be given what "they believe they need" because they have not been given what was supposed to be provided for them due to their sense of deprivation, neglect, and abuse. This emotional state of entitlement also works to protect the patient from both the difficult, emotional experiences of the primary anguish, and from the primary emotional explosion. I think this can become like a violent cocoon, from which the patient cannot move easily, and which halts the emotional development, preventing any potentially fulfilling relationships and hence creativity.

Clinical material of entitlement of "unconditional love"

I shall move to clinical material to demonstrate how a particular entitlement of "unconditional love" partly spares one from primary anguish and guilt, which in turn makes it impossible to develop an intimate relationship.

Ms L is in her mid-30s and was in her analysis for four years. At the beginning of the analysis, she was often silent or talked in a rather mechanical manner, as if her feelings were frozen. What then gradually emerged in the analytic process was her experience that her mother did not love her but hated her, since her mother felt that having Ms L had ruined her life completely. Ms L felt that her father was devoted to her and loved her, but when he was with her mother he turned his back on Ms L as if he had completely forgotten her. This left Ms L feeling totally isolated, excluded, abandoned, and emptied out, as if the world was falling apart.

Ms L often fluctuated between two states in the early stage of her analysis. In one state, she openly expressed her relief whenever she felt understood by me, as if she was actually on my lap. Yet if she felt I could not understand her as much as she wanted me to, or when the end of the session, the weekend and the breaks approached, she became increasingly hostile and hateful towards me, claiming that I did not care about her because she knew she was unlovable and worthless. She was often suicidal. When expressing her hostility and hatred of others and of me, she would shout in the room. With the volume of her voice, it felt to me as if she was claiming how big she was.

In the Friday session I shall present here, she began talking about a story in an adventure book for children where there were always people coming to stay with the main character – siblings, friends, and a girlfriend. She was aware that she did not have anyone like them in her life. Society had not given her anything very much. With a depressive tone of voice, she claimed that she could not see any point in her life. She added that she had watched a documentary of primitive tribes. A tribal chief had said that no one should have a child if it was not to be loved. A sense of deep sadness and pain prevailed in the room. I found myself almost feeling like crying for her.

I suggested that it seemed a part of her heart and soul that had been frozen had gradually thawed out, which brought up pain in a more real way. Therefore, the external cold weather and darkness (as it was in the middle of winter), and her experience with people who left her alone, including at the end of each session with me, hit her as an unbearable blow both physically and emotionally. At what I suggested, she became weepy and seemed pained, and was suddenly furious and resentful. She raised her voice excitedly, saying how people were not giving her what she really needed. They were just cockroaches who could not do anything for her at all. Fluctuating between a deep sense of sadness and pain on the one hand, and reproach, condescension, and bitterness on the other, she seemed to find this torturous stuckness unbearable. She appeared triumphant, strongly emphasising her need for unconditional love, without which she did not have any hope in life, and she wriggled on the couch as if she was fighting in the area of emotional contact.

I brought up the sense that the more pain and agony came to the surface the more vulnerable and unbearable she felt, as if she was falling apart in a terrifying manner. I added that she had to resort to the idea of unconditional love to protect herself, but it led her to feel more alone with pain. She became furious again and talked about how her mother had not loved her at all: she should have given her unconditional love. Shouting, Ms L said she wanted to slice up her mother and make her into a mass of meat, and she deserved this. The violent fantasy seemed to have two different meanings: on the one hand, her violence became more accessible to her own ego and to me; on the other hand, the fantasy seemed to have the effect of pulling her together, preventing her feeling of falling apart through pain, agony and emptiness, and through guilt for her destructiveness.

She emphasised how she was entitled to unconditional love. She went on to say that people must stay with her and continue to love her, no matter how destructive, condescending, insulting and violent she became to them. They must continue to love her. Although some people had been able to stay with her, no one had in the end been able to when she shouted at them about how worthless and useless they were. The world was just shit. I suggested that she seemed to feel as if I was destroying her by drawing attention to how her hope for unconditional love actually isolated her because any closeness and contact with others, including me in the sessions, might well deteriorate into pain and guilt. I added that her hope for unconditional love led her to kill me off and resulted in more despair.

This calmed her down and she fell into silence for a while. She then said that she knew she did not hate people as much as she had done before. Yet she did not feel she was wanted, especially when she was in pain and sadness. People just left her alone. That was what she at least perceived. I suggested that she also felt left alone by me by the approaching weekend, so that I was also not giving her what she needed. She became sad and told me that although her analysis helped her a lot, it had not and would not give her what she needed – "unconditional love". She could not accept that people, including me, would not stay with her when she needed them. She could not understand how people could leave her alone when she was in pain and dying. I felt she implied that I was not sacrificing myself enough.

Discussion for the clinical material: search for "unconditional love"

I shall start focusing on the role of the claim of "unconditional love" through the clinical vignette here. It is very clear that whenever she became more able to get in touch with pain, agony, and emptiness, which I think related to her subjective experience of deprivation in her early life, she either resorted to condescension, violent fantasy, or the longing for unconditional love, which she claimed she was entitled to have because she had not been given it in her life. She carried the hope that once she was given unconditional love it would wipe out all pain, agony, emptiness, fury, murderousness, and guilt, from which she would be completely free. Therefore, her search for unconditional love meant turning away from her own impulses and devastating primitive feelings.

I would also like to draw attention to the fact that whenever she felt understood, and people, including me in her analysis, could stay with her in her stormy emotional turbulence, it would cause intense primitive feelings of primary anguish, and a primary emotional explosion which felt unbearable, as if it was destroying her. Therefore, she would have to destroy those warm relationships instead. This caused an impossible dilemma and vicious circle. No matter how much she longed for love and care, whenever people around her tried to give her support by being devoted to her and making great efforts to stay with her, as in the analytic sessions, it would cause more devastating and unbearable feelings, which she had to destroy. This in turn caused more unbearable guilt. She could not help but drive away those who cared for her, or kill them off. This combination resulted in her conceiving people who tried to care as abusers who caused pain and agony. In this sense, the offer of love and care could only lead to further destruction, which made her feel that she was deprived of love again. This vicious circle would not lead to development and forgiveness. Instead, bitterness, fury and entitlement to unconditional love reigned, hampering any development.

However, it needs to be noted that her hostility and hatefulness towards people were mitigated and appeased in the analytic process, and she clearly mentioned that she did not hate people as much as before. What alleviated and made more manageable her hatred and hostility? I would like to discuss what can be an important factor in that process.

Forgiveness and compassion

Importance of forgiveness in emotional development

Klein emphasises the importance of reparation for emotional development – in order to deal with the depressive feelings that arise from destroying one's object, at least in phantasy (Klein, 1935). It is Rey who makes a link between reparation and forgiveness:

> [For reparation] forgiveness is a key concept, for nobody who has not forgiven can be expected to feel forgiven. Lack of forgiveness means the desire for revenge on the objects remains active and has not forgiven ... Only when the super-ego becomes less cruel, less demanding of perfection, is the ego capable of accepting an internal object which is not

perfectly repaired, can accept compromise, forgive and be forgiven, and experience hope and gratitude.

(Rey, 1986, p. 226)

Steiner develops Rey's idea:

... forgiveness is an integral element of mourning, and is therefore necessary for psychic growth. Forgiving others for their hurtful actions and forgiving oneself for having caused pain to others are crucial to moving on in life and to opening oneself to new experiences. An inability or unwillingness to forgive keeps one tied to the past and impedes development.

(Steiner, 2018, p. 206)

Steiner and Rey both think of the connection between forgiveness and the acceptance of imperfection and mourning. In other words, all things, or all people, including oneself, remain damaged, and one has damaged others to some extent. It needs to learn and accomplish to sustain both fulfilled and flourished aspects and damaged ones of his objects and himself, for which it has had to go through a lot of developmental processes as discussed already.

Compassion, forgiveness, and reparation through Buddhist Sutras

What can trigger and facilitate forgiveness in the human mind? This important and invaluable question reminds me of the ancient story of Ajātashatru in Buddhist Sutras; scriptures many of which are regarded as records oral teachings of Buddha. I shall visit the tale first. It has different versions in different Buddhist Sutras.[1] [2] [3] [4] I will quote the following aspects that are in common in all the different Buddhist Sutras and which relate to the current theme. I would like to divide the tale into four parts.

1   The parents attempt to kill Ajātashatru as a baby
2   The imprisonment and murder of his father and attempted murder of his mother
3   Remorse and persecutory guilt through physical illness
4   Forgiveness by Buddha

The parents attempt to kill Ajātashatru as a baby

Ajātashatru was a king of the Haryanka dynasty of Magadha in North India in the early 4th century BCE. He was the son of King Bimbisara. What is in common in all Sutras is that his parents tried to kill Ajātashatru as a baby, either at the point of his birth or immediately after, due to their fear that what they had done before – their murder and greed – might, by fate, lead the baby to kill them or become a monster. In one Sutra, the mother, the Queen, gave birth to him from the top of a tower, and when he was born he fell to the ground; he survived but his little finger remained broken, damaged.

Imprisonment and murder of his father and attempted murder of his mother

Ajātashatru grew up as arrogant, violent, greedy, and relentless. He was also told by one of Buddha's opponents that his parents had tried to kill him immediately after his birth. Due to his sense of entitlement and grievance against his parents, he forcefully took over the Crown from his father and imprisoned him in order to starve him to death. In the end, his father died. Ajātashatru was also murderous to his mother who tried to rescue her husband. He almost killed her, yet one of his ministers persuaded him not to by saying that there had been no king in all of history who had killed his own mother.

Remorse and persecutory guilt through physical illness

After the murder of his father and attempted murder of his mother, Ajātashatru's body become covered by masses of sores that emitted an unbearable odour, so no one was able to approach him. His mother was the exception. The Queen was in deep remorse for what she had done to Ajātashatru after his birth. She tried to look after him by tirelessly applying cream to his sores, which made him feel emotionally relieved, but his skin sores got worse. He started to feel deep remorse about the murder, and he told his mother that the sores were caused not by his body but his mind. Therefore, no one could cure them.

Forgiveness by Buddha

There are two different stories developed in different Sutras. In one story, the Queen became desperate because no matter how much she tried to look after her son, his sores did not get better. She went to Buddha in despair. His sincere attitude of listening to the Queen gradually helped her become aware, in a more emotionally real way, of her own crime of the attempted murder of her son and its consequences. Through Buddha's forgiving attitude, she managed to feel remorse and guilt. She went back to her son and resumed her care, which this time helped her son's sores improve.

There is another version of the story. Ajātashatru heard the voice of his father from Ten, the world above, which frightened him and his sores deteriorated. His father felt sorry for his son and wanted to rescue him, having forgiven him for the murder. His father's voice advised him to go to meet Buddha, and Ajātashatru did so. Buddha told Ajātashatru that he would stay with him until he was enlightened by forgiveness, which led Ajātashatru to come to terms with his own crimes and sins. Buddha mentioned his own sin because, although he had known that Ajātashatru would kill his father to become the king, he himself had not been able to stop it. If Ajātashatru would go to hell, Buddha himself must have the same fate. Buddha knew that human beings are fundamentally sinners, committing crimes in order to live. Only by coming to terms with one's sins and crimes can one reach enlightenment. Ajātashatru's skin disease improved and he came to terms with his committed crime.

Ajātashatru and Oedipus

There are a lot of similarities between this story of Ajātashatru and Oedipus. In both stories, the parents tried to kill their son through fear that he would kill them because of the crimes they had committed. The son survives and instead kills his father, which gives rise to a disastrous physical state: a lethal plague in Thebes in the story of Oedipus, and the skin disease in the story of Ajātashatru. Both are stories about seriously traumatised children who act out their murderousness, resulting in unbearable guilt.

What happens next is very different in the two stories. On the one hand, in the tale of Oedipus, Jocasta, the mother and later the wife of Oedipus, commits suicide, and Oedipus blinds himself when what's happened becomes clear. For both Oedipus and Jocasta, guilt, pain, and shame are so unbearable and persecutory that the emotional experiences cannot be processed. The only outcome is further physical punishment where Jocasta's body and Oedipus's perceptive organ – his eyes – are destroyed, so that they will not have to experience or even see their internal worlds and emotional experience. It can be said that in the myth of Oedipus a fatal plague happens far away from the characters, which implies that the projection of guilt is too distant to even touch it slightly. On the other hand, in the tale of Ajātashatru, both he and the Queen are able to move out of the unbearable persecution and concomitant physical illness, and come to terms with their crime of murder, their guilt and pain, and this leads to proper reparation. Therefore, the difference between the two tales is striking. I would like to discuss what facilitates Ajātashatru's development.

Facilitating object's behaviour

I would like to pay special attention to the *guilt* and the early trauma in Ajātashatru's tale. As we have seen, after the murder of his father and attempted murder of his mother, Ajātashatru develops skin sores which emit odours that prevent anyone from approaching him except his mother. His skin illness can be thought of as partly the expression of self-punishment due to his guilt for murdering his father, his sense of entitlement to the Crown and his attempted murder of his mother. The skin sores can be also construed as the re-emergence of his early life of emptiness and isolation, with the pain, agony, and despair of not being loved, but also of being hated and rejected by everyone, left alone with his wounds.

His mother's care for him seems to lead Ajātashatru to become more able to feel the guilt that gave rise to the persecution and hopelessness at the beginning, as "the sores were caused not by his body but his mind. Therefore, no one could cure them". His mother's later care for him after the encounter with Buddha in one story, and both his father's and then Buddha's forgiveness for him in the other version, facilitates his sense of remorse, opening a door for reparation. His early traumatic experience becomes less agonising and more manageable. Thus, he is able to stay with his guilt and early trauma without resorting to the physical symptom, so his skin illness is cured. One can say that his psychosomatic experience of skin sores would have its emotional representation through his experience with his parents and Buddha.

What then facilitates such an important emotional development? I think that neither the Queen nor Ajātashatru himself would have been able to stay with their own guilt, primary anguish, and primary emotional explosion, without the devotion and willingness of the objects to stay with them and empathise. I therefore would like to suggest that it is the compassion of objects that may be able to alleviate the primary anguish and make the primary emotional explosion less violent and destructive. As a result, guilt becomes less persecutory and punitive; the feelings become more manageable so that they can be experienced emotionally rather than expressed physically through psychosomatic symptoms.

Facilitating factor 1: compassion by objects

I would like to touch upon the psychoanalytic understanding of compassion. Freud suggests the origin of compassion:

> during the copulation in the primal scene he had observed the penis disappear, that he had felt compassion for his father on that account, and had rejoiced at the reappearance of what he thought had been lost. Moreover, the narcissistic origin of compassion (which is confirmed by the word itself) is here quite unmistakably revealed. (German "*Mitleid*", literally "suffering with")
>
> (Freud, 1918, p. 88)

This demonstrates that a boy actively projects his own fear and anguish of castration onto his father through his observation and feels the pain and suffering that he imagines his father would be experiencing through the identification with him. Therefore, he becomes relieved and blissful when his father's penis is not damaged but intact as if it was his own penis. Freud suggests the narcissistic origin of compassion in this process. For the boy seems to have been convinced that what he imagined in his illusion would be his father's actual experience. He did not differentiate between his father and himself. Therefore, he seems to feel there is no difference between his illusion and the fact.

I would also like to emphasise that the boy's reaction to his observation illustrates his passionate love for his father, which is part of the origin of his identification; being and becoming him. Compassion is therefore an emotional process where one is actively involved with an other's emotional suffering, putting oneself in their shoes with love and passion; this creates the state of "suffering with".

Eshel suggests that "Compassion, from the Latin *com*, 'with' + *pati*, 'to suffer', means to suffer with (and, I would add, to suffer within), to be present within another's suffering and become at-one with it" (Eshel, 2013, p. 933). It is Bion who emphasises the importance of compassion of analysts when he suggests that "I do not think we could tolerate our work – painful as it often is for both us and our patients – without compassion" (Bion, 1991, p. 522). I think that the psychoanalyst's compassion for his patient can be construed as his capacity to stay with and feel his patient's emotional experiences of primary anguish and the primary emotional explosion with guilt, while sustaining warmth and concern for his patient, which might be called passion and love for human beings. He is in a way "suffering with" his patient.

I would like to suggest that compassion has got different layers developmentally. As suggested above, its origin can be seen as narcissistic by passion and love while experiencing no separateness between himself and his objects. When the ego and the self develops maturely, he can be "suffering with" his objects by being and becoming them emotionally while sustaining the sense that they are separate and therefore what he imagines and feels they are experiencing in his illusion might not be their experience. I think this emotional awareness of differentiation between the two with compassion is an essential mental functioning as analysts.

I would like to add that compassion becomes more important for those whose traumatised experiences overwhelm their premature self in early development due to the level of pain and anguish that they are suffering. They often experience that they were not only unlovable but even a nuisance that would have destroyed their parents' life through the introjection of their primary neglectful and accusatory objects, which make their self-more fragile with self-loathing (Fairbairn, (1944 [1952]; Ferenczi, 1949). Steiner states:

> No longer pre-occupied with the exposure of traumatic memories, the task for the analyst became that of trying to receive and understand both

verbal and non-verbal communications from his patient and to recognise how trauma was experienced and responded to.

(Steiner, 2018, p. 563)

I think Steiner suggests the importance of analyst's compassionate willingness to be suffering with his traumatised patients through his attempt to understand their traumatic experiences emotionally. The analyst's compassion can be seen as an important facilitating factor for his patients' emotional development.

Facilitating factor 2: forgiveness by objects

I have discussed the potentially facilitating function of the object's compassion to help the patient tolerate and make more manageable the traumatised early experiences, along with the primary anguish, primary emotional explosion, and concomitant guilt. I would like to further explore the facilitating function of the object's forgiveness.

As I have discussed, forgiveness means one does not take revenge on others' hurtful actions but instead accepts that certain damage is irreparable. I think, unless one puts oneself in the perpetrator's shoes and "suffers with" him, one cannot reach a sense of forgiveness. Hence, I think forgiveness can be considered as a particular expression of compassion.

I would like to go back to my clinical experience with Ms L here. As the analytic process went by she started to say that she knew she did not hate people as much as she had done. What triggered such an important emotional shift in her? I would like to pay a special attention to the fact that while she kept on blaming, becoming contemptuous, and attacking others and me in her analysis relentlessly and ruthlessly, I did not lose sight of the underlying primary anguish that she would have felt was unmanageable or even threatening to her life emotionally. This owed to the fact that she had managed to communicate that disastrous emotional state to me. My emotional understanding of those experiences of her helped me put myself into her shoes, sustain the compassion of her and therefore remain able to forgive what she had been doing to me relentlessly. The compassion and forgiveness on my part enabled me to continue to attempt to understand her emotional experiences, without taking revenge or disregarding her feelings. They helped me see how her pursuit of unconditional love aimed to protect her from the primary anguish while giving her power through the entitlement which could be partly seen as an expression of her primary explosion. Yet her hope for unconditional love led her to kill me off and resulted in more despair, which intensified her primary anguish. This emotional understanding of mine about her state and my attempt to share them with her into words, to the degree of which I would have thought could be manageable, helped her become more able to see what was happening inside her in a more real way. I think this helped her become aware that her emotions and feelings would not destroy everything but be tolerable enough to lead the understanding, therefore emotional development. These might well have alleviated the primary anguish and mitigated the primary emotional explosion. Therefore, I think her degree of hatred and hostility towards others could have been ameliorated.

I would like to move on to see if there is any particular function for emotional development through the forgiveness of objects. In 1931, Kosawa, the founder of the Japanese Psychoanalytic Society, suggests there are two types of guilt following the tale of Ajātashatru (Kosawa, 1931): guilt from fear of punishment and guilt from being forgiven. He calls the former forced guilt and the latter spontaneous guilt – a state of repentance. He makes the further suggestion that spontaneous guilt for feeling murderous towards one's parents would be dissolved by the self-sacrifice of the parents.

Forgiveness: facilitating development or regression into omnipotence

What Kosawa suggests meets with my clinical experiences, where forgiveness by others can facilitate guilt. Yet I think there is some problem behind this. I would like to compare my own clinical experience of Ms L, who claimed she was entitled to "unconditional love", and the tale of Ajātashatru. Ms L pursued the state of "unconditional love" because she claimed it would save her from any sense of the unbearable emotional experience of primary anguish. She made a demand on her objects that they would have to accept and bear any violence from her and that they should still love her. She openly made a demand for sacrifice on her objects. I think the sense of guilt, the emergence of the need for others and of envy – all of which could be intensified if they persevered through her violence and unbearable feelings even for a while with compassion and forgiveness as that could evoke the sense of need for them inside her – would drive her to destroy the objects further in order to avoid such emotional experiences. She could not own or bear those difficult feelings yet.

Whereas when we look at the tale of Ajātashatru, what is significant and different to my patient, Ms L, is that he already started owning the feeling of guilt, despair and hopelessness. Yet Ajātashatru could not bear to metabolise such emotional experiences and instead developed the illness in his body – the skin sores. He experienced hopelessness and deep pain at what he had done and so his guilt remained persecutory. In his book *The Kyōgyōshinshō*, Shinran (1973), one of the most famous Buddhist monks in Japan in the 13th century, suggests that the reason why Ajātashatru became repentant with the help of the compassion and forgiveness of the Buddha, was that he had already begun accessing the difficult feelings in himself. It can therefore be said that he was at the threshold of accepting what he had done and the emotional experiences he had suffered, and he was moving towards remorse.

He was able to feel moved, touched, and cared for by his mother's and Buddha's compassion and forgiveness, which facilitated his emotional development of reparation and forgiveness of himself. Therefore, I suggest that the objects' forgiveness and compassion can facilitate the emotional development of reparation only when one starts accepting those difficult and unbearable feelings. At this point, one might be able to introject the objects' function into oneself to experience remorse and forgive the damage done.

However, if the primary anguish, the primary emotional explosion and its concomitant guilt, feel too monstrous and unbearable, the others' forgiveness might evoke these feelings too strongly and trigger regression, often malignant, as Ms L demonstrated. If an analyst only relied on his compassion and forgiveness, this might well drive a patient like Ms L and the analyst in a vicious circle, where the destructive omnipotent entitlement and excitement of the patient, along with the masochistic sacrifice of the analyst, could lead the couple into a sado-masochistic tie. I think that with Ms L, who gets stuck in manic and omnipotent reparation with entitlement, it is crucial for the analyst to become firm and robust enough to describe what the patient is doing and how it destroys any potential fruitful relationship, while both forgiving their relentless attack by them and being compassionate about the pain, agony, and utter emptiness, along with the rage, murderousness, and guilt. Therefore, I would like to suggest that the objects' forgiveness can lead to both directions.

I would like to summarise my argument that the objects' compassion and forgiveness are in general essential for the development of human minds, especially traumatised minds. The objects' compassion can help the primary anguish become less devastating and the primary emotional explosion and concomitant guilt become less destructive and persecutory. The objects' forgiveness can facilitate the subject's guilt for the damage done both in actions and fantasy. Therefore, the objects' compassion and forgiveness can help human beings develop towards proper reparation and creativity. Yet if one's main internal world is dominated by the perverse omnipotent demand of the object's self-sacrifice to spare oneself from any unbearable emotional experience, the object's forgiveness can exacerbate the demand and an eternal vicious circle arises with sacrifice and masochism.

Conclusion

I have discussed the importance of the state of forgiveness for the development of human minds that is essential to reach reparation proper. I have brought in my own clinical experience in order to describe what hampers the development towards forgiveness in terms of both the unbearable sense of guilt caused by the damage to the objects and the early trauma. Referring to the Buddhist tale of Ajātashatru, I moved on to look at how the objects' compassion and forgiveness can facilitate the subject's forgiveness. Finally, I discussed how compassion can alleviate pain, distress, and agony, and help hate, hostility, destructiveness, and murderousness become less violent and guilt less persecutory. Forgiveness can facilitate guilt. Yet for those who cannot bear guilt, forgiveness can only exacerbate the omnipotent demand for reparation and the entitlement. It is therefore crucial for the analyst to sustain a firm and robust attitude in describing the dynamics to the patient while keeping compassion in mind. I think the discussion of compassion and forgiveness is really important to understand the facilitating factors for the development of human minds; I hope this chapter can widen the interest and understanding of them.

Note

1 There are various tales of Ajātashatru in Buddhist Sutras. I will mainly follow and quote the three Sutras.
2 Tripiṭaka of Buddhism in India.
3 Mahaparinibbana Sutra, which is one of the Tathāgatagarbha sūtras of Mahāyāna Buddhism that originated in Andhra, India, and was substantially expanded in China and imported to Japan. It became the one of the main sutras in Buddhism in Japan.
4 Kanmuryoju Kyo (*The Sutra of Contemplation on the Buddha of Immeasurable Life*) is one of the Mahayana Buddhist sutras in Japan.

References

Akhtar, S. (2002). Forgiveness: Origins, Dynamics, Psychopathology, and Technical Relevance. *Psychoanalytic Quarterly*, 71(2), 175–212.

Bion, W.R. (1959). Attacks on Linking. *Int. J. Psych-Anal.* 40, pp. 308–315. Also in W.R. Bion, *Second Thoughts* (London; Karnac), pp. 93–109; and in *Melanie Klein Today I, Mainly Theory*, pp. 87–101.

Bion, W.R. (1991). *A Memoir of the Future*, III. London: Karnac.

Eshel, O. (2013). Patient-Analyst "Withness": On Analytic "Presencing," Passion, and Compassion in States of Breakdown, Despair, and Deadness. *Psychoanalytic Quarterly*, 82(4), 925–963.

Fairbairn, W.D. (1944 [1952]). Endopsychic Structure Considered in Terms of Object-Relationships. *Psychoanalytic Studies of the Personality*. London: Tavistock Publications Limited, pp. 82–136.

Ferenczi, S. (1949). Confusion of the Tongues Between the Adults and the Child. *Int. J. Psycho-Anal.*, 30, 225–230.

Freud, S. (1918). From the History of an Infantile Neurosis. *The Standard Edition of the Complete Psychological Works of Sigmund Freud, Volume XVII* (1917–1919): *An Infantile Neurosis and Other Works*. London: Hogarth, pp. 1–124.

Khan, M. (1963). *The Concept of Cumulative Trauma. The Privacy of the Self.* London: Hogarth, pp. 42–58.

Klein, M. (1935). A Contribution to the Psychogenesis of Manic-Depressive States. *International Journal of Psychoanalysis*, 16, pp. 145–174. Reprinted in *The Writings of Melanie Klein I*, pp. 344–369. London: Hogarth.

Kosawa, H. (1931). Two Kinds of Guilt Feelings – The Ajase Complex. *Japanese J. Am. Psychoanal. Assoc.*, 1(1), 1954.

Rey, J. H. (1986). Reparation. *Universals of Psychoanalysis in the Treatment of Psychotic and Borderline States: Factors of Space-time and Language*. London: Free Association Books, 1994.

Shinran, Gutoku Shaku. (1973). *The Kyōgyōshinshō. The Collection of Passages Expounding the True Teaching, Living, Faith, and Realizing of the Pure Land* (tr. Daisetz Teitarō Suzuki; ed. The Eastern Buddhist Society). Kyōto: Shinshū Ōtaniha.

Steiner, J. (1993). Revenge, resentment, remorse and reparation. *Psychic Retreats Pathological Organizations in Psychotic, Neurotic and Borderline Patients*. London: Routledge, pp. 74–87.

Steiner, J. (2018). The Trauma and Disillusionment of Oedipus. *The International Journal of Psychoanalysis*, 99(3), 555–568.

Winnicott, D.W. (1949). *Mind and its Relation to the Psyche-Soma. Through Paediatrics to Psycho-Analysis*. London: Hogarth and the Institute of Psycho-Analysis, pp. 243–254.

Winnicott, D.W. (1961). Theory of the Parent-Infant Relationship. *Maturational Processes and the Facilitating Environment*. Madison, CT: International University Press.

Winnicott, D.W. (1974). Fear of Breakdown. *International Review of Psycho-Analysis*, 1(1–2), 103–107.

Chapter 4

Revenge or forgiveness:
The Oresteia

Ronald Britton

Psychoanalysis has from its earliest days been interested in the mythology of the Ancient world and classical literature to add to its armoury of clinical understanding. The Ancient Greek tragedy *The Oresteia* by Aeschylus was described by Professor Gilbert Murray as an attempt to think out the problem of 'Sin, Punishment and Forgiveness' (Murray, 1946). This stimulated Melanie Klein to write a paper on the plays as part of her review of her own theories of the origin of the superego and its evolution into a conscience. Her paper was never properly finished and was published posthumously (Klein,1963). It is stimulating but not resolved or quite coherent: she gave us the ingredients but not the recipe.

One idea she had long proposed was that the precursor of the superego was a terrifying internal object transformed in optimal development into a moral conscience. She was therefore very taken by the transformation in *The Oresteia* of the monstrous, bloodthirsty Erinyes, persecutors of the guilty, into the Eumenides, as merciful judges. But in another version of mental development she had proposed that fearful, phantasy, monsters untransformed still existed submerged in '*the deep unconscious*', and not integrated into the 'superego' (Klein, 1958).

The implication of 'deep' meant that in normal life they played no part in conscious thinking nor in the dynamic unconscious, and had no direct nor indirect access to the ego. They could only force their way into consciousness when physical illness, psychosis or severe traumatic events seriously weakened the ego. Evidence of their shadowy existence was to be to be found in the imaginative drawings of small children, night terrors, delirium and nightmares.

We are still looking for a recipe for these ingredients, we have gained more ingredients from clinical practice and from greater knowledge of the culture and literature of the ancient world, its history and anthropology, and from the academic studies of classical literature, such as *The Oresteia*.

But before discussing *The Oresteia*, I want to quote from *Henry IV* which Shakespeare wrote a few years before he wrote *Hamlet*, a passage on the death in battle of a heroic leader in a rebellious uprising. His death might have begun endless reprisals. Shakespeare spoke from Hotspur's lips,

DOI: 10.4324/9781003364313-4

... Time, that takes survey of all the world,
Must have a stop.

These lines by Henry Percy famously reputed to be undefeatable, were in his dying speech, after he had been unexpectedly beaten by Prince Henry, heir to the throne. As he dies Hotspur bemoans the loss of his famed status as an undefeatable champion,

O Harry, thou hast robbed me of my youth!
I better brook the loss of brittle life,
Than those proud titles thou has won of me.
They wound my thoughts worse than thy sword my flesh
but thought's the slave of life, and Times fool!
And Time, that takes survey of all the world,
Must have a stop.

(Shakespeare, *Henry IV*, p. 275)

The thought that is 'the slave of life' is of hurt pride, resentment, shame and humiliation, and it is this that time must stop. The traditional stopper is vengeance, by bringing the offenders to punishing defeat. But in this play, at this point, Shakespeare produces another possibility: forgiveness.

Hotspur's gracious acceptance of his defeat does bring to a stop the rebellion: there will be no vendetta, forgiveness ends the day. This is graciously accepted by Prince Henry as he, in turn, forgives Hotspur's rebellious challenge to his position as Prince of Wales, heir to the throne.

This earth that bears thee dead
Bears not alive so stout a gentleman ...
Adieu, and take thy praise with thee to heaven.
Thy ignominy sleep with thee in the grave,
But not rememb'red in thy epitaph.

(Ibid., p. 275)

This is a tender burial, with ignominy sleeping in the grave and no epitaph of reproach or grievance, so their mutual forgiveness will let Hotspur enter the afterlife in grace.

Mutual forgiveness prevents the unquiet ghost from haunting the next generation with demands for vengeance. In contrast, Hamlet's father's ghost unequivocally demands that Hamlet should kill his uncle, Claudius, who took his life, his wife and his kingdom. Persecuting ghosts of wronged relatives demanding vengeance has a long, persistent, history in the literature of human ancestry. Even in the earliest Sumerian clay tablets of 5000 years ago much is written of restless ghosts, seeking revenge or justice.

In the Ancient Greek tragedy by Aeschylus, *The Oresteia*, performed 2000 years earlier than *Hamlet*, the ghost of his father Agamemnon, haunts Orestes. The god Apollo demands that Orestes avenges his father by killing his mother and makes clear that unless he does so Orestes will suffer endless torment.

The Oresteia addresses the argument by Aeschylus in favour of the evolution from the old rigid law of 'blood for blood' of the Titans, to the new Olympian ideal court of Zeus, where men will administer Justice and the automatic operation of a Law of recompense is corrected by the will of the Father God.

It consists of three plays: *Agamemnon* in which Clytemnestra murders her husband; *The Coephora* in which Orestes kills his mother as revenge; and *The Eumenides* which is of Orestes' trial for matricide.

The first play describes Agamemnon's return from his Trojan triumph and his murder by Clytemnestra his wife. The setting of the play is the Palace of the House of Atreus. The chorus, as in all the Greek plays, sometimes figure as commentators, sometimes as audience, sometimes as the voice of public opinion. In this first play, the chorus consists of 12 senior citizens of Athens.

Agamemnon returns home victorious from Troy, Clytemnestra keeps secret from him that his cousin Aegisthus is her lover, and she, with murder in mind, receives Agamemnon and seduces him into entering into the palace on a magnificent, red, silk carpet. This ominously betokens his death as he steps out of a luxurious bath onto a mat where he has one foot on the ground and one in the bath when Clytemnestra throws a fishing net over him and stabs him to death.

Meanwhile, Princess Cassandra, daughter of the Trojan King and slave/mistress of Agamemnon, has an important dialogue with the chorus. They know of her reputation as a foreteller of events but are sceptical of her powers. She was given by Apollo the gift of supernatural foreknowledge, but he added a curse that she would never be believed. This was her torment.

The scene begins with Cassandra telling the chorus of an overwhelming intuition she is having of terrible events that took place, generations ago, in this palace when Atreus (Agamemnon's father) was king. The curse on the House of Atreus was a consequence of the dreadful revenge Atreus took on his brother Thyestes who stole his wife. Atreus deceived his brother by inviting him to dine with him on a meal he had secretly cooked of Thyestes' children whom he had murdered.

The chorus knew this secret history and were impressed by her intuition of past events and they were therefore prepared to listen. She then foretells dreadful events about to take place in the palace which includes the murder of Agamemnon and then of herself. The chorus remains sceptical of her foretelling.

Cassandra then follows Clytemnestra into the palace and the chorus in a dilatory fashion is about to enquire within the palace about what is happening.

'*When*! *The great door swings open* revealing Clytemnestra, *who stands, axe in hand*, over the dead bodies of Agamemnon and Cassandra' (Murray, 1946, p. 96).

A dramatic argument follows between the chorus, appalled by her act, and Clytemnestra's cool justification of it.

The thrust of what she says is that revenge is overdue!

Her justification is twofold: first is that these events are destined by a chain of crimes in the House of Atreus. And second Agamemnon's murderous sacrifice of their oldest daughter Iphigenia in a ritual to get the gods to give his Armada a fair wind to Troy. In a passionate speech, she says:

> Against him no word was cried,
> When, recking not, as 'twere a beast that died ...
> He slew his child, my love, my flower of pain
> And hark what oath-gods gather to my side!
> by my dead child's Revenge, now satisfied.
>   (Murray, 1946, pp. 98/99)

It had to be done, she argues, to complete a threefold circle of vengeance, blood must have blood.

Aegisthus now arrives having heard the news, triumphant at becoming joint regent with Clytemnestra and avenged as the son of Thyestes. But he becomes enraged when the chorus of Athenian worthies mock his unmanliness, for depending on a woman to do the dangerous, dirty work. Furious, he says he is ready to make more bloodshed. But Clytemnestra stops him, and quells his anger,

> Nay peace, O best beloved!
> Peace and let us work no evil more ...
> What we did must needs be done.
> And if of all these strifes we now may have no more,
> I will kneel
> And praise God ...
>   (Ibid., pp. 110/111)

Her hope that they can reach a stopping point by bloody revenge, discharging debts and balancing the books, is soon demonstrably demolished by Aeschylus in the second play.

The Choephoroe or The Libation Bearers

It is seven years later and begins in a desolate place where the grave of Agamemnon is an anonymous, mound of earth.

Libations are food or drink given literally into the graves to comfort the dead who lie waiting to be admitted to the underworld, like a precursor of the concept of purgatory. The libation bearers act as the chorus they are slaves of Clytemnestra: with them is Electra, Clytemnestra's daughter by Agamemnon, who, resentfully, feels enslaved by her mother. They are bearing libations to Agamemnon's unceremonious, unmarked, shabby grave. The slaves hate her and Aegisthus who have ruled jointly for the last seven years. They speak bitterly, sardonically of their mission as libation bearers:

> So, we are sent, by her whom the gods hate,
> Here to propitiate / You, Mother Earth!
> To avert the stroke of Fate
> With pious blasphemy / With Clytemnestra's prayer!
> (Vellacott, 1959 p. 105)

They make clear their longing for the return of Orestes, Electra's exiled brother, to avenge his father and put things right. Together with his great friend Pylades, Orestes witnesses these oblations, having arrived secretly from Phocis. He identifies himself to his sister and to the chorus. They tell him of their grievances.

He confides to them he must avenge his father's murder under threat from Apollo, and he asks why the libations to his father's grave were ordered at this time by his mother.

They tell him:

> It was dreams, night walking terrors,
> That frightened the godless woman and made her send these gifts ...
> She dreamt that she gave birth to a snake ...
> She wrapped it in shawls and lulled it to rest like a little child ...
> She, in her dream, gave it her breast to suck ...
> With her milk the creature drew forth clots of blood.
> (Ibid., pp. 122/123)

Orestes interprets the dream as referring to *his* birth from '*the same place as the snake*', but he sees it *not* as enlightening him of his mother's fears, but as a call to action from his father, whom he believes is the author of the dream as a form of instruction:

> I must transmute my nature, be viperous in heart and act! The dream commands it: I am her destined murderer.
> (Ibid., p. 123)

He told the chorus more of the command from Apollo to avenge his father,

> His voice urgent, insistent, drives me to dare this peril, Chilling my heart's blood with a recital of threatened terrors, if I should fail to exact vengeance, like for like ...

Orestes' situation is clearly one of the alternative terrors of persecution. As Apollo says:

> many things rise from the earth to appease the angry dead ... for him who disobeys, the night hath Furies, shaped of his father's blood; ... the blind arrows of dead men ... And madness and wild fear out of the night, shall spur him, rack him, till out of all men's sight. Alone he goes.
> (Ibid., p. 124)

Aeschylus' powerful description of this potential torment is only equalled by the later description of the same Furies pursuing Orestes after he kills his mother. In both cases, it is described as driving him mad.

Oretses' plan for the murder is to deceive his mother and Aegisthus by representing himself and Pylades as travellers from Phocis who bring to her the news of the death of her son Orestes. He, like Clytemnestra, thinks vengeance will finalise the sequence. He muses on the third murder of Aegisthus as if it might be the last.

> Then shall the Curse have drunken of our gore
> Her third, last burning cup, and thirst no more.
> (Murray, 1946, p. 124)

Orestes and Pylades are welcomed as strangers and invited into the palace. The chorus is fully complicit in the plot and intercepts Orestes old nursemaid on her way to the palace. They do not tell her the truth but tell her she should summon Aegisthus to come quickly without ceremony and without his guards.

As Aegisthmus enters the palace Orestes kills him. The chorus then urges Orestes to kill his mother.

The confrontation of Clytemnestra and her son Orestes is the crux of the trilogy and it is dramatised at the most personal level and at the same time confronts the burning religious question facing Athenian Greece, does duty lie primarily to Mother Earth or to God the father Zeus, whose son Apollo orders Orestes to revenge his father's death.

Clytemnestra arrives to find Orestes has killed her lover Aegisthus: 'Oh! Dearest Aegisthus! Dead? Where was your strength?'

Angrily Orestes says, 'Was he dear, this man of yours? Then you shall lie with him / In the grave ...'

Clytemnestra says: 'Put down your sword, my son! My own child, see this breast ... your soft mouth / sucked from me the good milk that gave you life and strength.'

Orestes hesitates, 'What shall I do? To kill a mother is terrible, shall I show mercy?'

Pylades, like the chorus, has no doubts! And reminds Orestes of Apollo's threatening words, 'Make not an enemy of the gods', he says.

Clytemnestra pleads unsuccessfully and warns him of 'the hounding Furies of a mother's curse'.

Orestes replies: 'How shall I escape my father's curse if I relent?'

Clytemnestra accepts her death now as inevitable saying, 'The living only listen to the dead.' And then: 'My dream! Here is the snake I bore and fed.'

Orestes says: 'The terror in your dream told you prophetic truth. Unholy was your crime, unholy shall be your punishment' (Vellacott, 1959, pp. 136–137).

He then confronts the crowd with the dead bodies and justifies his actions. He has the approval of the chorus of bondswomen and his sister but already he feels the presence of the Erinyes, the Furies pursuing him who it is predicted will drive him mad:

> Therefore while I am still in my right mind,
> … I proclaim it was no sin to kill my mother …
> Apollo … revealed to me
> That if I did this deed I should be clear of blame.
> (Ibid., p. 141)

It is clear that Orestes is now persecuted by his horrific pursuers, the ghastly Erinyes (Furies), who are invisible to others but terrifying to him. He is said to be driven mad in all the versions of the myth; in this play, Aeschylus represents it as the relentless persecution of his flesh.

The chorus who had willed the murder, 'When shall the ancestral curse relent,

And sink to rest, its fury spent?' (ibid., p. 143).

The third play *The Eumenides* opens at the Temple of Apollo at Delphi with the Pythian Prophetess officially declaiming the lineage of the gods, from Mother Earth via the Titans to the Olympian Gods. This is a diplomatic cover-up of the tension between the followers of Mother Earth and the supporters of the new Olympic gods, led by Zeus, the father. The realisation that sexual intercourse is the origin of pregnancy and childbirth had led to a great upheaval in the ancient world. It raised the question of the social and religious status of the Queen's sexual partners in many cultures. The warlike conflict that ensued between matriarchal and patriarchal rule was current at the time that Aeschylus was writing the trilogies.

The Prophetess after this introductory speech enters the Inner shrine but recoils when she finds there, as horrifying regressions to the pre-Olympian order, the ghastly Furies, who were sleeping grouped around their prey, Orestes. He is a suppliant in the temple, blood-stained but with laurel leaves.

Apollo comforts Orestes but warns him that he will be pursued, and hunted by these ancient, ageless hags 'born for wickedness, hated by the gods and hating human thought'. He advises him to fly throughout the earth until he finds 'Pallas Rock and fold thine arms', around her image.

When they leave, the ghost of Clytemnestra appears dramatically berating the sleeping Furies for leaving her, 'among all the dead Dishonoured' ... 'I go Wandering in shame' ... 'there is none / Cares for a mother murdered by her son' (Murray, 1946 p. 207).

'Ye slumber! Wake! What task have you to do on earth save to work misery?' (ibid., p. 208). ...

The Furies are the children of 'Night' the dark sister of 'Mother Earth' who is worshipped as the giver of life, joy, and sustenance. The Furies say with pride,

> We were born for punishment
> Of all who live in light.

We can easily see the two sisters, Mother Earth and Night, as the fore-runners of the good and bad breasts of Melanie Klein's conceptual description of infantile phantasy to which we can add the new Olympic regime as a phallic idealisation. This is represented by Apollo who champions patrilineal descent, kingship and government by order and reason. He wants the sisterhood of the Furies abolished.

> 'We hound matricides into exile' the Furies proclaim.
> 'And when a wife kills husband, what of her?' replies Apollo.
> 'They are not kin; therefore such blood is not self-spilt', say the Erinyes.

He responds furiously:

> Then you dishonour and annul the marriage-bond
> Of Zeus and Hera, that confirms all marriage bonds
> And by your argument the sweetest source of joy to mortals.
> (Vellacott, 1959, p. 1 54)

It is a stalemate. The impasse leads to a referral to Pallas Athene as a mediator. She has been listening to Orestes whom she found clinging to her statue surrounded by the Furies who eventually defer to her to judge the case. She gains the same deference from Orestes.

However once in court the Furies as prosecuting counsel mockingly say,

> Doth Zeus count fatherhood so high a thing?
> Who cast in bonds his father and his king
> Old Cronus?

Apollo answers:

The mother to the child that men call hers
Is no true life-begetter, but a nurse
Of live seed. 'Tis the sower of the seed
Alone begetteth ...

To prove his point he claims,

There have been fathers where no mother is.

He goes on to cite Athena Pallas as a perfect example, born as she was from her father, Zeus, head,

thought -begotten ... no nursling of the darkness of the womb ...
(Murray, 1946, pp. 234–235)

The trial

The trial of Orestes on the charge of matricide is organised by Athena at the newly founded Areopagus with a jury of old, wise, Athenian citizens. They are to vote according to their conscience but she will have a casting vote if they are divided.

The Furies leader is the prosecuting counsel; Apollo is the counsel for the defence.

PROSECUTION: Did the prisoner kill his mother? He admits it. He must die.
DEFENCE: Apollo ordered him to kill, because she had killed her husband –
Why did you not pursue her?
PROSECUTION: A husband is not a blood relation
DEFENCE: If it comes to that, neither is a mother ... the human mother is in function exactly like Mother Earth. She provides the soil for the seed, she does not provide the seed itself.
PROSECUTION: A monstrous doctrine, to deny a mother's sacred blood!
DEFENCE: No more monstrous than to deny the bond between husband and wife.

(Murray, 1946, pp. 261–262)

Athena makes clear that the Athenian Judges should cast their pebbles in the guilty or not-guilty urn, if they are equal she has the casting vote and she uses it. And so it is done;

This prisoner, since the stones for ill and good / Are equal, hath escaped the doom of blood.

(Ibid., p. 240)

Her work is, however, far from finished as the Furies are not reconciled to the result, though they accept it as lawful. It is difficult to say what particular plea of Athena finally won the Erinyes over, and transformed them into the Eumenides (Kindly Ones). It included her recognition of their lineage and accepted their view of the vital importance of punishing crime, and she offered them a grand place to live in Athens where they will be respected as having authority by men as well as women.

> Athena: 'No house shall prosper save by aid of thee.'
> But only as she stipulates:
> 'If thou canst hold that spirit in reverence
> Which hears Persuasion and which thinks again'.
> (Ibid., pp. 245–246)

This is the contract: they give up their role of endless pursuit and persecution and have a splendid residence of justice: they have retained power and determine the fortune of the citizens. If anyone falls out of favour or is judged to be guilty, they can be persecuted.

The finale of the play is a Song of Blessing on Athens as the model city, their new home, sung by the two choruses, the former Furies, and the Athenian citizens in unison.

> Outpour the Chalice of Peace … the task is done.
> The Law that is fate, and the Father the All-Comprehending,
> *Are here met together as one.*
> (Ibid., p. 253)

It is the exemplification of the Athenian ideal, of the Olympian world, that Aeschylus believes has displaced the *Urdummheit* (Primal Stupidity) of the Titans. The senior male citizens, servants of Zeus are united with the fervent defenders of Mother Earth's morality, in the concept of judgement.

Discussion

'Time must have a stop' expresses the hope of Hotspur that his death will end the war and that attempts to reverse the loss of his status beyond the grave, will not happen. Aeschylus makes clear that the attempt to exorcise the resentful, restlessness of ancestral ghosts by vengeance balancing the bloody accounts is a failure: it becomes endless, repetitive revenge. His plays express the Athenian hope that if penitential suffering is served, and justice is done there will be an end to the conflict. Shakespeare in *Henry IV* suggests that mutual forgiveness and respect should end resentful retaliation: the ghost of Hotspur accepts defeat as an honoured ancestor without an epitaph demanding restoration.

The process of putting to rest ancestral ghosts is represented in psycho-analytic theory as some sort of settlement between ego and superego. It was the attempt to use the plays to re-examine her theories of the development of the superego that stimulated Melanie Klein to write her paper on *The Oresteia*. The notion that Olympian judgement evolved from Titanic blood laws, personified by the transformation of the Erinyes into the Eumenides echoed in her mind the archaic, cruel superego evolving into a moral conscience. However, only a short time before this she had been writing of archaic monsters buried forever in the 'deep unconscious', not playing any part dynamically in healthy mental function. This is unresolved in her paper. However, as in the play, it is as if these fearful creatures could be resurrected and are always a possible threat.

This 'deep unconscious' as envisaged by Melanie Klein is like Freud's 'System Uncs', timeless in the sense of being outside time. Time is a construct, whether conscious or unconscious of the ego, and like place always has a context. The superego and or the deep unconscious appears to be outside the boundaries of time and the ego's distinction of past, present and future and similarly free of the constraints of a specific context.

It is interesting that, like the trilogy itself, Melanie Klein's attempts at synthesis leave out of account the crucial figure of the murdered Cassandra, who as the mistress of prediction represents a crucial aspect of human thinking: *expectation*. In the superstitious this is treated as a magical prediction: it is not an expectation based on experience. In the blood laws, it is based on a crude sense of moral outrage. It is not 'ego' but 'superego' and it is a critical difference between them. Judgement, as an ego function, is an expectation based on learning from experience. The superego's claim to know the future is based on wishes, virtuous prescriptions, penitential suffering, or dread. The ego to be free and true to itself has to emancipate itself from the superego with its predictions which are neither based on experience nor reason but are pre-conceived and recurrent.

In the play, Cassandra appears on the scene like a Holocaust survivor, the child of the murdered Royal family of Troy, whose people have been totally destroyed in a genocide. She is casually killed and soon forgotten in the ensuing carnage her warning voice disregarded in Greece, as it was in Troy. Her voice in the turmoil of vengeful passion is unlikely to be heard.

That desire for revenge may be augmented by the acquisition of a lust for blood is eloquently described by Clytemnestra in the aftermath of murdering her husband. She claims that the arithmetic of successive crimes justifies her actions and hopes that they will put a stop to the incursion of the daemon that haunts the House of Atreus.

But like Macbeth, she pauses for a moment after her hope of fulfilment by revenge and has the thought: blood will have blood.

She becomes aware that the gratification involved in revenge might stimulate further blood lust:

The thrice-engorged Wrath;
From him is that ache of the flesh
For blood, born and increased,
Ere the old sore had eased
It oozeth afresh.

Clytemnestra, however, was sure that killing her husband was appropriate and justified, 'What we did must needs be done', she says to Aegisthus with no shame nor any expectation of guilt. She hopes it has ended the recurrent blood baths of the House of Atreus: 'of all these strifes we have no more'.

She is fearless, self-assured, doubtless and completely shameless. For her, the ego and superego are one. I am reminded by this of Freud's description in 'Libidinal Types' in 1931 of the 'narcissistic character type'. He said, 'for people like this: There is no tension between ego and superego (indeed, on the strength of this type one could scarcely have arrived at the hypothesis of a super-ego)' (Freud, 1931, p. 218).

Clytemnestra is ego as superego: her core instrumental self and her judging, moral self are 'as one'. Such absolute shameless, self-righteousness and total conviction are profoundly shocking to ordinary people, represented by the chorus in the play, who cannot credit it is as conceivable. Freud's further comments on the qualities of such 'narcissistic libidinal characters', are also exemplified by Clytemnestra. He wrote of them,

> they are ... independent and not open to intimidation. [Their] ego has a large amount of aggressiveness at its disposal in readiness for activity ... they are especially suited to take on the role of leaders. to provide stimulus for fresh cultural development or to damage the established state of affairs.

He added, they are also 'peculiarly disposed to psychosis if frustrated ... and they also present essential conditions for criminality' (ibid.).

The character of Lady Macbeth created by Shakespeare is very similar and her relationship with Macbeth is strikingly similar to that of Clytemnestra with her paramour Aegisthus. One can see Clytemnestra, conjured up centuries later by Nietzsche, when he pronounced 'God is dead', to be replaced by 'superman', or superwoman, as Clytemnestra or Lady Macbeth.

In contrast to this, Orestes is God-riven, persecuted by Apollo who insists he avenges his father's murder by killing his mother, yet fearful of doing so knowing he will be persecuted by the Furies acting on behalf of his mother's ghost. If we can liken Clytemnestra to Lady Macbeth, we could liken Orestes to Hamlet.

The meta-theological background to The Oresteia, when performed in Athens in 458 BC was the conflict between the worship of Nature, personified by Mother Earth, and Apollo as the representative of Intellect and Will under Zeus. Yet Apollo's *first* indignant response to the Furies' claim that the murder of Agamemnon by his wife is of little account as they were not blood-related, is that this is an attack on the great importance of marriage, and Zeus's supremacy as a father.

> How! Would you count as a light thing and vain
> The perfect bond of Hera and high Zeus? ...
> The fate-ordained meeting, breast to breast, of man and woman is a tie
> more sure ... if Justice guards it pure.

This sanctification of the marriage bond gets lost later in the heat of argument in the courtroom. But I think it expresses symbolically that the bond, the link of the internal parents is central to the structure of the superego and its relationship to the ego.

Yet, Apollo in the trial, lawyer-like, reverts to presenting the birth of Athena from her father's head, as evidence of sole patrilineal descent, challenging the matriarchal supremacy of the Titans represented in court by the Erynnes.

But who is the goddess Athena and from whence did she come? She was alone amongst the gods for giving her name to a city Athens, and not taking her name from a place.

Her origins in the myths were the subject of several versions; Plato identified her as derived from 'a place' elsewhere in an epoch when fatherhood was not yet recognised. The prevailing Greek myth at the time of Aeschylus was that she was born of Metis, a female Titan impregnated by Zeus who having seduced Metis swallowed her when she was pregnant. Subsequently, this gave him such a headache that Hermes, the divine messenger, relieved him by performing a craniotomy, so she was conceived in Metis but delivered from the head of Zeus. Athena was acceptable to the Furies as having a Titan maternal ancestry and to Apollo as motherless, born from Zeus' head. This diplomatic description we could describe as a good example of John Steiner's 'pathological organisation', or Freud's compromise formations, one that conceals profound basic, unresolved conflicts with intellectual, ostensibly reasoned solutions.

In the play, she remains as I have described her elsewhere (Britton, 1998) as 'Forever father's daughter', and the official voice of her father. 'Stern Daughter of the voice of God, O Duty!'

The resolution of the trial with Orestes' acquittal is seen as a triumph of Athenian justice.

'The Law that is fate, and the Father the All-Comprehending, / *Are here met together as one.*' Sing the Chorus of Athenians in a procession celebrating the end of the trial.

The triumphalism of this ending probably reflected the Athenian mood at the time. *The Oresteia* was produced shortly after the Greek victory over the

Persians at the battle of Marathon in which Aeschylus was a soldier. It was a short-lived mood, banished in Athens after defeat by Sparta, in the Peloponnesian wars, and by the populist risings in Athens against the Aeropagus, the wise Court envisaged in the play.

In the last words of the plays, Aeschylus represented his hope that in Athens *justice* wisely dispensed, could be the alternative to revenge. Justice, meaning measured punishment, does not satisfy the aggrieved: it needs forgiveness to overcome the instinctual wish for retaliation. Forgiveness needs another ingredient, '*caritas*', as St Paul used it, meaning affectionate, neighbourly love. The Latin *caritas* has another dictionary meaning: 'high price', 'value', respect, 'appreciation'. This accords with the emotional experience of being forgiving, and of feeling forgiven, of generously, absolving a debt for the sake of love or appreciation. This is part of Apollo's claim that the bond of man and woman, unified in parenthood is '*a tie more sure*' than blood. Yet the passionate sense of attachment to 'Mother Earth' and her sister Night, fiendishly represented by the Erynnes is transformed into the Eumenides by kindness and a capacity for second thoughts. It could be that the strength of attachment to Night was outdone by attachment to Mother Earth, the good breast more than the bad breast.

Aeschylus was hoping to introduce us to an internal conscience that contains compassion and reason not in opposition but in alliance. It is what Freud and Klein had in mind in their hope that in human development a forgiving conscience might evolve out of some very rough justice. I think it probably requires a relationship between the subjective self (ego) and a superego complex comprised of an internal maternal object and of a paternal internal object, a triangle of relationships in which optimally the internal parents are at peace with each other.

When they are at war the central self is divided by its incompatible attachments: in extreme situations, the individual feels compelled by obedience to conflicting murderous figures. The self is haunted by the fear of persecution from one direction or the other. We might call this an Orestes complex, an internal, infernal, eternal triangle first met with in Athens, not altogether unlike the complex afflicting his neighbour Oedipus in Thebes.

I have been impressed in my psychoanalytical experience by a number of cases where patients had an unconscious drive *to repair* ancestral (parental) marital severance by trying to sustain marital success in their own lives, with repeated acts of forgiveness as reparation.

We also meet it in re-enactments that take place in the transference-countertransference interactions Can we make peace and stimulate forgiveness between our internal parental objects as we failed to do in childhood? The answer could be by identification, this time re-enactment in a good cause! Perhaps it happens also in the retelling of old tragic stories but this time with a happy ending.

Maybe by identification an opportunity is created to exercise forgiveness between two important internal objects who can no longer provide it for themselves. This seems to me to be the basis of the archaic forerunner of later religious practices plus the provision of libations for the restless dead in their graves. Clytemnestra was belatedly and unsuccessfully trying to appease the ghost of Agamemnon in his unmarked grave with libations in the second play of the trilogy. The chorus clearly thought that without remorse this hypocrisy would not work. In Christianity, though it has been contentious since the Reformation, the same wish has in a more abstract form lingered on with prayers for the dead who can no longer pray for themselves.

I think that Shakespeare was particularly interested in the idea that serious parental conflict means the child's world is so disordered even the seasons are changed. At the outset of *Midsummer Night's Dream*, Oberon, King of the Underworld and his Queen Titania are quarrelling over the possession of an infant boy. This has such repercussions that the summer is changed into winter and vice versa for everyone. Nature is at war with itself and all our compass bearings are reversed.

As Titania says to Oberon:

> The spring, the summer,
> The chiding autumn, angry winter change
> Their wonted liveries: and the mazed world,
> By their increase, now knows not which is which.
> And this same progeny of evils comes
> From our debate, from our dissension:
> We are their parents and original.
> (Shakespeare, *Midsummer Night's Dream*, p. 111)

This is, however, a play where dissension and forgiveness are repeatedly enacted, and re-enacted. So happily, we find it on the library shelf where '*Comedies and Romances*' are placed, together with *Winter's Tale*: but without forgiveness, we would have found it on the *Tragedies* shelf alongside, *King Lear* and *Othello*.

References

Britton, R. (1998). *Belief and Imagination*. London: Routledge.

Freud, S. (1931). 'Libidinal Types'. *S.E. XXI*. London: Hogarth, 1951.

Klein, M. (1958). 'On the development of mental functioning', *The Writings of Melanie Klein*, Vol. *III*, ed. R. Money-Kyrle. London: Hogarth Press (1975).

Klein, M. (1963). 'Some reflections on the Oresteia' *The Writings of Melanie Klein*, Vol. III, ed. R. Money-Kyrle, London: Hogarth (1975).

Murray, G. (trans.) (1946). *Aeschylus 'The Oresteia'*. London: Allen & Unwin Ltd.

Shakespeare, W. (1969). *Henry IV*. Complete Shakespeare, Histories. Harmondsworth, Middlesex: Penguin.

Shakespeare, W. (1969). *Midsummer Night's Dream*. Complete Shakespeare, Comedies & Romances. Penguin.

Vellacott, P. (trans.) (1959). *Aeschylus 'The Oresteia'*. Harmondsworth, Middlesex: Penguin.

Chapter 5

Cry havoc and reconciliation

David Millar

Introduction

Connection is a strange thing. In the sciences and the arts, pain and frustration at the loss of connection is part of a process of discovering new ways of seeing what is going on. In life, loss of connection with our loved objects is immensely painful.

> When God at first made man,
> Having a glass of blessings standing by;
> Let us (said he) poure on him all we can;
> Let the worlds riches, which dispersed lie,
> Contract into a span.
> So strength first made a way;
> Then beautie flow'd, then wisdome, honour, pleasure:
> When almost all was out, God made a stay,
> Perceiving that alone of all his treasure
> Rest in the bottome lay.
> For if I should (said he)
> Bestow this jewell also on my creature,
> He would adore my gifts in stead of me,
> And rest in Nature, not the God of Nature:
> So both should losers be.
> Yet let him keep the rest,
> But keep them with repining restlesnesse:
> Let him be rich and wearie, that at least,
> If goodness leade him not, yet wearinesse
> May tosse him to my breast.
> (Herbert, 1957, p. 134)

It is the connection to goodness and its loss that creates the repining restlessness that George Herbert describes in *The Pulley*. If we return to something resembling our connection with the breast at the beginning, it may well

DOI: 10.4324/9781003364313-5

be weariness that gets us to rest. However, there is something else. Connection to goodness and its catastrophic loss create havoc. I mean havoc in its Old English, medieval French sense, where *cry havoc* is a shout that went up to pillage the enemy during defeat in battle; something essential to havoc is thoughtless possession and the taking over of the other through action.

In *A Psychoanalytical View of Biblical Myth* (Millar, 2001), and in *A Connecting Door: Why We Need to Go On Asking Questions and Being Asked Questions* (Millar, 2022), I have written about connection and its catastrophic loss in the context of creativity and its invasion by an internal tyrant, a warfare from which there is no release. In the present chapter, my aim is to illustrate further the deep and wide significance of the theme.

Let me begin with the notion that I call hardened myth. The idea can be put as follows. Hardened myth is a kind of idealised, paranoid belief system, transmitted through the generations over the centuries, within the Judaeo-Christian tradition. It covers up a subjective experience of connection and its catastrophic loss; with an underlying catastrophic belief that God, the group's ideal object, has made a destructive attack on the group's connection with goodness as a punishment for badness.

In hardened myth, exclusive possession of goodness and virtue is asserted by a group, which identifies with a tyrannical aspect within its wider tradition and culture. Guilt, worthlessness, badness, inferiority, vulnerability and fallibility are split off and projected into a devalued near-foreign group. The near-foreign group becomes the unforgivable un-forgiven, accused and blamed for loss with virtuous hatred. For the Jewish group, the unforgivable, un-forgiven near-foreign group is the Samaritans; for the Christian group, the unforgivable, un-forgiven near-foreign group is the Jewish group. History shows a repetitive pattern where hardened myth, submerged and dormant for long periods of time, springs back with vengeance.

Two pictures of the Fall

Next, I describe a personal communication from Ignês Sodré to John Steiner, regarding the connection and its catastrophic loss, quoted at the Melanie Klein Trust Conference on 14 June 2014 (Sodré, 2014; Steiner, 2020).

Ignês Sodré describes the Fall from a psychoanalytic point of view with the dawning of the Oedipus situation: a kernel of conflicts, with hard-to-bear feelings of jealousy, rivalry, envy, shame, guilt and hatred, where reality insists on the relinquishment of the ideal object as a concrete possession. Sodré writes:

> The ideal object always causes some humiliation at the moment of the first realisation of separateness because as the object is seen more realistically, i.e. no longer as a possession and with the idealisation gone, the Fall is too great.
>
> (Sodré, 2014)

Any response that challenges the idealisation may lead to a feeling of catastrophic collapse in which the disillusionment opens up a gap between the self and the object: a gap that to start with is filled by Chaos, leading to panicky feelings of falling into a terrifying unknown. Normally the mother's love saves the day, since it creates a link and is felt to rescue the baby from the abyss.

(Ibid.)

But if this fails and the pain, humiliation, and fear are unbearable, the "horizontal" gap between self and breast becomes a "vertical" gap with only two positions, triumph or humiliation. The longing for love is replaced by a longing for power. The patient inhabits an up and down universe in which strength fuelled by hatred is idealised and love is seen as weak and contemptible.

(Ibid.)

Ignês Sodré is describing two kinds of Fall from a psychoanalytic point of view; she gives two different pictures of loss of connection. In both images, loss of connection is too great – "the Fall is too great" – but loss of connection is qualitatively different.

In the first picture, where the child's sense of connection, of belonging around good experience, is invaded by bad stuff, he or she chucks it out, screams it out, pees it out, shits it out, but "normally, the mother's love saves the day, since it creates a link and is felt to rescue the baby from the abyss".

Incremental disillusionment – through the mother's love that creates a link and is felt to rescue the child from the abyss – contains the child's omnipotence. It opens a connecting door to the oedipal situation, where we experience hard-to-bear feelings and internal conflicts, where ambivalence – our positive, loving feelings and negative, hateful feelings towards a person or situation – is managed, where the ideal object as a concrete possession is relinquished, and where mental capacities develop further to allow diverse, rich, new connections in a complex world. Melanie Klein, Ronald Britton, and Dana Birksted-Breen describe the development from different angles.

Melanie Klein wrote in *Lectures on Technique*:

I hold the view that feelings of sorrow, guilt and anxiety are experienced by the infant when he comes to realise to a certain extent, that his loved object is the same as the one he hates and has attacked and is going on attacking in his uncontrollable sadism and greed, and that sorrow, guilt and anxiety are part and parcel of the complex relation to objects which we call love. It is from these conflicts that the drive to reparation springs, which is not only a powerful motive for sublimations, but also is inherent in feelings of love which it influences both in quality and quantity.

(Klein, 2017, p. 37)

Ronald Britton (1989) describes the coming into existence of what he calls a third position of self-observation in triangular space. It enables the self to make judgements based on the authority of experience, and subject to modification, different from the superego that claims parental and ancestral authority. It is not a concrete possession. Britton describes it as within the ego and vulnerable to invasion by a tyrannical superego (Britton, 2003). If we think we possess a third position then it has already become part of an idealised, paranoid belief system.

Dana Birksted-Breen (1996, 2016) describes the internalisation of a "penis-as-link" in its "structuring and linking function", configured as a tripartite world of mother – linked with but different from father – and child that promotes mental space and thinking. An internal "penis-as-link" in its "structuring and linking function" normally belongs to the development of men and women. Through the internalisation of "penis-as-link", in its structuring and linking function, we become able – in a fuller sense – to treat a symbol, which is not the thing it symbolises, as if it is the symbolised thing, carrying its emotional charge. It makes it possible for "guilt and anxiety [to become] part and parcel of the complex relation to objects which we call love". It makes it possible to relate to an idea, to explore it but be separate from it.

In addition, I think the relinquishment of the ideal object as a concrete possession brings into existence ego ideals which bear the particularities of culture, place and time. They invite not imitation, which is destructive of identity, but experimentation that can contribute to achieving the means that offer real choice – bringing change to the boundaries of the self and what the self is capable of.

However, in Ignês Sodré's second picture of the Fall, a picture of connection and its catastrophic loss, omnipotence is not contained.

> ... the pain, humiliation, and fear are unbearable, and the "horizontal" gap becomes a "vertical" gap, with only two positions, triumph or humiliation ... longing for love is replaced by a longing for power ... an up and down universe in which strength fuelled by hatred is idealised and love is seen as weak and contemptible.
>
> (Sodré, 2014)

Whatever the external or more objective reality, the mother's love does not create a link that saves the baby from falling into a terrifying unknown, full of panicky feelings. The baby's subjective experience is a destructive attack by the mother on his or her connection and communication with her. Ronald Britton writes that Wilfred Bion "made it clear that the inability of the mother to take in her child's projections is experienced *by the child* as a destructive attack *by her* on his link and communication *with her* as his good object" (Britton, 2015).

The linguist George Lakoff and philosopher Mark Johnson (1980) contend that the fundamental ideas of the human animal are structured by systems of what they term "conceptual metaphor" – grounded, shaped and constrained by embodied experience embedded in social interaction. They argue that metaphorical thought is ubiquitous in our mental life, mostly unconscious, with a central role in abstract thought; that metaphors are fundamentally conceptual in nature, and that metaphorical language is secondary.

They see the heart of conceptual metaphor as inference; that we systematically see patterns between one conceptual domain and another conceptual domain. These patterns are what they call structural metaphors; and the correspondence across conceptual domains is what they call metaphorical mapping. Ronald Britton calls these analogical patterns "models in the mind".

In Ignês Sodré's second picture, falling into a terrifying unknown creates models in the mind "with only two positions, triumph or humiliation ... an up and down universe in which strength fuelled by hatred is idealised". The child, experiencing a destructive attack by the mother, hears her shout *cry havoc* and responds in kind, with vengeance, without thought, creating havoc.

This picture is connected with the formation of an abnormal kind of superego, an internal tyrant. Edna O'Shaughnessy (1999) writes that its "dangerous aim is to dissociate the ... [self], to attack the link with the object ... since it is upon the link with the object that the safety of the ego depends" (p. 863). As we see in hardened myth, models in the mind organised around an internal tyrant, may be handed down the generations over centuries.

I think we all carry, to a certain extent, experience of both kinds of the Fall. We inhabit a limited and limiting world, where feelings of sorrow, remorse, guilt, and reparation, together with being forgiven and forgiving, have their part. And we inhabit a different, idealised, paranoid world, organised around an internal tyrant, where the ideal object as a concrete possession is not relinquished; a world committed to self-sufficiency and attacks on mutual dependency, where havoc created by connection and its catastrophic loss is repeated.

An internal tyrant can appear in different guises. It is a spurious, threatening higher power that is felt to deliver authoritative truth. It holds out the promise of some kind of permanent state of wellbeing, a dream-like state, *and* demands propitiation. Its propitiation means the sacrifice of our longing for love; that is for caring and being cared for profoundly by others. Substituted is a longing to feel powerful and untouchable, which generates rigid and cruel hierarchies organising our minds, and social relationships, and which disturbs the desire to know what is going on, that is to say, our curiosity.

When loss and deprivation threaten, they bring painful feelings of sadness, meaning having to face, against our will, the need to recognise and mourn what is lost and gone forever and how that has come about. Only then are we able to think about what we might be able to do to repair the damage. However, loss and deprivation also reverberate with the experience of connection and its catastrophic loss buried deep in our minds, threatening us with horrible, bad, inescapable feelings. An internal tyrant is more or less asleep inside all of us, threatening to come back to life with a vengeance, and, under pressure, where we feel insignificant and helpless, we may give in to occupation.

In the remainder of this chapter, I want to give some illustrations of where a depressive coming-down from a "vertical" gap – sometimes seen after the destruction and havoc of war – brings about interactions in psychic reality from which emerge a transition. A transition is a psychological notion, in contrast to change, which is something more external or objective (Hall & Stokes, 2021). The idea of transition is itself a depressive state of mind, a flexible position. It is vulnerable to invasion by an internal tyrant. I realise that this is a rather loose, even vague notion but, I hope, profitably so.

Recapitulation

In *Evil and the God of Love*, John Hick (1966), philosopher and theologian, shows how in the surviving literature of the 100 years or so after Jesus' disciples' experience of connection and its catastrophic loss – Jesus was violently executed by the Roman occupation, followed later by the destruction of Jerusalem by the Empire's armies – and the putting together of the New Testament, there is no common way of thinking about sin and evil. Then there emerges in Christianity a majority report (the Latin tradition) and a minority report (the Greek tradition).

Hick describes how the majority report goes back to Augustine in the 4th/5th century CE. The majority report sees the connection and its catastrophic loss as a consequence of our ancestors', Adam and Eve's, blameworthy disobedience; a fall from an original state of perfection, followed by God the Father – the un-relinquished ideal object as a concrete possession – demanding propitiation. In this idealised, paranoid, belief system, without the perfect sacrifice of the Son to placate God the Father, all of us human beings would be in hell – the unforgivable, un-forgiven in a melancholic place where connection to goodness and its catastrophic loss is repeated with vengeance forever and ever. On the other hand, if we submit to a sacrifice of our unique selves with our own feelings and ideas, we are promised to share in a triumphant, concrete resurrection.

The majority report remains dominant in Western Christianity through and beyond the Reformation. Geoffrey Lampe (1964) writes in *Soundings – Inquiries in Christian Understanding*.

> When we turn from the New Testament to read what the Thirty-nine Articles of the Church of England tell us about the death of Christ, we

find ourselves abruptly plunged into a very different atmosphere ... Something has happened to the good news of the love of God ... Now it has become a message that the estrangement was on the side of God. God was at enmity with us, rather than we with him. He has been reconciled to us by the death of Christ.

(Lampe, 1964, pp. 179–180)

Hick traces the "minority report" back to Irenaeus, Bishop of Lyons, from the late 2nd century CE. The difference between the majority and minority reports is not black-and-white, but the minority report conveys the notion of a developmental journey. Irenaeus has the idea of the incarnation as a "recapitulation" of the creation of man after the image and likeness of God (Stevenson, 1987). Hick describes this as "the point of view that was to characterize the Greek as distinct from the Latin Fathers" (1966, p. 217).

I see Irenaeus' idea of the incarnation as a recapitulation as a notion of a recapitulation of connection to goodness and its catastrophic loss, through whatever medium – resonating with the notion of a depressive coming-down from a "vertical" gap. The idea opens a connecting door to a picture, a hypothesis, of a message of the good news of the love of God delivered to a limited and limiting world impregnated with uncertainty.

Hick describes how versions of the minority report keep popping up over the centuries. I think it resurfaced in the 1960s, in the reparative atmosphere of the ecumenical movement, and the second Vatican Council, after the destruction and havoc of the war. It is a moment where imagination shook loose many things, where the young discovered more of their own liberty, and where a new generation in Germany took upon their shoulders the weight of the horror, murder and terror of the Holocaust – the defining experience in the 20th century of connection to goodness and its catastrophic loss, creating havoc – the remembrance of which their parents and elders had suppressed.

Remember Enniskillen

On Remembrance Sunday, 8 November 1987, in Enniskillen in Northern Ireland, the Provisional IRA, ruthlessly cruel and murderous, but also belonging to the deeply-layered opposition to oppression by the British state – with its long history of connection and its catastrophic loss – planted and detonated a 40lb bomb in the town Reading Rooms behind the cenotaph. The explosion killed 11 people and injured 64. The blast buried 60-year-old Gordon Wilson, a draper, and his daughter, Marie, 20, a nurse. In an emotional television interview with the BBC only hours after the bombing, Gordon Wilson said:

We were both thrown forward, rubble and stones and whatever in and around and over us and under us. I was aware of a pain in my right shoulder. I shouted to Marie was she all right and she said yes. She found my hand and said, "Is that your hand, Dad?"

Now, remember, we were under six foot of rubble. I said, "Are you all right?" and she said yes, but she was shouting in between. Three or four times I asked her, and she always said yes, she was all right. When I asked her the fifth time, "Are you all right, Marie?" she said, "Daddy, I love you very much". Those were the last words she spoke to me.

She still held my hand quite firmly and I kept shouting at her, "Marie, are you all right?" but there wasn't a reply. We were there about five minutes. Someone came and pulled me out. I said, "I'm all right but for God's sake my daughter is lying right beside me and I don't think she is too well". She's dead. She didn't die there. She died later.

The hospital was magnificent, truly impressive, and our friends have been great. But I miss my daughter, and we shall miss her, but I bear no ill will, I bear no grudge. She was a great wee lassie. She loved her profession. She was a pet and she's dead. She's in heaven and we will meet again.

Don't ask me please for a purpose. I don't have a purpose. I don't have an answer. But I know there has to be a plan. If I didn't think that, I would commit suicide. It's part of a greater plan – and God is good. And we shall meet again.

I have lost my daughter, and we shall miss her. But I bear no ill will. I bear no grudge. Dirty sort of talk is not going to bring her back to life. I shall pray for those people [the IRA bombers] tonight and every night. May God forgive them.

Gordon Wilson, grieving and facing the reality of the loss of his daughter Marie, says "No" to destructive, violent revenge that obstructs thinking and furthers a vicious circle of havoc. He does not forgive the bombers but, looking to his ego ideals, says he will pray for them every night. "May God forgive them".

Many different, complex, interacting factors contributed to the Good Friday Agreement, but I think one thing is a depressive coming-down following the havoc of Enniskillen. The BBC later said that the IRA's attack on Enniskillen shook the IRA "to its core".

Gordon Wilson's words, with the authority of his own experience, long-remembered, were stepping-stones on a long path of the painful questioning of what was going on, of perseverance, painful compromise, and of politically fixing things well enough at a multi-national level, that led to the transition of the Good Friday Agreement.

Following Brexit, enough collective political will and determination has remained to find ways, however messy, to prevent a sacrifice of the Good Friday Agreement. But this "recapitulation" requires constant work and attention. There is always the threat of occupation by an internal tyrant and havoc.

Misogyny and the Marschallin

After Menelaus, King of Sparta, loses Helen to Paris, a prince of Troy, Menelaus' powerful brother, Agamemnon, leads the Greek forces in an invasion. Homer's *The Iliad* describes how, from the start, the merciless Olympian gods descend to demand propitiation. To propitiate the goddess Artemis and get a wind to allow the invasion fleet to sail, Agamemnon "places his neck beneath the harness / of what had to be" (Aeschylus, 2018). He gags and sacrifices Iphigenia, his and Clytemnestra's daughter.

The havoc brought by the invasion of Troy continues in the third play of Aeschylus' trilogy *The Oresteia*, where the young prince Orestes, son of Clytemnestra, comes to Athens to beg sanctuary from the goddess Athena after he has murdered his mother, who had axed Agamemnon to death in retribution for his killing of their daughter.

Emily Wilson (2020), Professor of Classical Studies at the University of Pennsylvania, argues that the ideology of the trilogy is misogynistic. Wilson writes:

> Each of the three plays is radically different in style, mood and action. But each centres on female anger and female grief at violent loss of life and the willingness of family members to kill one another. The trilogy is about language and the mysterious will of the gods, about tyranny, freedom and political change, and about a slow path to maturity for one young man (Orestes) and an entire culture. That "maturity" turns out to involve the subordination of women and of the family, which is conceived as feminine, to enable the creation of a political community like real-life historical Athens, in which male citizens use the law courts and the institutions of democracy to legislate for structures of power that can contain, marginalise and silence other members of the community – women, immigrants and enslaved people.
>
> (p. 9)

In the third play:

> The jury is split and Athena breaks the tie in favour or Orestes … Clytemnestra was accused of having a heart like a man. Electra, in desperate grief, obsessed over her dead father and absent brother, and resented her mother. Athena takes the pattern of female male-sympathisers even further: she has the militaristic, dominant heart of her father, Zeus, and insists that the sunlit, male-dominated world of politics will, from now on, prevail over the underground, ancestral-rights of the female Furies
> …
> These dense plays are concerned with a transition from a world of mystery to a world of history, from war to peace, from myth to reality, from aristocratic households to the democratic society of contemporary

Athens ... But, most fundamentally, the trilogy uses all these interwoven narratives to tell a story that justifies the triumph of men over women. The institution of the all-male democratic law court, presided over by its male-biased judge, is presented as the only possible solution to the endless violence of the earlier world, one in which the experiences and voices of angry, wronged, grieving women were allowed to matter as much as those of men.

(p. 10)

On the afternoon of Sunday 8 January 2017, I attend a new production of Richard Strauss' *Der Rosenkavalier* at Covent Garden, where Renée Fleming is in the role, it seems for the last time in London, of the passionate Viennese aristocrat, the Marschallin, in her early 30s. I am drawn into the to-ing and fro-ing of her deep feelings around valuing and feeling valued – jealousy and resentment brought by realisation of the inevitability that her young lover, Octavian, sung by a mezzo-soprano (Alice Coote), will one day fall in love with a younger woman. The younger woman who triggers her deep feelings is Sophie von Faninal (Sophie Bevan), a young, nouveau riche girl, fresh from the convent, ordered by her tyrannical father into marriage with the frightful Baron Ochs auf Lerchenau, the Marschallin's cousin.

The Marschallin's deep feelings include her oedipal desires to have and possess everything but also, I think, bring into the open her hatred of a very bad experience she had been unable to mourn – the system of misogyny in which she has grown up, and which she has so skilfully managed. She reflects on how she herself was taken out of the convent and married (part of the system of misogyny) – for the first time questioning what is going on.

I too can recall a young girl, who was ordered, fresh from the convent, into holy wedlock ...

How can it really be, that I was once little Resi, and that one day I shall be an old woman. How can this come about? How can our dear Lord make it so? When I am still the same person. And if he must make it so, why does he let me see it all so very clearly? Why does he not hide it from me? It's all a mystery, so very much a mystery.

(Strauss, 2009, p. 74)

The Marschallin is disturbed by her curiosity, by her questioning. Why does she have to know? Why does she have to connect with her hard-to-bear feelings? Why can it not stay a mystery? Why does she have to see that misogyny is no mystery of God but a hateful system now once again threatening to invade and take over? Nonetheless, her reflections and questioning are part of a "recapitulation" where she becomes able to think of her own responsibility in all this: "And we are here to bear it. And in the 'how' there lies the whole difference".

However, the threat of havoc is never far from the surface of Strauss' opera. It comes to a head, as feelings between Octavian and Sophia develop, with the scenes of havoc, alongside comedy, which ends with the Marschallin sending off Baron Ochs auf Lerchenau, with his noble ideals of blood, genes, and sex, with his tail between his legs. But the danger of occupation by an internal tyrant is only off-stage. Never has the dark side of this "comedy for music" been in plainer view than that Sunday afternoon, less than three weeks before the ascension of Donald Trump to the White House.

However, the end of the opera is a moment of a depressive coming-down. The Marschallin uses her social position and charm to protect Sophia from her tyrannical father and an arranged marriage; different from her own parents' lack of understanding of the transition from girlhood to womanhood. It opens a connecting door to Octavian and Sophia committing themselves to each other. I think this act of reparation emerges from a "recapitulation" of connection and its catastrophic loss where the ideal object as a concrete possession is relinquished. But this verdict of reality brings a painful transition for the Marschallin, which we hear in the beauty and sadness of the final trio – Renée Fleming, Alice Coote and Sophie Bevan.

The beauty and sadness takes me from my to-ing and fro-ing, my own remembering, to "a sure and certayne hope" (Cranmer, 1910) of the current of life that creates the love that rides the river that raises the new (Clarke, 2016); "a sure and certayne hope" that is always vulnerable to invasion by tyranny.

Two kinds of Return in Rembrandt's painting – Judas Repentant Returning the Pieces of Silver (1629) and The Return of the Prodigal Son (1666–1669)

Judas Repentant Returning the Pieces of Silver (1629) shows the moment in the scene where Judas has just thrown the coins he received for the betrayal of Jesus in front of the priests in the Temple, the seated high priest in the centre of the composition turning away.

Christopher Brown, An Van Camp and Christiaan Vogelaar (2019) write:

> The painting is a key document of Rembrandt's early hesitant development: the many changes he made as he tested out his idea on paper and, later, on the panel itself, reveal that he struggled to arrive at a composition that satisfied him.
>
> (p. 196)

On 27 April 2020, in a series *Museums in Quarantine*, BBC 4 broadcast a programme made the previous month, written and voiced by Simon Schama on the exhibition *Young Rembrandt* before the Ashmolean Museum closed its doors following the outbreak of COVID-19.

I want to quote Schama's words about *Judas Repentant Returning the Pieces of Silver*, which I found enlightening and moving.

> Judas returning the pieces of silver he received for betraying Christ. A break-through picture that made him famous also moved the Secretary of the Prince of Orange, Constantijn Huggens, to certify the Miller's son has the real thing.
>
> "All honour to thee, Rembrandt", Constantijn Huggens wrote in ecstatic admiration when he saw this picture.
>
> What did he see that so moved him?
>
> He might have talked about the light ...
>
> But the destination of that light – the face and body of Judas himself was what so moved Huggens to describe it thus;
>
> Screaming, begging for forgiveness

- devoid of all hope
- his gaze wild
- his hair torn out by the roots
- his garment rent
- his hands clenched until they have lost circulation
- his whole body writhing in pitiful hideousness

This humane treatment of the infamous Judas was unprecedented.

Judas was usually painted as the embodiment of evil – a demon of treachery – so this in a way is revolutionary.

Physically it is not a big painting but he knows what he is doing – all about emotional compression – ratcheting up the intensity – something profound, huge, cosmic is happening on a modest surface.

We know little about Rembrandt's early life. But I think the something profound, huge, cosmic, happening on a modest surface, which Simon Sharma describes, conveys a sense of an experience deep within Rembrandt of connection and its catastrophic loss, where any flickering flame of hope is snuffed out, permeating this painting.

In the 1660s, Rembrandt's glory days in the Dutch Republic were long over. As he was painting *The Night Watch* in 1642, Saskia, his great love and his wife, lay dying, and their little boy Titus had just been born. The loss seems to have brought some kind of breakdown. Rembrandt made etchings and drawings but stopped painting for almost a decade. He had a difficult and complicated relationship with Geertje Dircx, a woman who could become very angry, but who he treated badly. And the accumulation of debt that Rembrandt did not manage culminated in 1656 with his insolvency declared in Amsterdam Town Hall. His possessions and magnificent home were sold. What havoc and humiliation.

There were two further losses. Hendrickje Stoffels, Rembrandt's second great love, the model for some of his great paintings – excommunicated by the Reformed Church for "practising whoredom with the painter Rembrandt" – died from the plague in 1663. And his son Titus was buried on 7 September 1668, just 26 years old.

But Gregor Weber (2014a, 2014b) describes how in these last years something remarkable happened. Rembrandt was a searching artist who was constantly experimenting.

> The concept of making contemplation and introspection the dominant themes of his compositions led Rembrandt to an innovative solution. His new approach involved packing the psychological power of the entire story into a single person.
>
> (Weber, 2014a, p. 235)

> The pictorial concept of inner conflict takes on a new form and meaning in Rembrandt's late work. In a sense he reduces the factual information that is important in "reading" the story being presented ... But the less information is incorporated in a picture, the more open it is to projection by the viewer ... Quite apart from anything else, this approach to representing emotions gives the viewer a greater role, even projecting his own emotions into the figures as they follow their fate.
>
> (Ibid., p. 250).

The Return of the Prodigal Son is dated about 1666–1669. The painting hangs in the State Hermitage Museum, St Petersburg. It is the largest painting produced in the final years of Rembrandt's life.

In a visit to the Hermitage in December 2004, I am drawn back many times to look at *The Return of the Prodigal Son*, with the radiant dark red of the father's cloak. I do not want to let it go.

> The son, dressed in rags, is on his knees in front of his father; one shoe has slipped off his foot to reveal dirt and calluses. The father leans over his son and gently embraces him with both hands. Visually, his arms form a diamond shape framing the head of his son. The reactions of the figures gathered around are calm and thoughtful. The figure on the far right is possibly the Prodigal's brother; in the parable, he responds with jealousy to his brother's return, but here his face – like those of the other two men – is calm and thoughtful, even serene.
>
> (Weber. 2014b, p. 264)

That shoe that has slipped off the son's foot to reveal dirt and calluses! The son – who had wanted his inheritance so badly, demanded it, and now experiences being insignificant – has returned weary, walking and walking from havoc. He is like the thousands of refugees from Syria, Iraq, and Afghanistan, fleeing worsening fighting and chaos, lack of food and lack of employment. Angela Merkel – *Wir schaffen das* (We will manage this) – kept open Germany's borders. It was a moment, but a moment that mattered.

I think Rembrandt's late work emerges from a recapitulation of connection to goodness and its catastrophic loss, where his ideas and passions come together in a depressive coming-down to create something new, a different kind of return to *Judas Repentant Returning the Pieces of Silver*. Looking at *The Return of the Prodigal Son*, I see love create a link that makes it possible for the son to return from the abyss, where a third position keeps open the borders; a moment of reconciliation that achieves the means that offer real choice – always vulnerable to invasion by an internal tyrant.

Acknowledgement

I am grateful to Denis Flynn for drawing my attention to this meaning of *cry havoc*.

References

Aeschylus (2018). *The Oresteia*. Translated by Oliver Taplin. New York: Liverite.

Birksted-Breen, D. (1996). Phallus, Penis and Mental Space. *The International Journal of Psychoanalysis*, Volume 77, pp. 649–657.

Birksted-Breen, D. (2016). Phallus, Penis and Mental Space. In: *The Work of Psychoanalysis: Sexuality, Time and the Psychoanalytic Mind* (pp. 126–138). London: Routledge.

Britton, R. (1989). The Missing Link: Parental Sexuality in the Oedipus Complex. In: *The Oedipus Complex Today*. Edited by John Steiner. London: Karnac.

Britton, R. (2003). The Ego and the Superego. In: *Sex, Death and the Superego: Experiences in Psychoanalysis*. London: Karnac.

Britton, R. (2015). The Triangular Model. In: *Between Mind and Brain: Models of the Mind and Models in the Mind*. London: Karnac.

Brown, C., Van Camp, A., & Volgelaar, C. (2019). *Young Rembrandt*. Oxford: Ashmolean Museum, University of Oxford.

Clarke, G. (2016). *Swans. Selected Poems*. London: Picador.

Cranmer, T. (1910). At the Burial. *First Prayer-Book of Edward VI. 1549*. Compiled by Thomas Cranmer. In: *The First and Second Prayer Books of King Edward VI*. London: Dent.

Hall, J., & Stokes, J. (2021). *Changing Gear. Creating the Life You Want After a Full-on Career*. London: Headline Home.

Herbert, G. (1957). The Pulley. In: *The Metaphysical Poets*. Introduced and edited by Helen Gardner. Harmondsworth, Middlesex: Penguin Books Ltd.

Hick, J. (1966). *Evil and the God of Love*. London: MacMillan.

Klein, M. (2017). *Lectures on Technique by Melanie Klein*. Edited with critical review by John Steiner. Abingdon, Oxon: Routledge.

Lakoff, G., & Johnson, M. (1980) *Metaphors We Live By* (with a new afterword, 2003, pp. 243–274). Chicago and London: The University of Chicago Press.

Lampe, G. (1964). The Atonement: Law and Love, In *Soundings: Essays Concerning Christian Understanding*. Edited by A. Vidler. Cambridge: Cambridge University Press.

Millar, D. (2001). A Psychoanalytical View of Biblical Myth. *The International Journal of Psychoanalysis*, Volume 82, pp. 965–979.

Millar, D. (2022). *A Connecting Door: Why we need to go on asking questions and being asked questions*. New York: International Psychoanalytic Books.

O'Shaughnessy, E. (1999) Relating to the Superego. *The International Journal of Psychoanalysis*, Volume 80, p. 863.

Sodré, I. (2014). A Personal Communication from Ignês Sodré to John Steiner, quoted at the Melanie Klein Trust Conference, 14 June 2014.

Steiner, J. (2020). *Illusion, Disillusion, and Irony in Psychoanalysis*. London: Routledge.

Stevenson, J. (1987). *A New Eusebius. Documents Illustrating the History of the Church to AD 337*. Second Edition. London: SPCK.

Strauss, R. (2009). Notes & Libretto Act 1 Der Rosenkavalier (German and English). Richard Strauss as Der Rosenkavalier, Renée Fleming as the Marscallin, Munchner Philharmoniker, Conductor Christian Thielmann. London: A Unitel Classica production under exclusive licence to the Decca Music Group Ltd, p. 74.

Weber, G. (2014a). Inner Conflict. In: *Rembrandt: The Late Works*. London: The National Gallery.

Weber, G. (2014b). Reconciliation. In: *Rembrandt: The Late Works*. London: The National Gallery.

Chapter 6

Revenge and resentment in the 'Oedipus situation'

John Steiner

There has been a great deal of interest recently in the problem of resentment and grievance. In considering the way grievance is maintained and the defensive reasons for its persistence, we have come to understand how it can appear to be held onto at all costs and how the analyst may be experienced as a threat, trying to take something precious away from the patient. There is often an addictive quality and perverse gratification that adds to the hold which grievance has on the personality. At the same time, the patient comes to fear that the relinquishment of the grievance would lead to collapse and catastrophe and it seems to provide a sense of integration and protection from breakdown (Feldman, 1995). A related view of grievance comes from the work of Spillius (1993) who described what she called impenitent envy, that is, envy leading to a hatred that is felt to be justified and does not lead to regret or guilt. She links this type of envy to grievance, which also has this impenitent quality.

My own concern has been to try to look at the relationship between resentment and the wish for revenge that arises when the patient feels injured and wronged. My contention is that when such injuries are felt to be unfair they give rise to a wish for revenge that is accompanied by extreme hatred and destructiveness. Because of this, the patient believes that it is too dangerous to seek vengeance openly and directly in action. Instead, the destructiveness is controlled and expressed in indirect and often hidden ways.

I have previously described this situation in terms of a 'psychic retreat' to which the patient can withdraw where he is protected from the dangers of an open attack on his objects. In this way, the hatred is bound in a complex organisation and the sense of hurt and wrong forms the focus of grievance. Sometimes revenge is repeatedly thought about in phantasy but sometimes even the idea of entertaining vengeful thoughts is felt to endanger the patient's need to remain in the right. Nevertheless, the chronic disguised hatred, often suffused with sadism, is extremely destructive and is often felt to be vengeful by the object on the receiving end. It also provokes retaliatory acts which keep the cycle of hurt and revenge alive. In short, I argue that when revenge is felt to be unacceptable it is transformed into grievance and forms the focus of a psychic retreat.

DOI: 10.4324/9781003364313-6

I will first consider some features of revenge that may help us to differentiate it from the hostility and destructiveness which may arise in other circumstances. One striking characteristic is the sense of right, of justice, of duty and of devotion to a cause, which accompanies the quest for vengeance even in those individuals who appear to be consumed with hatred. When the patient feels himself to be the wronged victim, he is free from anxiety and guilt; in Spillius's terms, he is impenitent, and he justifies his hatred in a variety of ways. Indeed, it is often seen as a duty that he feels obliged to shoulder.

It is sometimes possible to trace the way in which the quest for vengeance begins as a demand for justice, but it seems to be taken over by a more malignant destructiveness of an insatiable kind. An example is provided by the short novel called Michael Kohlhaas, by Heinrich von Kleist (1777–1811) (Kleist, 1978). In this story, set in the sixteenth century and based on a real event, a horse dealer, Michael Kohlhaas, becomes embroiled in an incident when he refuses to pay an illegal levy to a baron for passage across his land. The baron detains two of his horses while he leaves to take up the matter with the authorities. Justice is denied him because of corruption and on his return he finds the horses neglected and his groom abused. In the process of seeking redress, he destroys his business and his marriage, burns down the baron's castle, murders its innocent inhabitants, and incites a revolt that lays waste much of the country. He is eventually executed for excessive and unlawful vengeance even though his original claim was just. It is as if the initial motive was based on respect for justice but was taken over by an insatiable destructiveness, which appears to be nothing less than an expression of the death instinct.

So, although vengeance may initially be linked to the pursuit of a just cause, the enactment reveals how it can be taken over by motives based on envy that will not be satisfied until self and object are totally destroyed. In so far as he or she has a sense of this, it is understandable that the patient is concerned to prevent its enactment in an object relationship.

The wish for revenge is therefore a complex one which often begins as a desire to preserve the good object and the patient's relationship with it. When the child feels betrayed by its good objects, a painful confusion between good and bad impulses results. In these situations, the patient's attachment to his primary objects is sustained by a profound split in which the object is idealised and love and loyalty to it demands the projection of all badness onto a persecutor. When the self, the good object, or the relationship between them is injured, it is the good object that seems to demand revenge and the patient feels it is his duty to respond as a means of restoring and preserving the lost idealised relationship. When the analyst does not support this view he threatens the ideal relationship and he is identified with the bad object who cannot be forgiven. Revenge is the antithesis of forgiveness and the patient insists that the object cannot be let off the hook until it has been forced to confess and atone for the injury done.

In a state dominated by grievance, revenge is repeatedly played out in phantasy, sometimes consciously but, as I have suggested, often unconsciously. In both cases, it is prevented from being openly expressed and even in phantasy it has a peculiar quality of unreality that is typical of psychic retreats. The result is that a direct and violent attack on the object is avoided but instead a powerful impasse is produced where development is obstructed and where destructiveness is denied. Britton (1995) describes these phantasies as inconsequential and I have previously linked them to Freud's mechanism of fetish formation in which a fact is both accepted and disavowed at the same time (Steiner, 1993).

Another characteristic of grievance is connected with the terrible sense of unfairness that is felt when the object does not behave in the way the patient believes he deserves. This type of disappointment is typically suffered in the 'Oedipus situation', which introduces the child to new realities that are experienced as profoundly shocking and can lead to a deep sense of hurt, of injustice and of betrayal.

The 'Oedipus situation', as envisaged by Klein, includes what Freud considered in the context of the primal scene, that is, the sexual relation between the parents, both as perceived and as imagined by the child. It is the reality of this relationship that introduces a third object into the two-person dyad and this is traumatic for a number of reasons, but it is particularly provocative of revenge because it shatters the assumption of the exclusive relationship between mother and child that so often forms the basis of a prior narcissistic object relationship. Environmental failures and traumatic intrusions from disturbed adults clearly play a crucial part in determining the extent of the trauma but the situation itself is one where hurt and a sense of wrong are inevitable.

The wounds are experienced as injuries to the self but also as attacks on the idealised good object, in the first instance the mother, who is felt to have been abducted against her will. The oedipal child therefore feels he has to defend his mother against the persecution of bad objects. Any challenge to this view threatens a near-delusional possession of the mother and is felt to be an attack. Knowledge of the psychic reality of the relationship between the parents is felt as a blow to omnipotence tantamount to a castration threat from a malignant powerful father motivated by envy and hatred. Such castration threats may lead to the dissolution of the Oedipus complex, as Freud described (1924), but leave behind a deep sense of injustice and violation that fuels the wish for revenge. The child feels that he is forced to give up his incestuous wishes towards his mother because of the cruel authority of the father, but he does not recognise the justice of this demand, and although he may redirect his sexual desires and inhibit his hatred and vengeance he is left with feelings of grievance, which make him look forward to a time when he can enact revenge and achieve the oedipal gratification he was denied.

Freud describes how the child finds a solution to this situation by making an identification with the abusing figure and this is well illustrated by Sophocles' *Oedipus at Colonus* in which Oedipus ill-treats his sons in the same persecutory way that his father ill-treated him (Steiner, 1990, 1993). In my view, this kind of identification often represents a disguised way of expressing grievance against the original persecutor.

The sense of wrong experienced is made more painful if it follows a period of seduction by the primary object, who may have colluded in fostering the belief that oedipal intimacy is desired by the mother as well as the child. The result is that when this fantasy collapses the child feels that a promise has been broken, so that he is not only wronged but betrayed. It is often at this point that the demand for justice turns to the thirst for vengeance. While the child can believe that his mother played only a passive part in his betrayal she can remain loved and desired. When the parents are seen to be accomplices in the child's betrayal they both become the objects of hatred and envy.

In this situation, self-deception is difficult to avoid. The sense of right is easily transformed into an assumption of righteousness as the original split needs to be strengthened by the projection of bad feelings, especially of guilt, into the third object. In this way, the betrayal by the mother is denied and the belief is re-established that she will see the error of her ways and return to the idealised relationship.

I believe that this persecutory version of the attempt to resolve the 'Oedipus conflict' is universal and gives rise to a psychic retreat based on grievance. At the same time, it seems to me that alongside this type of solution an alternative scenario exists that is also universal and that can lead to growth and development if the patient can emerge from the retreat. One might call this the depressive solution to the 'Oedipus conflict' and it also leaves the patient with major problems to be negotiated. Paradoxically, it arises when the patient is able to find the strength to rebel against parental authority and to enact his wish for vengeance both in phantasy and in a moderated form in his actual relationships, specifically in the transference. This requires that the patient is able to emerge from the psychic retreat and face his feelings towards his objects as they are revealed both through phantasy and in his actions.

If, instead of being defeated by a powerful father, the child, in phantasy, has successfully challenged the father, he comes to realise that he also hated the mother who betrayed him, and that the attack was directed against both parents, and in particular, on the relationship between them. At its most malignant it was driven by envy, and attacked all those differences which are represented by the facts of life.

When the patient is able to emerge from the psychic retreat where unreality reigns, he comes into contact with psychic reality. If he comes to have a belief in the psychic reality of phantasies and takes what happens in phantasy seriously, then the fact that the destructive attacks on the object have occurred in a dream or day-dream does not mean that they can be dismissed as unreal. They are, for a time, experienced as something that has actually happened, although it is also distinguished from the concrete situation of enactment in the external world. The result is that the patient is able to acquire a conviction of the reality of his wishes and he takes seriously the subjective belief that, as a result of his hatred, his whole world has been destroyed. Even though the revenge has been perpetrated in phantasy, it is a phantasy with consequences that does affect object relations in the real world. The individual has to face what we think of as the depressive position, in particular what was described by Klein in terms of the 'loss of the loved object': 'when the ego becomes fully identified with its good internalised objects, and at the same time becomes aware of its own incapacity to protect and preserve them against the internalised persecuting objects and the id' (Klein, 1940).

These states are filled with despair and represent the depths of depression that have to be surmounted if reality is to be faced and development is to proceed. We are not clear what it is that enables such mental distress to be tolerated but the dilemma arises in the transference as the patient tries to negotiate an alternative to the impasse that the psychic retreat based on resentment represents. If he emerges from the retreat to face the current psychic reality, he has to acknowledge that in phantasy he has attacked and destroyed his good objects in acts of vengeance that leave him and his objects devastated. Only then can he face the task of reconstructing his world and setting in motion the long and painful task of finding forgiveness and of making reparation. When he finds the pain and cost of this move to be too high, the patient will retreat to the protection of an omnipotence that enables him to re-establish a possessive control of the ideal object and to disguise his vengeful hatred.

I will first try to illustrate the way that the impingement of the 'Oedipus situation' can lead to hatred and how it gives rise to resentment if it is not acknowledged and expressed. My patient, Mr D, only rarely and briefly allowed contact of a meaningful kind. He worked as a research fellow in a cut-throat academic climate in which rivalry was at times deadly. He habitually entered new situations with a flourish and was encouraged and praised, but he could not sustain the promise and excitement that resulted and his projects repeatedly collapsed. He had become seriously depressed at university when he was first promoted and later sacked as an editor of a student newspaper. He feared a recurrence of the depression and sought analysis chiefly to avert this. In fact his situation at work was becoming increasingly precarious, partly because he could not bear criticism, so that numerous clashes with his superiors led to a furious reaction that he had to suppress to ensure his survival.

His personal involvement in the rivalry was denied, as too was his jealousy of an older sister who was not academic and was married with a young baby.

He recognised the pleasure that his sister gave his parents but saw this as something that he would easily surpass as soon as he was able to bring off his research success and with its aid acquire the kind of wife of whom his parents would approve.

A great deal of time was spent in planning moves to different departments, to different countries, and even to different fields of research, and although in fantasy these led to triumph over his colleagues and teachers he saw them as reparative rather than vengeful, and he denied any hatred towards those who constantly appeared to overlook his importance and to prevent his advancement.

I want to concentrate on a session in which he began by describing a meeting that took place in the office next door to his on the previous day. It was in the senior lecturer's room and he was not invited, which rubbed in the fact that he no longer had a place in the department. Later he had a serious talk with the senior lecturer who gave him advice about how to handle himself better. He was told that he made impulsive decisions that were not to be trusted and the patient responded compliantly by agreeing that this was absolutely correct and by expressing gratitude for what the department had done for him. This can be viewed as a submission to a powerful father, but in fact it was clear from his frequent disparaging remarks about this lecturer and about the department that he thought of himself as superior and that he was holding his tongue until he could show them all how he would succeed in a different setting.

He went on to speak excitedly, but with some lack of conviction, about his new prospects and research plans, but he added that he thought I would be disappointed in him since I would view these as a repetition of a cycle and see him as 'back to square one'. He had broken off the relationship with his old girlfriend over a year previously but continued to phone her and discussed his new jobs and new girls with her in great detail. Now he complained that he had left a message for her and she had failed to phone him back. He wondered if it was because he had recently spoken about his masturbation, which had come up in the analysis. I think he expected her to admire the way he was able to use his analysis to talk about things that others found embarrassing but instead she had said 'how disgusting'.

I made several interpretations in the course of the session, that centred around the idea that the underlying situation that he could not bear was one in which the meeting held in the next-door office reminded him of my independent existence and of times when he felt small and excluded. I had in mind that if he could recognise and express his hatred and wish for revenge, he might be able to recognise the attacks he made against me and that it could lead to a move towards emergence from the retreat and a contact with his regret and wish to put things right with me. In this instance, such a move seemed too great an injury to his pride and was quite out of the question.

The patient's reaction to the senior lecturer was excessively deferential and compliant. Not only did he deny his rage but he agreed with the criticisms that were made of him. He was shortly to be dismissed and this is why he was not invited to the meeting. He saw it as both a punishment for his arrogance and excessive ambition and a lesson he had to learn in order to curb his true feelings. He was similarly deferential in his treatment of me in the sessions and in both cases it was clear that his rage could not be expressed. I was never sure if he had to curb his violence because he feared that I would be destroyed by it or if he was convinced that I would retaliate with such severity so that he submitted to avoid castration or death. The result was that his vengeance, being unexpressed, was transformed into resentment and grievance.

When his projects collapsed this patient felt so betrayed and so wronged and defeated that his identification was with a sadistic, punitive, vengeful but essentially weak father, which led him to treat others in the same way that his father treated him. He wanted to avenge the wrongs done to him but did not feel strong enough to express his hatred openly. As a result, he gave up his ambitions towards his primary object but did not give up his hope of revenge, and turned to new objects with his ambition and aim essentially unchanged.

This was clear in his constant excited search for new projects, which had a manic quality as he appeared to identify with an omnipotent and savage father. Although intended as reparative projects that would put things right with his family, these always seemed to lead to disaster and to a collapse that led to the cycle having to be repeated. It was this that he recognised when he thought I would be disappointed with him and see him as 'back to square one'. This was why he was unable to relinquish the psychic retreat based on grievance and tolerate any meaningful psychic change.

I am ashamed to admit that I could not find satisfactory clinical material of an instance where a resentful impasse can soften to allow a successful move towards a depressive solution of the 'Oedipus conflict' and this is why I turn to literature for an example. Nevertheless, I believe these instances are clinically real and important although very difficult to describe. Often they are fleeting and both patient and analyst may come to doubt whether they are genuine. Sometimes, after a more-than-usual virulent attack, the patient may notice that I look tired or even unwell. A recognition that I am considerably older than the patient has realised has produced another shift that has led to a lessening of resentment and envy.

These moments often follow periods of intense hatred in which the analyst has been cruelly attacked. If the attacks can be tolerated and properly analysed rather than condemned, resentment can give way to remorse and a move towards reparation can begin. Often this takes the form of forgiveness both on the part of the patient for the analyst's faults and shortcomings and on the part of the analyst, who must share this process and give the patient the sense that psychic reality does not have the moralistic unforgiving quality that it so often acquires. In the same way, an open attack by the patient may enable the analyst to escape from a paralysis of guilt and defend himself more vigorously. This may in turn enable him to feel regret and guilt, allowing him to climb down and initiate a more forgiving atmosphere.

I will try to illustrate what I mean by looking briefly at the case of the relationship between the young David Balfour and the older Alan Breck in Robert Louis Stevenson's novel, *Kidnapped*. The dangerous, arduous, and painful journey that these two are forced to undertake has many parallels to that which patient and analyst endure with each other. Of the many themes explored, revenge is prominent and the quarrel between the two heroes, which is the high point of the novel, shows both the difficulty of avoiding resentment and the need to enact it as revenge, in order to surmount it.

A repeated theme is the violence of the hatred between rival groups, whether these be between Scots and English, Highlanders and Lowlanders, Celts and Saxons, Presbyterians and Catholics, or rival clans, in this case particularly the Campbells and Stewarts.

On the one hand, there is the first-person narrator, David Balfour, representing lowland Scotland, who tries to be fair and reasonable, believes in the process of law, and in the moderating influence of religion. In contrast, Alan Beck is romantic, proud, loyal, cynical, and forthright. Of the two, Alan is the more violent, full of hatred and always talking of vengeance. When David mentions his friend Mr Campbell, Alan cried that he hated all that were of that name.

> I know nothing I would help a Campbell to unless it was a leaden bullet. I would hunt all of that name like black-cocks. If I lay dying, I would crawl upon my knees to my chamber window for a shot at one. Ye ken very well that I am a Stewart, and the Campbells have long harried and wasted those of my name.

He explains the various persecutions suffered by the Stewarts, who were dispossessed from their land and were even forbidden to wear a kilt. That his constant harping on revenge was based on love and loyalty to his family is emphasised when he proudly claims that 'the one thing they couldnae kill was the love the clansmen bore their chief'. I often find that I feel the attacks of the patient most painfully when it is not me but my 'chief' who is attacked, usually psychoanalysis, Freud or Klein.

This is the background to the quarrel between the friends that forms the climax of the book and illustrates the way in which David's resentment builds up into a self-justifying system of argument, which entraps him in a self-destructive state from which he is at first unable to emerge. What makes this chapter so moving is that he is finally able to express his rage and his hatred and, through this expression, find a way of admitting his need for Alan. This in turn allows Alan to respond and to express his remorse and regret at his part in the quarrel.

The two have aided each other and have endured great hardship and danger since David was kidnapped, but at this point David has been unable to resist the temptation to indulge in secret speculations that he could save himself if he abandoned his friend. This makes him feel guilty and disloyal and he begins to hate himself as well as Alan. The situation is made more acute by the fact that Alan tricked David into lending him his money, which he gambled away. Again there are parallels with analysis, where the desire to break off treatment is common in these situations of impasse and so too are accusations over money, notably about the fee, paying for missed sessions etc., which fuel the resentment.

David and Alan become more and more exhausted by the hardship of the journey. To begin with, David withdraws into silence.

> For a long time we said nothing; marching alongside or one behind each other, each with a set countenance; I angry and proud and drawing what strength I had from these two violent and sinful feelings: Alan angry and ashamed, ashamed that he had lost my money and angry that I should take it so ill ... During all these horrid wanderings we had no familiarity, scarcely even that of speech. The truth is that I was sickening for my grave, which is my best excuse. Besides that, I was of an unforgiving disposition from my birth, slow to take offence, slower to forget it and now incensed both against my companion and myself.

For three further days, Alan remained largely silent but polite and helpful, but after another short outburst of bitterness he seemed to forgive himself for the affair of the money; 'cocked his hat again, walked jauntily, whistled airs, and looked at me upon one side with a provoking smile'. Next, he started to taunt David, calling him Whig, the term he used for supporters of the English King, and teased him for his tiredness.

David knew it was his own fault but he was unable to repent and he began to dwell on fantasies of lying down and dying on the wet mountain.

> My head was light perhaps; but I began to love the prospect, I began to glory in the thought of such a death, alone in the desert, with the wild eagles besieging my last moments. Alan would repent then, I thought; he would remember, when I was dead, how much he owed me, and the remembrance would be torture. And at each of Alan's taunts, I hugged myself, 'Ah!' thinks I to myself, 'I have a better taunt in readiness; when I lie down and die, you will feel it like a buffet in your face; ah what a revenge! ah, how you will regret your ingratitude and cruelty!'

The idealisation of death as the ultimate revenge is a theme familiar to analysts and involves a kind of unreality since the patient is both dead and also alive and enjoying the pleasure of revenge, as in fantasies of being present at one's own funeral.

David continues,

> All the while I was growing worse and worse. The stitch in my side was
> hardly bearable. At last I began to feel that I could trail myself no far-
> ther; and with that, there came on me all at once the wish to have it out
> with Alan, let my anger blaze, and be done with my life in a more
> sudden manner.

He complains to Alan about his insults, and returns with even harsher ones
himself, demanding that he speak in a civil way of the King and of the
Campbells.

> 'I am a Stewart—' began Alan. 'Oh' says I, 'I ken ye bear a king's name.
> But I have seen many of those that bear it; and the best I can say of them
> is this, that they would be none the worse of washing'.

The attacks on both sides are on the family name and their loyalty to it is
challenged. Alan finally says, 'This is a pity. There are things said that cannot
be passed over'. David had intended just this and drew his sword as if to
settle the matter through violence, knowing full well that against the
experienced swordsman he stood no chance.

Alan cries, 'Are ye daft? I cannae draw upon thee David, it's fair murder'.
Being further provoked he draws his sword but throws it to one side saying,
'Na, na,—I cannae, I cannae'.

David continues,

At this the last of my anger oozed all out of me; and I found myself only
sick, and sorry, and blank, and wondering at myself. I would have given the
world to take back what I had said; but a word once spoken who can
recapture it? I minded me of all Alan's kindness and courage in the past, how
he had helped and cheered and borne with me in our evil days; and then
recalled my own insults, and saw that I had lost forever that doughty friend.
At the same time, the sickness that hung upon me seemed to redouble, and
the pang in my side was like a sword for sharpness. This it was that gave me
a thought. No apology could blot out what I had said; it was needless to
think of one, none could cover the offence; but where an apology was vain, a
mere cry for help might bring Alan back to my side. I put my pride away
from me. 'Alan!' I said; 'If you cannae help me, I must just die here'. 'If I die
ye'll can forgive me, Alan? In my heart, I liked ye fine even when I was the
angriest'.

'Wheesht, wheesht', cried Alan, 'Dinnae say that! David, man, ye ken—'
he shut his mouth upon a sob, and began to help David to lean upon him.
Again he came near sobbing. 'Davie, I am no right man at all; I have neither
sense nor kindness; I couldnae remember ye were just a bairn. I couldnae see
you were dying on your feet; Davie, ye'll have to try and forgive me'.

'Oh man, lets say no more about it' said David, 'we're neither one of us to mend the other—that's the truth'.

> The reconciliation is not based on denial but on a recognition of psychic reality; it is not just an acknowledgement of wrongs done but also of difference and of dependence. Reparation can begin with forgiveness but only after a belief in what has happened is achieved since a belief cannot be relinquished unless it is first fully acknowledged.
>
> (Britton, 1995)

Of course, such developments are always unstable, easily turning once more into resentment. Even after the above scene Alan goes too far in a patronising direction and offers to carry David on his back. David rejects this provocatively by claiming that he is a good 12 inches taller than Alan.

> 'You are no such thing. There may be a trifling matter of an inch or two; I am no saying that I'm exactly what you would call a tall man, whatever; and I dare say', he added, his voice trailing off in a laughable manner, 'now when I come to think of it, I dare say y'ell be just about right. Ay, it'll be a foot, or near hand; or maybe even mair'! 'Alan', David cries, 'What makes ye so good to me? What makes ye care for such a thankless fellow?' 'Deed I don't know', said Alan. 'for just precisely what I thought I liked about ye, was that ye never quarrelled;— and now I like ye better!'

I believe that Stevenson is right that the two great sins, the obstacles to emergence from the psychic retreat based on resentment, are anger and pride. He is also astute when he suggests that they serve a function in times of stress as when David explains that he drew what strength he had from these two 'violent and sinful feelings'.

A great deal has been written on hatred and we recognise that when its roots lie in envy it can become such a destructive force against development in the self in the object and in particular in the relationship between them. We seem to understand pride less well. When David comes to claim his inheritance from his wicked uncle Ebenezer, he learns that the two brothers, his uncle and father, had loved the same woman. This rivalry was solved by a deal in which David's father won his mother but had to live in poverty, while his uncle was recompensed with the family fortune and the family name and estate. This he holds on to as a miser and has David kidnapped to prevent him from making a lawful claim. Ebenezer's sense of identity turns on pride and depends on the possession of wealth, property and title. David too, when he is enraged at the wrongs done to him by Alan, is at first too proud to admit his dependence, and his pride seems to give him a determination that would rather see him dead than humiliated.

Sometimes, in these cases, pride seems to be based on anal mechanisms, and retention and hoarding are turned to as a substitute for feeling loved. Holding on to anal contents may be an act of loyalty to an object felt as protected as well as possessed and controlled, and also as a way of avoiding dependence, humiliation, and shame. Sometimes phantasies of anal riches give rise to a sense of strength and independence, in phantasy being represented as an internal penis or serving as a vertebral column supporting the patient and helping him to deny his need for others. The threat of loss of this source of strength is felt as an anal attack, as a castration threat, or a robbery, and leads to an intensification of resentment, sometimes with a conviction that survival depends on the combination of resentment, pride and hatred.

What precisely leads to the opportunity to emerge from such states is difficult to describe. Perhaps the pain and exhaustion that lead David first to glorify his death as the ultimate revenge can later lead him to admit his need for help. I believe that a resolution could not have happened if his anger had not led him openly to draw his sword and attack Alan. Many patients believe that the demand on them is to give up the grievance and submit in order to become compliant and conformist. We do not understand the factors that enable someone to move in precisely the opposite direction and to pluck up the courage to emerge from the retreat and have it out; one could say have it out with a vengeance. In some cases, this leads to a conviction that the child will destroy the parent, but David's sense of reality was intact and he knew such an attack was suicidal. The change seemed to have resulted from some internal process in David that enabled him to test the nature of his object through experience rather than phantasy. This change also had consequences for the relationship between David and Alan, since it enabled the older and stronger man to recognise that he was dealing with a child and hence to desist and to climb down.

David and Alan did not suffer the kind of disturbance of personality that characterises many of our patients, and yet the basic mechanisms are, I believe, similar, and such moments do occur in an analysis, where too, the move to forgiveness may be initiated by either the patient or the analyst. Perhaps it is the stronger partner who has to climb down, and a more open attack enables him to do so. Perhaps the analyst's capacity to emerge from the paralysing depression occasioned by his guilt, as happened to Alan when he got over stealing David's money, is another factor. Something seems to give way with the exhaustion of a long struggle, and pride is relinquished and replaced by acknowledgement of psychic reality, including a mutual, but not equal, dependence. Out of this, forgiveness can arise, and can allow an emergence from the psychic retreat to face the reality of the relationship. The patient I described earlier could not pick up some equivalent of David's sword and attack me directly. Perhaps he was too proud, perhaps he was too convinced he would be the stronger and that he would annihilate me if he emerged from the retreat. There are many imponderable aspects of this situation which makes for a difficult but interesting analytic task that offers a challenge to further research.

References

Britton, R. S. (1995). Psychic reality and unconscious belief. *Int. J. Psychoanal.*, 76: 19–23.

Feldman, M. (1995). *Grievance.* Unpublished manuscript.

Freud, S. (1910). A special type of choice of object made by men. *S.E.* 11.

Freud, S. (1924). On the dissolution of the Oedipus complex. *S.E.* 19.

Klein, M. (1940). Mourning and its relation to manic-depressive states. *Int. J. Psychoanal.*, 21: 125–153. Reprinted in *The Writings of Melanie Klein*, Vol. 1. London: Hogarth, 1975, pp. 344–369.

Kleist, H.von. (1978). *The Marquise of O and other stories*, trans. D. Luke & N. Reeves. London: Penguin.

Spillius, E. B. (1993). Varieties of envious experience. *Int. J. Psychoanal.*, 74: 1199–1212.

Steiner, J. (1990). The retreat from truth to omnipotence in *Oedipus at Colonus. Int. J. Psychoanal*, 17: 227–237.

Steiner, J. (1993). *Psychic Retreats: Pathological Organisations of the Personality in Psychotic, Neurotic, and Borderline Patients.* London and New York: Routledge.

Stevenson, R. L. (1886). *Kidnapped.* London: Penguin, 1994.

Chapter 7

"She waited, Kate Croy": the villain's tragedy

On Henry James and Forgiveness

Ignês Sodré

Summary of the novel:

The *Wings of the Dove* tells the story of Milly Theale, a young American heiress stricken with a serious disease, and her effect on the people around her. She travels to Europe with her companion, Mrs Susan Stringham, a widow; she passionately wants to live as much as she can. In London, they meet Susan's old friend, the wealthy Mrs Maud Lowder, and her niece, the beautiful Kate Croy, who befriend her. Kate is secretly engaged to Merton Densher, who Milly had met, and fallen in love with, when he visited New York. Aunt Maud wants Kate to marry an impoverished aristocrat, Lord Mark; she would give Kate her money to make this possible (though she wouldn't help her to be able to marry Densher, a journalist). In London Milly enjoys great social success; she had chosen to go there, after starting her European tour in Switzerland, to see a famous specialist, Sir Luke Strett, because she fears she may die very soon. Kate finds out about this illness, and devises a plan which involves Densher: she wants him to woo and marry Milly, so that when she dies he will inherit her fortune, making it possible for them to marry. Milly rents a Palazzo in Venice to which she and Susan move, and where she will soon die. Kate, Aunt Maud and Densher are invited to come; Kate and Aunt Maud leave, and Densher stays, and he and Milly become very close. Sir Luke Strett visits her; then when Lord Mark comes to see her and tells her that Kate and Densher are secretly engaged. Milly gives up fighting for her life and dies, having first forgiven Densher. She leaves her fortune to him, but he refuses it. Kate realises that he secretly loves Milly, although he still wants to marry her, and their relationship ends. (The reader might also want to watch Iain Softley's accomplished 1997 film adaptation.)

The Wings of the Dove (1902) recounts the story of two young women – two tragic heroines. The "Dove", Milly Theale, is modelled on Henry James' beloved cousin Minny, who died of tuberculosis when she was 24; Milly, condemned to the same cruel fate, has a "passionate yearning to live while she might"; she falls in love, but discovers before she dies that this isn't reciprocated. The other, Kate Croy, who will eventually become the villain of the story, experiences mutual passionate love, and creates a plot designed to protect it so it will last forever; in the end, she tragically suffers the cruel death of this perfect love. In the drama of forgiveness, Milly will be the forgiving, Kate the unforgivable, and Merton

DOI: 10.4324/9781003364313-7

Densher, Kate's secret lover, who Milly falls in love with, will be the forgiven. The novel starts and ends with Kate Croy, who is also the creator of its title: it is she who gives Milly the name "Dove".

In his 1909 preface to *The Wings of the Dove*, Henry James discusses the structure of the novel and what he felt was his failure to get the balance right in relation to the different parts of the book and the different characters; I thought he was unconsciously apologising to Milly Theale, his tragic heroine, for giving so much space, and love, to her "sister" Kate Croy. Kate and Milly are rivals for Densher's love. In the preface, they seem to be rivals for their author's love as well.

In Henry James's first (1894) sketch of the novel, Kate Croy is conceived much more as the "heartless and scheming" villain in a melodrama; Milly Theale as her passively suffering victim, a "figure of excruciating agony". "She is equally pathetic in her doom and in her horror of it. If she could live just a little; just a little more – just a little longer. She is like a creature dragged shrieking to the guillotine – to the shambles" (Brooks, 1976, p. 179). As the novel develops, the characters become much more complex, their consciousness examined in great depth: the ultimate demonstration of what James developed to the utmost power of his genius in his last three masterpieces. The question of innocence and guilt – the moral battle between good and evil – is presented in the most intricate way. Milly (like Minny) has enormous strength of character and courage; and we do understand what motivates Kate to create her villainous "plot".

Henry James' preface to the 1909 New York Edition, and the writing of *The Wings of the Dove*.

The preface starts:

> *The Wings of the Dove*, published in 1902, represents to my memory a very old – if I shouldn't perhaps say a very young – motive; I can scarce remember the time when the situation on which this long-drawn fiction mainly rests was not vividly present to me. The idea, reduced to its essence, is that of a young person conscious of a great capacity for life, but early stricken and doomed, condemned to die under short respite, while also enamoured of the world; aware moreover of the condemnation and passionately desiring to "put in" before extinction as many of the finer vibrations as possible, and so achieve, however briefly and brokenly, the sense of having lived.
>
> (p. 3)

> … The last fact was the real issue, for the way grew straight from the moment one recognised that the poet essentially *can't* be concerned with the act of dying.
>
> (p. 4)

Henry James' "old and young" motive is his wish to portray his beloved cousin Minny: her strikingly vital, original personality combined with her betrayal by fate. "Death at the last, was dreadful to her; she would have given anything to live" (2003, p. 484). Milly, who has Minny's personality, will be betrayed by her friends; this, at the end, will make her lose her indomitable wish to live.

That this poet "can't be concerned with the act of dying"— both the moment of death and all the physical suffering that must have preceded it — is understandable as this would have required him to imagine Minny's death from TB: she already had haemorrhages before he left the USA, and the gruesomeness of the condition and her appalling suffering would have been unbearable. Throughout the novel, Milly's illness remains unnamed and mysterious.[1] One imagines also that writing the book could have been an attempt at making reparation for his guilt at having abandoned her, as well as his gratitude for inheriting a treasure from her in his inspiration for the novel.

The central point of re-visiting the novel in his 1909 preface is the explication of what he felt were, or could be seen as, his failures: the structure that doesn't entirely follow the plan (referred to as done "in good faith", interestingly), the centre is located later than it should have been (in Book 5), the last part of the novel is "foreshortened", "deformed" (p. 13). Kate's presence dominates Book 1; Densher, and her relationship with him, are at the centre of Book 2. Milly only makes her appearance in Book 3. Her "almost full-blown consciousness" only appears in Book 5.

Defending the choice of starting with, and giving so much space to, Kate Croy:

> If [Milly's] impulse to wrest from her shrinking hour still as much from the fruit of life as possible, if this longing [for a life "quite dazzlingly liveable"] can take effect only by the aid of others, their participation ... becomes their drama too – that of their promoting her illusion ... from motives and points of view, of their own.
>
> (p. 5)

> ... there could be no full presentation of Milly Theale as *engaged* with elements amid which she was to draw her breath in such pain, should not the elements have been, with all solicitude, duly prefigured. If one had seen that her stricken state was but half her case, the correlative half being the state of others as affected by her (they too should have a "case", bless them, quite as much as she!), then I was free to choose the half with which I should begin ... yet it was nonetheless visibly my "key" ... that though [Milly] should form my centre, my circumference was every wit as treatable.
>
> (p. 8)

... from the moment I had comfortably laid the ground provided in my first Book, *ground from which Milly is superficially so absent.*

(p. 7)

... the whole preliminary presentation of Kate Croy *absolutely declined to enact itself save in terms of amplitude.*

(p. 9)

Book V re-adopts the previous centre, Milly's now almost full-blown consciousness. I had by this time all the choice of those [who would] brush that surface with a dark wing.

(p. 9)

And, back to discussing form, he again reassures Milly, touchingly, of his love for her:

the author's instinct [is] everywhere for the *indirect* presentation of his main image ... which proceeds, obviously, *from her painter's tenderness of imagination about her* ... So, if we talk of princesses, do the balconies opposite the palace gates ... rake from afar the mystic figure in the gilded coach as it comes forth into the great *place.*

(pp. 15–16)

The curtains open on a scene of a young woman who is at her father's lodgings waiting for him to arrive for a meeting with her. We see her despondency, we hear her thoughts, we visit the room which describes not only his circumstances but also his character. I will take it here as a description of the hateful, untrustworthy father in her inner world. Her mother has died: the depressed, impoverished victim of this cruel father. In the novel, we will see a transformation in this bright, beautiful young woman, Kate Croy, who becomes the villain in a cruel plot of her own devising. I will suggest that she unconsciously identifies with this unforgivable object, whilst steeling herself away from an identification with a loving but horribly damaged depressed mother. Kate creates her plot so as to ensure the survival of her perfect love (she says to Densher, her lover, with "extraordinary beauty", "I engage myself to you forever" (p. 93)). In Kate's story, it is the impossibility of bearing a triangular relationship which will end up killing that which she was trying to preserve forever. In terms of internal reality, we could conceptualise this totally symmetrical relationship which excludes all others as a perfect union with a loving mother pre-catastrophic fall from illusion (as Steiner (2020) has described).

An examination of the first paragraph of the novel:

She waited, Kate Croy, for her father to come in, but he kept her *unconscionably*, and there were moments *at which she showed herself, in the glass over the mantel, a face positively pale with irritation* ... It was at this point, however, that she remained; ... moving from the shabby sofa to the armchair upholstered in a glazed cloth that gave at once – she had tried it – the sense of the *slippery* and of the *sticky* ... [S]he had from time to time taken a brief stand on the small balcony ... *The vulgar little street offered scant relief from the vulgar little room; its main office was to suggest to her that the narrow black house-fronts, adjusted to a standard that would have been low even for backs, constituted quite the publicity implied by such privacies.* One *felt* them in the room exactly as one *felt* the room in the street. Each time she turned in again, each time in her impatience ... she *tasted* the faint flat emanation of things, the failure of fortune and of honour. To feel the street, to feel the room, to feel the table-cloth and the centre piece and the lamp, gave her a small salutary sense at least of neither shirking not lying. This whole vision was the worst thing yet ... *and for what had she come but for the worst? She tried to be sad so as not to be angry, but it made her angry that she couldn't be sad. And yet where was misery, misery too beaten for blame and chalk-marked by fate like a "lot" at a common auction, if not in these merciless signs of mere mean stale feelings?*

(James, 2003, p. 22, my italics)

She waited, Kate Croy: This is a very powerful beginning (I think of *Call me Ishmael*). Not "*Kate Croy waited*".[2] Kate waits and waits and waits ... until the last line of this long novel – finally not to get what she has been waiting for: to achieve a union with her loved object forever. In this first scene, she is waiting "for her father to come in, but he kept her unconscionably": waiting for a cruel and irresponsible father, who only loves himself; "*unconscionable*" describes his character. But this word – the 15th word in the first line of the novel, will be shown to be the perfect word for Kate Croy's secret plot to deceive her innocent, dying, friend, Milly Theale.[3] The first paragraph refers not only to Lionel Croy's past behaviour, but also to what he is about to do: to sell his daughter to her wealthy Aunt Maud.

"*Her face pale with irritation*": Irritation is a feeling you want to get rid of, scratch out; unlike anger, it is impotent, contemptible (an "ugly feeling"[4]). Looking at herself in the mirror, she gets no reassurance: her face reflects what she is seeing; she is imprisoned, body and mind, in ugliness. She feels over-identified with her father: she is "inside" him, inside his atmosphere; but he is also too much "inside" her, contaminating her with the ugliness of his character. The *slippery* and the *sticky* appear simultaneously: two qualities of the Bad Lap, apparently opposite, but horribly intertwined, conveying the impossibility of ever feeling lovingly held: ... "*shabby, wanting in freshness, low even for backs*". Kate *feels* the street, *feels* the room, *feels* the tablecloth; she *tastes* "the emanation of things, the failure of fortune and honour".

"Feeling" and "tasting" are important, in addition to seeing, and, we imagine, smelling; she is, against her will, imbibing the atmosphere of the bad object, which is being projected into her through all her senses, including under her skin. She is forced to introject it, as well as being claustrophobically "inside" it. She is irritated, but cannot get rid of it, and this makes her ugly: full of "mean stale feelings".

The last words of this paragraph:

> ... and for what had she come but for the worst? She tried to be sad so as not to be angry, but it made her angry that she couldn't be sad. And yet where was misery, misery too beaten for blame and chalk-marked by fate like a "lot" at a common auction, if not in these merciless signs of mere mean stale feelings.

Her insightful observation that she is unable to feel sad makes it possible for us to imagine that Kate's fear of poverty is the fear of sinking into an identification with the poor, unloved, ill mother.

I think this is "the worst" in Kate's sense of herself. In the beginning, she struggles against this sense of miserable meanness and internal poverty (her father's moral failure, her mother's depression); gradually she comes to idealise the state of strength which comes from the internal split between her preservation of the ideal world of romantic love and the betrayal of her friendship with Milly.

This is the end of Kate's conversation with her father:

> "Well then good-bye papa".
> "Of course you understand that it may be for long".
> Her companion had hereupon one of his finest inspirations. "Why not frankly forever? ... if I offer you to efface myself it's for the final fatal sponge I ask, well saturated and well applied".

(p. 31)

The first paragraph encapsulates an enormous amount of information in relation to Kate Croy's state of mind which, I suggest, ultimately leads to a horrible identification with the bad internal object; this will make it possible for her to *become* the villain, and shows James' profound psychological understanding of his character. Her father appears very little in the novel; this encounter with him is fundamental for our understanding of the plot: Kate as a betrayed child, whose father, with no thought, let alone regret, sells her forever. A father who it is impossible to forgive; who behaves, always, unconscionably. Kate, his daughter, will, unconsciously, create the plot which is the centre of the novel.

Her trajectory in the novel towards conceiving the plot to betray Milly is slow; doubt and uncertainty are left to Densher. Escaping poverty is the stated reason for the plot, even though Densher, a bright and ambitious journalist, is not a pauper. Beauty is held onto through the passionate love between her and Densher. Her tragedy is that this is what she will finally lose.

Densher

James introduces Densher as difficult to place: a gentleman, educated, generally sound, generally civil; "*yet, though to that degree neither extraordinary nor abnormal, he would have failed to play straight into an observer's hands*". He would look "*vague without looking weak – idle without looking empty*". The word *unconscionable* appears again, with a much lighter meaning: he is sitting, and *throws* [his head] *suddenly back and, supported behind by his uplifted and interlocked hands, place him for unconscionable periods in communion with the ceiling, the tree-tops, the sky.*

From John Steiner's (1990) paper on forgiveness:

> The main thesis in my paper is that the goodness of the object is sought for two distinct aims. It can be used to get immediate relief by doing away with the bad feelings and evading responsibility and guilt, or it can be used to help the patient face psychic reality, take responsibility for his actions, accept his guilt and embark on the task of reparation. These two divergent paths occur repeatedly in different areas of development and fundamentally reflect the conflict between the pleasure principle and the reality principle.

Connecting this formulation to *Wings*, we could say that Densher apparently accepts some responsibility and guilt, and attempts to make reparation through refusing the inheritance; however, throughout the novel, as he becomes more and more aware of the plot: he will marry a dying girl in order to inherit her fortune – he constantly has an internal conversation in which he forgives himself: "At least I wasn't lying!": in Steiner's words, "It can be used to get immediate relief by doing away with the bad feelings and evading responsibility and guilt". Later it will be clear that this involves a great deal of self-idealisation.

When Kate and Densher are talking about Aunt Maud as "Britannia of the Market place", Kate says: "She fixed upon me herself, settled on me with her wonderful gilded claws". Densher replies: "You speak ... as if she were a vulture". Kate: "Call it an eagle – with a gilded beak as well, and with wings for great flights" (p. 61). But Densher knows that their murderous conspiracy involves vultures: Kate and he are birds of prey. (It is interesting also to think of Henry James's use of a real person as inspiration for the novel – a question novelists often have to negotiate, both consciously and unconsciously; and here of course because it involves great love of, and also abandonment of, his heroine. The novelist, in his internal world, is both eagle with golden claws, and vulture feeding from the dead.)

It is only in the last part of the novel, when the main characters have all gone to Venice, that Densher – finally! – fully understands Kate's plot:

KATE SAYS: "You'll have a free hand, a clear field, a chance – well, quite ideal".

DENSHER REPLIES: "Your descriptions – her 'ideal' was such a touch! – are prodigious. And what I don't make out is how, caring for me, you can like it".

KATE: "I don't like it, but I am a person, thank goodness, who can do what I don't like".

(p. 311)

But she is wrong about who she is. And at the end, when Densher sees what they have done, and loves Milly, and therefore isn't Kate's puppet, the situation becomes intolerable for Kate. Her belief, fundamental for her psychic equilibrium (Joseph, 1989), in the continuity of his perfect love for her, breaks down when she is faced by a rival. She is not the person she had imagined she was.[5]

Milly

Henry James had described Milly as "a creature with her security hanging so by a hair, couldn't but fall somehow into some abysmal trap" (p. 6).

Milly is first introduced through the eyes of her travel companion, Susan Stringham, whose maiden name is Shepherd.

> Mrs. Stringham was never to forget ... her own first sight of the striking apparition: ... the slim, constantly pale, delicately haggard, anomalously, agreeably angular young person, of no more than two-and-twenty summers, whose hair was somehow exceptionally red even for the real thing ... and whose clothes were remarkably black even for robes of mourning ... She was alone, she was stricken, she was rich, and in particular was strange.
>
> (p. 77)

Milly's mourning was "multitudinous": she had lost everyone in the world. (Minny Temple had lost both parents, as well as four of her eight siblings, in her childhood.)

At the beginning of Book 3, Milly and Susan are in a hotel in the mountains in Switzerland; Milly had left early in the morning alone for a walk. Susan follows her from a distance, and sees her sitting on a ledge over an abyss. Knowing that she is very ill, Susan's first thought is that she might be considering suicide. And then:

> If the girl was deeply and recklessly meditating she wasn't meditating a jump … She was looking down on the kingdoms of the earth [but] it wouldn't be with a view of renouncing them.
>
> (p. 88)

> … a view of great extent and beauty, but thrown forward and vertiginous … had gone straight down, till it was all before her.
>
> (p. 89)

Henry James is referring to Milton's Paradise lost (1990):

> The world was all before them, where to choose.
> Their place of rest, and providence their guide:
> They hand in hand with wand'ring steps and slow,
> Through Eden took their solitary way.
>
> (p. 441)

Adam and Eve were moving from Paradise to Reality (Steiner, 2020) where they would live but will also die. They went "hand in hand" into the world; as the novel continues, Milly will be tricked into believing she wouldn't have to be alone for her "solitary walk".

Although Susan quickly dismisses the question of suicide, this is of great importance in Henry James' mind, in relation to the two other women who are surely in the background of the novel: his sister Alice, who was thinking of suicide when she was a teenager (with her father's approval: he "reassured" her that this was her choice) and who became an invalid for most of her life (Strouse, 1980). And his close friend Fenimore (the writer Constance Fenimore Woolson), who committed suicide by throwing herself out of a window (an abyss) in Venice (surely a crucial motive for the choice of Venice for Milly's place of death) made him feel very guilty. Fenimore was a very close friend for many years, he shared her house in Italy; it was clear that she had wished for more intimacy and permanence in their relationship; to some extent, he had abandoned her to her death.[6]

Rosemary Davies (2020) has an illuminating view on this scene, and on Milly's personality:[7]

> Forgiveness is complex in the novel. And envy comes in its way. Milly in mourning black, but seemingly in New York, partying, is envied for her assumed capacity to love all those lost objects listed at the beginning of the novel. I agree that, like the real life Minny, she is exceptional and unique but isn't she too much the idealised object who disguises some rage? For example the episode of her on the ledge, looking as though she might jump. Did she know that her devoted companion would witness

this and feel afraid? She wanted to experience the "abysses" but there is a possible attempt to evoke fear in others, perhaps a deceit.

Davies is right to remind us of Milly's (split-off) rage: does she want Susie, her Shepherd, to be afraid for her? to think of suicide? And what does Milly mean, when she says later, "I want abysses!"?[8]

Thinking about Milly's rage makes sense of a violent, gruesome "French Revolution" image[9] that comes to her mind when she visits the famous specialist Sir Luke Strett in London to consult him about her illness. She trusts him immediately, and it is clear that he likes her and respects her; later he visits her in Venice. But in this first consultation, she sees pity in Sir Luke's attitude: pity is experienced as an attack on her. She wants to hide her suffering, to go on being strong and brave:

> [Sir Luke's] desire to let the patient down easily. When that was the case the reason, in turn, could only be, too manifestly, pity; and *when pity held up its tell-tale face like a head on a pike, in a French Revolution, bobbing before a window*, what was the inference but that the patient was bad? He might say what he would now -*she would always have seen the head at the window*; and in fact from this moment she only wanted him to say what he would.[10]
>
> (p. 150, my italics)

This image is surely the result of immense rage:

> She had simply given it to him so, *and this was all that would ever pass between them on the odious head.*
>
> (p. 152, my italics)

Of course, she had seen pity in Susie's eyes, too; which would support Davies's reading of the scene. And she consciously decides not to show her fear and fragility, so as not to see pity in her companions' eyes; she will be brave, and consciously chooses to disguise herself as the typical American Girl for this purpose. As Davies points out, Milly is a complex character, consciously capable of deceit.

I think Milly needs to become, in her own mind, an idealised version of herself to be able to re-emerge, albeit temporarily, from "turning to the wall" to turn to Densher to forgive him – possibly trusting that there is a real loving bond between them. But also being able to *feel*, in her fear and suffering, that she is loving and not vengeful? an unconscious "deceit" through which she can split off her vengefulness, envy, jealousy, and merge with an idealised, eternally forgiving, internal world mother, an ideally loving Dove.[11] In Kimball's words: "It is Milly who later recognises the image of the dove as 'revealed truth' and feels that 'it lighted up the strange dusk in which she had lately walked' … the dove, with its wonderful wings, is the symbol of her final solution" (1968, p. 268).

The Bronzino scene

This is a very important scene at the centre of the book. Lord Mark, Kate's suitor, who is also interested in Milly (for her wealth) invites Kate, Milly and Susan to a large party in his castle, Matcham. He asks Milly:

> "Have you seen the picture in the house, the beautiful one that's so like you?"
> "She was the image of the wonderful Bronzino".
>
> (p. 137)

> … she found herself, for the first moment, looking at the mysterious portrait through tears. Perhaps it was her tears that made it just then so strange and fair – as wonderful as he had said; the face of a young woman, all splendidly drawn … and splendidly dressed; a face almost livid in hue, yet handsome in sadness and crowned with a mass of [red] hair, was a very great personage – only unaccompanied by a joy. And she was dead, dead, dead.
>
> (p. 139)

> Of course her complexion's green" she laughed; but mine's several shades greener.
>
> (p. 140)

At the end of this scene, Milly asks Kate to "render a great service tomorrow": "It's a secret one – nobody must know. I must be wicked and false about it". She asks Kate to accompany her on her visit to Sir Luke Strett.

The end of the novel

Milly had found out from Lord Mark that Kate and Densher were secretly engaged to each other; she refuses to see Densher and "turns to the wall"; however, just before he leaves Venice, she agrees to see him, and forgives him.

After Milly's death, Kate and Densher meet occasionally, still in secret: they "wondered in neighbourhoods sordid and safe … not to talk of what they *might* have talked of" (of Milly and what they have done to her) (p. 400).

Densher has a secret love for Milly (which Kate partly guesses, partly imagines because of her rivalry with Milly as deserving of love):

The secret ... was that he was aware of how, while the days melted, something rare went with them ... The thought was all his own ... He kept it back like a favourite pang; left behind him, when he went out, but came home again the sooner for the certainty of finding it there. Then he took it out of its sacred corner and its soft wrappings; he undid them one by one, handling it, as a father, baffled and tender, might handle a maimed child.

(p. 402)

... "he should never, never know what had been in Milly's letter" – "his imagination had extraordinarily filled [it] out and refined" "the revelation the loss of which was like the sight of a priceless pearl cast before his eyes into the fathomless sea ... or the sacrifice of something sentient and throbbing".

(p. 402)

Densher's secret relationship with Milly the forgiver has a lot to do with self-idealisation. He goes back secretly to "a favourite pang" — he has transformed the horrible attack on "a maimed child" (the centre of the cruel plan) into a pleasurable, tender self-idealising phantasy that he has wrapped himself in. (James had described "wrapping himself" in his memory of Minny.) Kate and Densher planned to sacrifice a "sentient and throbbing" "priceless pearl". He wasn't the passive spectator of a "revealed" loss.[12]

At the beginning of the last scene of the novel, we know that Densher had posted to Kate, without opening, an envelope from New York, which he knew contained legal documents of the inheritance and a letter from Milly.

When Kate comes to his flat, she shows Densher that the seal of the envelope is broken. He says it had been up to her to decide not to send it back "intact and inviolate" (p. 403). She then throws the envelope into the fire.

They talk about Milly, remembering that they had called her "stupendous". Kate smiles, but Densher's eyes fill with tears (p. 406).

Kate:

"There's but one thing that will save you from my choice ... Your word of honour that you're not in love with her memory"

"Oh – her memory!"

... "don't speak of it as if you couldn't be. I could in your place ... Her memory's your love. You *want* no other".

"I'll marry you, mind you, in an hour"

"As we were?"

"As we were"

But she turned to the door, and her headshake was now the end. "We shall never be again as we were!".

(p. 407)

Kate turns to the door, as Milly had turned to the wall. "We shall never be again as we were!" The novel ends with the death of hope.

She would have married him without the money if he had proved to her that she was still his love: "as we were": meaning he "wants no other".

Kate Croy's tragedy

The novel starts with the striking phrase "She waited, Kate Croy", which I chose for my title: hers is a tragedy of waiting, from the first till the last word in the novel (the end of her existence in our minds), for the consummation of a perfect love that would last forever, only to lose it in the end. In the process we will observe her transformation into the villain of the story: in her obsessive clinging to the perfect love phantasy, she will betray the loveable young woman whom she has befriended.

The inseparable ideal couple has a perfect, and perfectly symmetrical, relationship, as in the scene when they fall in love at a party:

> The chance had come – it was an extraordinary one – on the day she first met Densher, and it was to the girl's lasting honour that she knew on the spot what she was in the presence of ... Densher's perception went out to meet the young woman's and quite kept pace with her own recognition.
>
> (p. 48)

They had met just before her mother's death.

> "The young man had affected her as detached, as awfully at sea"; then "she had had her equal consciousness that within five minutes something for each of them had happened ... it wasn't simply that their eyes had met; other conscious organs, faculties, feelers had met as well. And when Kate afterwards imaged to herself the sharp deep fact she saw it, in the oddest way, as a particular performance. She had observed a ladder against a garden-wall and had trusted herself so to climb it to see over it the probable garden on the other side. On reaching the top she found herself face to face with a gentleman engaged in a like calculation at the same moment, and the two enquirers had remained confronted on their ladders. The great point was that for the rest of the evening they had remained perched ... and indeed during the time that followed Kate at least had had the perched feeling – it was as if she was there aloft without a retreat".
>
> (pp. 48–49)

Although in the recognition of their potential for a perfect love they are above the wall that separates two gardens, ultimately the phantasy of sharing one unique blissful garden together (Steiner, 2020), which she had waited for since the beginning of the novel, could never be realised.

At the end, Kate feels their love is ruined because his "love-in-memory" is unbearable to her. She needs the exclusive two-ness of "how they were". The "unconscionable" plot would work only if they were of one mind: mutual loyalty to perfect love, totally symmetrical, had remained the only motivation for his relationship with Milly: this would be the only barrier against intolerable jealousy and loss and guilt. Although Densher has reason to feel guilty, by not taking full responsibility he projects it into Kate; he has made an attempt at (manic) reparation by rejecting the money, and he also forgives himself through self-idealisation. The forgiving Dove is not only a "maimed child": she is also an ideal internal mother who forgives a murderous child.

Kate offers Densher a way out of the impasse: he must promise her, convincingly, that he isn't in love with Milly – which he doesn't do. And even though Kate tends to be seen as only interested in money, when Densher offers to transfer the inheritance to her, she doesn't accept it.

Thinking about Kate and Milly being rivalrous sisters (which they seem to be in James' mind in his introduction) we could imagine that, unconsciously, the more ego-syntonic the murderous plot becomes, the more it develops in external reality, the more Kate's own goodness and love (as in when she describes to Densher her despair at her poor mother's fate) would be projected into the ideal perfect sister: Milly would become richer and richer in goodness and loveableness. Without the perfect love and the universe of "on top of garden ladders high above the party" (above the whole world) Kate wouldn't be able to bear the guilt that would be really unbearable: she has "become" her father. Kate needed Densher to share her Garden of Eden phantasy (powered by the unconscious belief of a fusion with an Ideal Object) but he has a mind of his own – Densher, after all, is not her puppet – so perfect love is lost forever. The reality of others – or we could say, Reality itself, is the triumphant rival.[13]

In the Idealised Two relationship – originally perfect baby/perfect breast merged together – no "mean feelings" exist: jealousy, envy, and terror are split off and belong to the "other" universe. This is the blessed relationship of falling in love, re-cognising the object who re-cognises you: these two people were made for each other, (originally this baby and this mother were made for each other) – a perfect match.[14] The belief in the perfect match with Densher had caused Kate to commit a heinous, unforgivable crime – she paid the highest price to protect it, and now it is lost forever.

Forgiveness

Henri Rey (1986) gave the capacity for forgiveness a place of central importance in psychic development when he wrote,

> Repeated attempts with my patients have led me to consider that for-
> giveness is a key concept, for nobody who has not forgiven can be
> expected to feel forgiven. This leads to desire of revenge towards the
> object to remain active and therefore the feeling that the object still seeks
> revenge and has not forgiven … Only when the super-ego becomes less
> cruel, less demanding as well, of perfection, is the ego capable of
> accepting an internal object which is not perfectly repaired, can accept
> compromise, forgive and be forgiven, and experience hope and gratitude.
>
> (p. 226)

Rey talked about forgiveness in Kleinian theory through his profound
understanding of its connection with the process of reparation. Grievance
and vengefulness powerfully undermine the capacity to make real (as
opposed to manic) reparation; and consequently perpetually threaten the
stability of the good, loving object in internal reality. Here I would like to
add to Rey's formulation that "nobody who has not forgiven can expect to
feel forgiven" the thought that, simultaneously, in a virtuous circle, nobody
who has not felt forgiven can be expected to forgive. His understanding of
the role of the cruel superego and the need to transform it is of course central to the work of psychoanalytic clinicians; the working through of persecutory anxieties will lead to a firmer establishment of the benign superego,
(originating, according to Klein, from the introjection of the Good Object)
who would be forgiving to the ego: a parent able to forgive the child for her
murderousness. The opening of psychic space for the ego's acceptance of an
imperfectly repaired good object is part of the process that will lead to
mutual forgiveness and the possibility of hope and gratitude: a virtuous circle
could replace the vicious circle of revenge and punishment which leads to
despair. Terror of the persecuting, guilt-projecting damaged object leads to
an imprisonment at the threshold of the depressive position (Roth and
Sodré, 2015), where love for the object and love from the object (and
therefore the possibility of forgiveness) are perpetually threatened.

Examining the 1909 preface, I thought of James' need to be forgiven by his
beloved cousin Minny, who is the inspiration for this book. The writer's guilt
about using a real person for the creation of a character is well illustrated by
Kate's words about "Britannia of the market place": Densher thinks of a
vulture; Kate denies this by describing an eagle with "gilded claws" and
"gilded beak". James' success and fame were not just narcissistically gratifying: he lived by his pen, and needed to sell his books. But I think James also
needed to be forgiven for showing, in his writing, such devotion to Milly's
rival Kate.

I then examined the ways in which the question of forgiveness is central to
"Wings", and how this appears in the character, personality, and vicissitudes
of the three central characters: Milly the forgiver, Densher the forgiven, and
Kate the unforgiven/unforgivable.

Densher, as we have seen, both accepts some responsibility and denies his guilt; in his weakness and compliance, he goes along with Kate's sinister plan without completely seeing it until near the end; he projects his guilt into her, and constantly forgives himself: "I'm not lying!" (Steiner, 1990). Finally, he feels forgiven through his loving Milly, making concrete reparation by refusing the inheritance, and, mostly, by self-idealisation: he "wraps" himself and Milly in a cloud of forgiveness and ideal, ethereal love.

James confronts us with the pain, terror, and loneliness of Milly's situation. Through his narrative we are able to imagine that Milly dies in a state of Grace, as a soaring Dove: a forgiving state, in which feeling loving, and, although betrayed, also believing in Densher's real loving feelings, temporarily makes it possible for her to turn away from the wall to forgive him.

Being able to feel full of loving feelings (rather than bitter, vengeful, full of hatred) would have made Milly light, able to soar, for a moment unburdened by terror – forgiven as she forgives, forgiving as she feels forgiven (the point of Grace: the certainty of being loved by God; in Christianity, the point of bedside confession and religious forgiveness, which we can imagine as a moment of belief in an idealised relationship with God). Whereas Kate is left with the burden of ugliness, of guilt, in her own mind unforgivable.

Milly accepts the name Dove as a disguise: a Dove can be "perched on a finger", showing herself innocent of the knowledge of deception, and as if unaware that she is already dying – so as to avoid the cruel "kindness" of other people's gaze. In the last scene where Kate, and the reader, see her, in her beautiful white dress, priceless pearls and brilliant smile, she also triumphs in her innocence: she soars over the abyss of death and the abyss of corruption.

In relation to Kate and Densher, we saw that "perching" is a crucial word: in Kate's mind, Kate and Densher perched high up above the world, contemplating the bliss of the Garden of Eden are, in Kate's mind, above guilt; the world of the perfect ideal couple is pre-Fall, pre-sin: perfect mutual love excludes jealousy, envy, even murderousness and betrayal; destroying "otherness", triangularity, separation and separateness, baby and breast are merged in eternal bliss. When this is destroyed by the presence of the ideal, idealised, rival, Kate's world is destroyed. She doesn't choose to accept the money, which would make her free to find a new partner. Love has ceased to exist, and she will choose Matcham, where she will be, unlike Milly who will be loved forever, "dead dead dead". In her mind Kate will remain unforgivable; though in our minds as readers, who deeply, and therefore compassionately, understand her, she will be forgiven.

Notes

1 Leon Edel (1987) in his classic, insightful biography linked Milly's mysterious illness and the creation of Sir Luke Strett, the London specialist who isn't able to

cure Milly but helps her to live as much as she can with the ideal specialist James never met in reality: as if in phantasy an ideal transference object. Young Harry James, aged ... and suffering from an "obscure wound" was taken by his father to visit a famous specialist in New York, who "pooh poohed" his suffering: when helping to put out a fire, her had suffered what he felt was a wound in his back which he never recovered from. Edel linked this with the fact that Henry James Senior had, as a boy, had lost a leg due to being in a fire (pp. 59–61).

2 The alliteration K/C adds a hardness to the name. "Croy", which suggests crow, links her with Mme Merle in "Portrait of a Lady": "merle" is a blackbird in French. She is the precursor to Kate as the betraying woman who involves the heroine in a cruel plot. The alliteration also emphasises the crow connection: "Caw ... caw ... caw", the crow's voice.

3 The next time this word appears, in Book 2, it is used to describe the behaviour of her lover, Merton Densher (who is being introduced to us). But there it has a much lighter meaning; and we will find out that Densher is seduced into participating in the secret plot, but constantly has misgivings, and repents at the end.

4 "Irritation" is described as one of the "ugly feelings" (envy is another one) in Ngai's (2005) interesting book. A good name for miserable "mean stale feelings" (in a simple contrast: a lion, with his ferocious destructive rage, is "noble", not "ugly").

5 Compare Mme Merle in *Portrait of a Lady*: she partly managed to "be that person" by arranging the marriage of Isabel to Osmond; on the other hand, she knew Osmond would never love Isabel – it is an established fact that Osmond is unable to love (with the exception of his narcissistic love for his (their) daughter Pansy).

6 Colm Toibín (2005) and Lyndall Gordon (2012, pp. 314–316) describe an extraordinary episode of Henry James trying to "drown" Fenimore's clothes from a gondola in the middle of the night).

7 Personal communication. I'm very grateful to Rosemary for her generous sharing of her insightful readings of "The Wings".

8 This brings to my mind a 12-year-old boy I saw nearly 50 years ago, who had cystic fibrosis and, unbeknownst to his parents, knew he was going to die soon: He jumped from the roof of their garage, to "prove that he wouldn't die" and came to his session, unharmed and triumphant (having frightened his parents, who thought he had fallen). His motive was complicated: to project his fear into his parents and therapist (who weren't saving and protecting him); to prove he wouldn't die, to prove his death was in his control; and as a suicidal gesture, or attempt; a mixture of rage, terror and despair at this cruellest of fates.

9 In his first sketch in his notebook of 1894 (where Kate is decidedly villainous from the beginning) James describes Milly as "equally pathetic in her doom and her horror of it ... She is like a creature dragged shrieking to the guillotine" (Brooks, 1976, p. 179).

10 Is "the head at the window" also Quint's head in "The Turn of the Screw"??

11 Jean Kimball links abysses and wings: "her liability to slip, to slide, to leap, to be precipitated by a single false movement ... into whatever was beneath". She sees the Dove as deliberate disguise (p. 277) "her will is free; she is never simply passive". But also: "On the intuitive level, however, the dove is the symbol for the struggle of Milly's soul or her personality to rise above annihilation".

12 Henry James describes Densher as a "bland Hermes" but Hermes is also connected to death. The association between Hermes and the underworld is related to his function as a god of the boundary between life and death; a deity who guides souls of the dead to afterlife. His image was commonly depicted on gravestones in classical Greece (see Byatt and Sodré, 2004).

13 In an excellent paper on "The Wings of the Dove" Jill Boswell (2005) describes this Oedipal triangle from Milly's point of view: "The idea of [Kate and Densher] gazing so 'beautifully' at each other takes hold of her: she now sees this aspect of Kate as 'the "other", the not wholly calculable'". "Milly goes on to reflect that she is not merely being pushed out, but placed 'on the edge of a great darkness'" (p. 1165).

14 Henry James's choice of "Matcham" for Lord Mark's castle refers to Milly and the woman in the Bronzino portrait "matching". But as Kate's ultimate destination it is ironic: Kate's love is "dead dead dead" like the woman in the portrait.

References

Boswell, J. *"Missing what was true: Problems of seeing and knowing in Henry James' The Wings of the Dove"*. *IJPA* 86(4), 2005: 1161–1173.

Brooks, P. *The Melodramatic Imagination. Balzac, Henry James, Melodrama and the Mode of Excess.* New Haven and London: Yale University Press, 1976.

Byatt A. S. and I. Sodré. "On Writing Madness". In *Madness and Creativity in Literature and Culture*, edited by C. Saunders, and J. MacNaughton, 202, 221. New York: Palgrave, 2004, pp. 202–221.

Davies, R.Personal communication, 2020.

Edel, L. *Henry James: A Life.* New York: Harper Collins, 1987.

Gordon, L. *Henry James.* London: Virago, 2012.

James, H. *The Wings of the Dove.* New York: W. W. Norton, 2003.

James, H. "Preface to the 1909 edition" of *The Wings of the Dove*. In H. James, 2003, 3–16.

James, H. "Notes of a Son and Brother". In H. James, *The Wings of the Dove* 2003, 484.

Joseph, B. *Psychic Equilibrium and Psychic Change.* Edited by Feldman M. and Spillius, E.London: Routledge, 1989.

Milton, J.Paradise Lost. In *The Complete English Poems*. London: Everyman's Library, 1990.

Kimball, J. "The Abyss and The Wings of the Dove: The Image as a Revelation". In *Henry James*, edited by Tanner, T. London: Macmillan, 1968.

Ngai, S. *Ugly Feelings.* Cambridge, MA: Harvard University Press, 2005.

Rey, H. *Universals of Psychoanalysis in the Treatment of Psychotic and Borderline States.* Edited by Magagna, J. London: Free Association Books, 1986.

Roth, P. and Sodré, I. "The Terror of Love". Paper presented at the English-Speaking Conference, 2015, Unpublished.

Steiner, J. "Envy, Resentment and Forgiveness". Paper presented at Pitlochry, 1990, Unpublished.

Steiner, J. "The Garden of Eden Illusion: Finding and Losing Paradise". In *Illusion, Disillusion and Irony in Psychoanalysis.* London and New York: Routledge. 2020.

Strouse, J. *Alice James: A Biography.* Cambridge, MA: Harvard University Press, 1980.

Tanner, T. *Henry James. Selections of Critical Essays*, London: Macmillan, 1968.

Toibín, C. *The Master.* New York: Simon & Schuster, 2005.

Chapter 8

Contessa perdono!

Mozartian sexual betrayal and forgiveness

Francis Grier

In three of Mozart's operatic masterpieces, *The Marriage of Figaro* (1786), *Don Giovanni* (1787) and *Così fan tutte* (1790), the dynamics of sexual betrayal and forgiveness are all central. Forgiveness is at the centre of *Figaro*, but is not manifestly important in *Don Giovanni* and *Cosi fan tutte*, though I shall argue that variations on its theme are in fact at the psychological core of those operas. I will assume a basic knowledge of the music and plot on the part of readers. My main focus will be on *Figaro*, but I will also add some thoughts initially about the other two operas. Mozart particularly focuses on couples: in *Figaro*, the Count and Countess, Figaro and Susanna; in *Don Giovanni*, Giovanni and whichever woman he is seducing and betraying; in *Cosi*, the two young couples of Fiordiligi and Guglielmo, Dorabella and Ferrando. Quite why these operas circle repeatedly around betrayal and forgiveness cannot be known for certain. Mozart's librettist for all three operas was Lorenzo da Ponte, not famed for his profundity. I would speculate, nevertheless, that forgiveness and betrayal were of central emotional significance to both collaborators, at least unconsciously; but I will not discuss any biographical dimension. Space also prevents me from discussing da Ponte's input, though if I write as if the psychological intentions were all Mozart's, readers should bear in mind that the librettist, too, made a major contribution.

The psychoanalysis of forgiveness

I will first set out some psychoanalytic thoughts about the place of forgiveness in couple relationships. Couples have to be able to forgive each other, even if only pragmatically, because it is impossible for partners within a long-term couple relationship not to fall out, over matters great and small. Betrayal is impossible to avoid. In a triangular relationship, moments will inevitably arise in which, from the point of view of one person, the other two will be seen as ganging up and excluding the one. This active exclusion often equates, at least in the mind of the excluded one, with betrayal. The act of falling in love may sometimes feel as if the partners have discovered a non-

DOI: 10.4324/9781003364313-8

triangular relationship, perfect and ideal, most obviously symbolised by the honeymoon couple. But this is an illusion: the third parties still exist, and the very fact that during honeymoons such care is taken to shut the bedroom door so firmly on the outside world is evidence of the fear of its spoiling intrusion. Nevertheless, for the time being, the two lovers may act as if they are an indivisible unit, excluding a world of third parties, perhaps unconsciously fearing their envy of the loving, sexual couple. As time passes, the partners begin to re-establish links with those in the third position. Now just who the partners are making up a couple, and who is in the excluded third position, begins to become much more fluid. The scene is set for felt betrayals, small and large. Betrayal also infamously arises from within the private, sexual sphere: a child may be born: then, inevitably, the question arises, which family members are felt to couple up with whom, and who experiences betrayal?

These issues are elemental and universal. I wrote about them in the introduction to *Oedipus and the Couple* (Grier, 2005a), in which I proposed that, in psychoanalysis' founding myth, we could see Laius and Jocasta as desiring a permanent honeymoon state, forever enjoying each other in non-procreative, essentially narcissistic sex. The fear and hatred of the third party, little Oedipus, can be seen as shared by both sexual parties – not just Laius the father, but also by Jocasta the mother who colluded with her husband in casting the boy out. She may have softened his sentence from immediate death, but she was complicit in his feet being cruelly pierced and left to die on the mountainside. I also suggested that Oedipus's life in Corinth symbolises the civilised life most of us try to lead in which, through splitting and repression, we turn a blind eye to the disturbances emanating from the unconscious, whereas Oedipus' return to Thebes and the events there symbolise precisely the inevitable encounter with those disturbances. I wonder whether the dramatic action of these Mozart operas could be imagined as taking place in a version of Thebes? We, the audience, join the characters in leaving the securities of Corinth to risk the dangers, but also the truth of the instinctual life, of Thebes. Not that Mozart's Thebes is the same as Sophocles' in its overt violence and murderousness, though *Don Giovanni* most obviously traverses the not-so-very-different emotional territory. Nonetheless, their comic, optimistic surfaces camouflage the utterly serious internal unconscious phantasy life, involving the return of the repressed, the id, and, finally, the ceaseless battle between the life and death instincts.

Matters of betrayal are at the heart of the human condition, particularly when viewed through the lens of the oedipal constellation. John Steiner has theorised two paths through the Oedipus complex (Steiner, 1999). In Freud's version, the paranoid-schizoid path, the son feels betrayed by both parents, but fear of the father's violent threat of castration pushes the boy to abandon his rivalry with his father and to set aside his possessiveness of his mother, instead moving – through coercion – to loving and identifying with his father and learning to love his mother affectionately, inhibiting through repression his sexual feelings for her. However, in the depressive position journey through the Oedipus complex, in addition to the foregoing, the boy has to face betrayal at a much deeper level. His feeling is that his mother has betrayed him. She has given him to understand – perhaps literally – that he was the centre of her universe of love: now she turns away from him and turns in love towards his father – not through fear of her husband's threats of violence, but because she wants to. The boy has to see that it's the father his mother desires, not him.

This is the elemental and universal human situation of betrayal, humiliation, and shame. The boy is no longer His Majesty but is very much The Baby, scorned, belittled, and patronised. Hatred follows, inevitably, hatred of both parents. In phantasy, the boy punishes them with cruel tortures and torments. In time, he realises that these hateful parents are also the parents on whom he depends, who love him and whom he loves. Yet in his hatred he is damaging them bitterly and ferociously. In time he can begin to mourn his violent attacks, he can begin to own his hatred as well as his love, and he may move towards reparation. The most crucial step is that of forgiveness. He will need to be able to forgive his father for seducing his mother. He will need to forgive his mother for her betrayal. He will need to forgive his father and mother together for their joint betrayal and for his humiliation. He will need to forgive himself for the violent damage he has wrought in phantasy – and, sometimes, in action – on his father, on his mother, and on the combined couple of his mother and father. He will then need to accept his real place in the family hierarchy as usually in the third, junior position and begin to move from a primarily narcissistic to a primarily object-related position.

I have followed convention in theorising from the point of view of the boy. But, from the perspective of forgiveness and betrayal, the situation is not so different for a girl. She, too, will have thought of herself as being the apple of her mother's eye, possibly even more so her father's, and she, too, will experience the parents' sexual love as a fundamental betrayal.

How does reparation, and specifically the part of reparation, which is forgiveness, come about? Partly from the innate character of the child, a capacity not to hold onto grievances, and a drive to move more towards the life instinct than the death instinct. But partly also through the parental response. There's a world of difference between parents who may be immune to their child's suffering these deep oedipal pains, or who may actively mock the child, and parents who can identify and sympathise with their child's dilemma.

Powerful papers have been written expressing doubt as to the psychoanalytic value of forgiveness. Smith (2008) asserts that it is a non-psychoanalytic term, a kind of Christianising, distorting import. He considers it redundant, in that some degree of forgiveness occurs naturally as a result of the psychoanalytic process and does not need to be singled out as of special, distinct value. He particularly challenges the notion that forgiveness has anything distinctive about it. Lansky (2009) has written quite extensively about forgiveness, particularly in relation to shame which he considers its opposite. In response, Smith suggests that Lansky's definition of forgiveness involves so many sub-terms that it proves what a foggy, indistinct notion it is. He follows Schafer (2005), who suggests that forgiveness is usually only partial, and implicitly involves denial, whereas the psychoanalytic process should undo denial and the forgetting that is often held to accompany forgiveness, so that an analysed person will be more in touch with and remember rather than forget his non-forgiving feelings.

In the opposite camp, authors endorse the value of forgiveness, particularly Akhtar (2002), Cavell (2003) and Bishop (2006). I have been particularly interested in an unpublished paper by Rachel Blass (2019), in which she sees revenge as the corollary or counterpart to forgiveness:

> Nor is forgiveness equivalent to forgetting. Forgiveness in the Kleinian literature usually refers to a state in which we acknowledge the harm that has been inflicted and yet places that harm in a context that, despite the harm, allows for love. Thus, forgiveness might mean seeing harm in the context of the limitations of the one who inflicted the harm. This forgiveness acknowledges and empathizes with the frailty of human beings. Forgiveness might also mean seeing harm in the context of the sorrow and repentance now felt by the one who inflicted the harm, or in the context of the love of which he may be capable if given the chance.

This quotation strikes me as clearly relevant to the quality of the Countess's forgiveness of the Count, and, in its negative form, in the non-forgiveness which marks the emotional territories of *Don Giovanni* and *Così fan tutte*. The plots of all three operas are also fundamentally marked by betrayal, which I consider to be the inevitable forerunner and trigger for any potential forgiveness. Lansky (2001) pairs forgiveness with shame, and Blass with revenge, but it seems to me that shame and revenge are themselves consequent upon the unbearable emotions arising from betrayal, unavoidably integral to the elemental triangular childhood – and human – situation.

Don Giovanni – and revenge

Don Giovanni and *Così* were both written after *Figaro*. I wonder whether, consciously or unconsciously, Mozart may have reacted against the optimism and predominantly loving world of *Figaro* by subsequently illustrating much bleaker narratives. In *Don Giovanni*, we enter a world in which forgiveness makes its impact by its absence, or, more accurately, by its refusal. This is obvious with regard to Giovanni's seduction and betrayal of the aristocratic ladies Donna Elvira and Donna Anna. They and their gentlemen, be they lovers or fathers, have been shamed and want revenge, not forgiveness. But I wish to focus on the non-aristocratic, pastoral interlude, Giovanni's attempted seduction of Zerlina.

The music in this section is of surpassing freshness. Mozart obviously intended quite consciously to write in a contrasting, freer style from the more elaborate, complex idiom he had been employing hitherto for the aristocrats who have all been battling with tragic emotions. In the famous duet, *Là ci darem la mano*, Giovanni aims to seduce the young peasant woman, Zerlina, on the eve of her wedding to Masetto. This is no overtly grand seduction scene. The sweetness of the music here is justly famous, but what is happening is far from sweet. As Rusbridger has shown (2008), Giovanni keeps turning himself, chameleon-like, into whatever type of suitor is most likely to gain sexual victory. The implication of the music, in which, by the end of the duet, Giovanni and Zerlina are singing in perfect harmony, clearly suggests that Giovanni is succeeding, and is only thwarted by Donna Elvira's sudden arrival. Giovanni's ploy to rid himself of Masetto's presence has been to send him off to make further wedding arrangements. This cynical strategy continues: he will dance with Zerlina under the pretence of blessing her marriage, and then try to rape her. Later he will beat up Masetto. The implication is that Zerlina would have been fully sexually seduced if external forces had not intervened, and she later has to apologise to Masetto. I want to emphasise again, though, that this is seduction in a very pastoral, simple musical language. The music possesses a very quiet erotic quality, not at all intensely romantic or passionate.

I wonder whether Mozart's unconscious imagination may have been fired by an interpretation of Giovanni as a baby and then young boy, full of rage at being supplanted by his father in his mother's affections, and acting out a scenario in which he manages to supplant the potential father, Masetto, with the mother, Zerlina, at precisely the stage in which they are in the act of forming a sexual couple: getting married. The beautiful simplicity of the music suggests a possible link in Giovanni's mind to the special child–mother, one-to-one relationship, recalled, and, of course, mightily developed in the current sexual context. Simple perhaps, but also elemental, in both its manifestations as simple (peasant) child–mother music but also as the music of lovers. Father is absent, or, better still, present but demoted to an extremely all-but-excluded third position, where he can only look on impotently at the "real couple", i.e. mother–son. This interpretation offers a deeper explanation of Giovanni's subsequent furious beating of Masetto: beneath the political narrative of the arrogant aristocrat beating the presumptuous peasant there is a hidden story of the baby, now an adult, indulging in the gratification of beating his father as he never could when he was small.

So this superficially pastoral interlude is, in fact, the vehicle for Giovanni's violent narcissistic aggression and grievance. He desires to get between the parents, spoil their intercourse, castrate father and in his place have intercourse with mother. The sweetness of his revenge is increased if the woman does not have to be raped but submits willingly to her own desire, thus reinstating the early mother who loved her baby boy not only spiritually but also physically and erotically – at least, from his point of view, and, quite possibly, albeit unconsciously, from hers as well.

This will teach the parents to have sex, worse still, loving sex, and exclude small Giovanni. Shame accompanies revenge in its central place (Lansky, 2001): Giovanni's envious motive is that Zerlina and Masetto will each endure overwhelming shame which will spoil forever the innocence of their marital love. Giovanni's superficial quietness hides, but simultaneously expresses, an overwhelming, rage-filled grievance and refusal to forgive. Here is the full unconscious phantasy of attacking, spoiling, and damaging the parental couple, emerging in hate-filled triumph, its glory enhanced by its simple, utterly deceptive pastoral beauty. Here is a mind set against forgiveness of either father or mother, or of the couple, or of the self. No reparation. They will burn with shame, just as he did. It is a fully anal triumph: Giovanni's plan is to leave the peasant couple smeared – in the nicest possible way – in excrement. Perhaps, we can speculate, that is just how little Giovanni felt his parents treated him. Perhaps they did – or, perhaps he, and others like him, absolutely could not tolerate the bedroom door being shut on him, and his demotion from His Majesty the Baby to the third point in the family triangle.

Musically and psychologically, in this quasi-pastoral interlude, Mozart makes his audience work hard, paradoxically at that part of the opera where we are most tempted to relax. The music is mainly marked by an absence of conflict, and we easily find ourselves seduced (along with Zerlina) by Giovanni's simple love-song, after the tempestuous music and drama of the first part of the opera. Subsequently, the external and internal drama harmonise musically: the dramatic feelings of the characters are accurately represented in the intense music, and vice versa. But in this section, all is reversed. The simple, lovely pastoral music camouflages something hideous, hidden in plain sound, before our ears. There is no musical expression of this envious assault. Why not? We are forced by Mozart – but quietly and willingly – to witness a cynical manipulation of a young peasant woman and her peasant husband, designed precisely to spoil their sexual love. Mozart here chooses to reproduce a situation met with often enough in the external world, in which the surface promises beauty, whilst simultaneously it is diabolically spoiled on an unseen – and, in music, unheard – level. We, the audience, are given the task of identifying with all the characters: with Zerlina as she is seduced; with Masetto as he is not so much fooled as forced sadistically to turn a masochistic blind eye and a deaf ear to the seduction of his bride, given the immense power of the older aristocrat; with Giovanni, as he gratifies his lust for the infantile pleasure of enviously splitting the couple and spoiling their love; with Leporello, Giovanni's servant, as he watches in a defensively detached, comical view of the frailties of human nature; and, finally, we have to identify with our own audience position, watching impotently as this particularly nasty variation on the theme of envious betrayal is enacted before us.

Forgiveness enters the final scene in its most fundamentally negative form. Giovanni is given the opportunity to repent – and, presumably, to be forgiven. The offer comes from the remorselessly revengeful superego ghost of the father killed by Giovanni as he attempted to protect his daughter. Giovanni's refusal to repent submissively represents the narcissistic iron which has not merely entered his soul but now inflexibly governs it. Yet his refusal elicits our admiration, as he remains the son who, confronted with his father's violent castration threat, refuses to submit and pretend to a love that is actually motivated by fear. There's nothing depressive here, this is a fully paranoid-schizoid atmosphere. There can be no reparation and no meaningful forgiveness. Mozart's music expresses this: strong, resolute, inflexible, threatening, and, in sexual terms, misogynistically phallic. There is no penis-as-link with its appreciation of the feminine (Birksted-Breen, 1996), including forgiveness, merely a never-ending drama of subjugation. If there is a Freudian oedipal drama which resonates with this murderous hostility between symbolic father and son, it is the story of *Totem and Taboo* (Freud, 1913), in which the father is indeed killed so that the sons can get hold of the women. In that story, however, the sons relent after the father's death, feeling and owning their guilt, implicitly moving towards reparation and forgiveness. Don Giovanni refuses to make this move, remaining as a son in an elemental and eternal stand-off with the father.

Cosi fan tutte – and remorse

With *Cosi fan tutte* Mozart seems to take one step even further away from the predominantly loving world of *The Marriage of Figaro* than he had in *Don Giovanni*. Many, including Beethoven, have flinched from and castigated its cynicism. The plot is designed to show how the reality of romantic, sexual love is far more shallow than its ideals pretend. In the absence of the beloved, the subject will seek a different object, however much she – for this is particularly an opera that attacks femininity in both sexes, and its embodiment in women – protests to the contrary. If the Commendatore in *Don Giovanni* embodies one kind of superego, Don Alfonso incarnates quite a different variety. His paternal ethics are marked precisely by a cynical disbelief in faithful love. Don Alfonso is the high priest of betrayal, insisting it is inevitable, normal, nor in any ultimate terms to be mourned, but accommodated. If anything needs forgiving, in his worldview, it is the naïveté with which young people cling to the illusion of faithful sexual love.

I am not sure if his misogyny is blunted or enhanced by the maid, Despina, who becomes his collaborator. She seems to be purely and comically light-hearted, which I suspect represents Mozart's lighter view of the matter, whereas Don Alfonso may represent Mozart's own more bitter sarcasm camouflaged as irony. The opera swipes at foolish romantic idealism, and can be seen as a step towards a liberating realism in the field of sexual love. The plot gives Mozart the opportunity to musically portray a whole range of intense feelings. There are wonderful expressions of narcissistic injury, shame, humiliation, excitement, arousal, and triumph between the two crossed pairs of lovers. You could see the opera as a riff on the paranoid-schizoid version of the Oedipus situation. The young men take on Don Alfonso, but find to their cost that he indeed knows better than they do the real nature of romantic love, as they learn the painful lessons at his hands of the shallowness of their, and the girls', infantile infatuation dressed up as ideal love. They suffer intense narcissistic humiliation. The young women fare similarly, though there is a patronising assumption that they are unlikely even to progress in furthering their knowledge of the human condition as far as the young men, since, after all, they are but female.

However, in the midst of all this idealised disillusionment, there is one major exception. Fiordiligi is the one character who enters the depressive position. In an exceptional aria, she painfully explores the complexities of her new emotional position after she has fallen in love with her friend's fiancé. Profound ambivalence and remorse tear her apart, as she realises how her new love is spoiling her old love, and how this damage is changing her sense of herself at a fundamental level. She asks her fiancé for forgiveness: "Per pietà, ben mio, perdona all'error di un'alma amante" (In pity's name, my dearest, forgive the misdeed of a loving soul). She is fully distressed and disturbed by the depth and confusion of her feelings and thoughts. This is the aria that neither Don Giovanni nor the Count can ever sing, as neither of these phallic men have the internal strength of this young woman to own the truthfulness of their emotional situation, particularly the damage they are wreaking.

Musically, Mozart expresses this not only through the extraordinary beauty of her melodic line, but also through her virtuosity. Her particular musical partners for this aria are the two horns, from whom Mozart demands equal virtuosity, as this aria extends and extends itself. The sound world is unique in Mozart's dramatic writing. The horn carried associations in his era to the masculine pursuit of hunting. So the instrument naturally evoked for its contemporary audience something of the forest, the mythological Germanic wild world, and, for Fiordiligi, her discovery of male sexuality and all it does for her femininity. Ironically, whilst this aria expresses verbal regret at the hurt she is causing her man, the rampant horns suggest that unconsciously, and simultaneously, she just cannot stop herself from joyously exploring maleness. The boldness of the music also implies her growing enjoyment of her own inner masculinity through her journey simultaneously through depressive anxiety and male eroticism: she sings ever more strongly, employing coloratura virtuosity, as she faces her disturbingly mixed feelings pulling her simultaneously in completely different directions.

This is a highly charged, romantic and sexual picture, both in terms of the eroticism of the male phallic elements underlying the female vocal line, symbolising the young woman's awakening to intense sexual desire and interest in the male, and its occurrence in the most reflective and serious music of the entire opera, symbolising Fiordiligi's journey to the heart of the depressive position and hence towards genuine maturity. In terms of operatic composition, this 1790 aria prefigures Wagner's style of writing for the orchestra a hundred years later. He would typically compose highly complex instrumental and harmonic configurations, often symbolising deep unconscious conflicts, underpinning the singer's vocal and verbal line usually expressing conscious emotions. Verdi found his way to a similar operatic compositional technique. In this Mozartian aria in particular we see the embryonic emergence of this compositional technique of portraying the conscious onstage and the unconscious in the orchestral pit.

Cosi has only the most superficial sense of reparation at its end, in line with Don Alfonso's particular brand of wisdom. Dorabella, Guglielmo and Ferrando seem all to have hardened their narcissistic defences in reaction to the unexpected events, but we, the audience, sense that for Fiordiligi things can never be quite the same again. When she asks Guglielmo to forgive her, she is actually singing to herself, so within her aria she is particularly exploring self-betrayal and the possibility of self-forgiveness. She finds herself in completely new, different, disturbing and dangerous emotional territory, in the arena of catastrophic change (Bion, 1965; Grier, 2005b). Likewise, Mozart, as he writes her central aria: he, too, is exploring new compositional territory, dramatic, vocal, instrumental, harmonic, structural, as he nears the end of his short life, presenting us with an experimental aria which prophesies the future direction of opera. I would speculate further that Mozart's response to the impact of his heroine's emotional dilemma might imply that – however much he may have defended himself against emotional assaults by donning the defensive garb of superego cynicism – like his young heroine, his defences perhaps often failed, and, to our inestimable benefit, he could not help himself from responding from the life instinct within him.

The Marriage of Figaro – and the moment of forgiveness

Ironically, Mozart may have set himself the most difficult task in the first of these operas, when, in *The Marriage of Figaro*, unlike its successors, he engaged with the theme of betrayal and forgiveness positively and optimistically. From curtain-up, the dramatic action moves inexorably towards its climax at the end of Act IV, the Countess's forgiveness of the Count. The theme of betrayal and forgiveness is explicitly at the core of the drama. Whilst Beaumarchais's text deals primarily with the political dimension –

hence giving the place of the primary role, even the play's title, to the Count's valet, Figaro, a servant who will outwit his aristocratic master, holding him to the new vision of human equality between classes – Mozart's music essentially expresses the emotional dimensions both of the individuals and their various interpersonal relationships.

Variations on betrayal and forgiveness are ubiquitous. Anticipating the narrative's climax, the Count is shown as completely unforgiving to the Countess when he suspects her of a liaison with the teenage Cherubino. The Count has hypocritically been scheming to arrange his own liaison with the Countess's maid, Susanna, the fiancée of Figaro. The Count has also been busy liaising with the young daughter of the gardener, Barberina, a sexual interest he shares – to his fury when he discovers it – with Cherubino. Even in Act IV itself, a fresh variation occurs, when Figaro mistakenly believes Susanna to be deceiving him with the Count. Figaro – despite all his modern liberal views – delivers an impassioned hate-filled diatribe against woman-the-betrayer in the form of his fiancée. He, too, has to be forgiven by Susanna: forgiveness is seen to be operating on both upper- and lower-class levels. The actual betrayers in all these situations are the males: they have to ask forgiveness; the females may choose to confer it – or not.

The music in all these situations shares the sparkle and wit of Beaumarchais's text, and, more to our point, is consistently marked by emotional intensity. The Count's character can be seen as a – mainly – comic version of Don Giovanni. Mozart is superb in depicting both the Count and Don Giovanni as hopelessly egocentric, full of infantile entitlement and quick to feel keen narcissistic injury and grievance. The Count's aria "Hai già vinta la causa!" expresses precisely his excitement, fury, and determination for revenge in retaliation for what he sees as treasonous machinations against his aristocratic self-importance – Mozart perhaps particularly enjoyed portraying His Majesty the Baby. This baby is all up for revenge: forgiveness is not on his horizon, partly because the notion that he might himself be the one who needs forgiving does not occur to him. The Count remains fixed in a paranoid-schizoid oedipal state of mind throughout the opera until, surprisingly, the moment when he is forgiven by the Countess.

Almost all the motivations of almost all the personalities are almost always narcissistic. Composer and librettist invite us to laugh – more kindly than in *Cosi*, usually with an affectionate irony – at the characters. But there is one exception. It is ironic that, in this opera whose manifest intention, following Beaumarchais, is to promote the cause of the servant classes and to demote the aristocracy, the ultimate hero is the Countess. This is not quite due to her aristocratic lineage, but because of the fullness of her personality as we see it develop through the opera. This is of fundamental importance, because, at the dramatic climax, the moment of forgiveness would surely not impress us to the same degree if the Countess were either a superego figure or merely a lady of idealised purity.

At her first entry, we are immediately impressed with the depth of her emotion as she sings of her feeling of loneliness. Her longing for the love she used to enjoy with her husband in her aria, "Dove sono i bei momenti", has long been recognised as perhaps Mozart's masterpiece amongst his soprano arias. So far, however, she is dramatically conventional, as an idealised, righteous, and betrayed, aristocratic wife. In the course of the ensuing drama, however, two unexpected developments occur. She becomes engaged in a lesbian relationship with her servant, and there are hints that she allows herself to become aware of erotic feelings towards a teenage boy.

My assertion of the Countess's homosexual relationship with Susanna is not supported by the libretto. There she is limited to becoming the happy co-conspirator with the wily and witty Susanna, though always remaining the senior partner in terms of class. However, listen to the music, and you will hear that the two women become utterly equal, as their two soprano lines bend and twist around each other, taking turns on top and underneath. This is music of incomparable beauty, but it's also music expressive of sublimated erotic interplay. The supreme example is in their letter-writing duet: "Sul-l'aria ... che soave zeffiretto". The particular quality of their two-some is enhanced by the implied man in the excluded third position, the deliciously mocked Count. So this is a case of the music even more than the words furthering the narrative. Ironically, perhaps, it is particularly the political aspect of the plot – the politics of gender and class – which is thereby developed, normally not the terrain of music. In terms of betrayal and forgiveness, it's also ironic that both the Count and Figaro storm angrily about their women's supposed infidelities with males, little suspecting that both women's closest erotic relationship is actually with each other, even if it remains unconscious and is signalled only through the music. Would we say that no forgiveness is needed here, because no betrayal was noticed?

Similarly, the Countess's possible erotic response to the attractions of a teenage boy, Cherubino, her godson, is only just implied by the script. She becomes incipiently aware that, although she finds it ridiculous and insulting that the Count suspects her, she nevertheless does begin to find Cherubino disquietingly erotic. Even more daring (in the text) and disquieting (to the Countess), she finds him – as does Susanna – particularly attractive when they cross-dress him as a girl. The gender dynamics here are truly and wonderfully complex, because there's also the fact that Cherubino, the priapic adolescent boy dressed as a girl is actually sung by a girl, or, rather, a young woman.

By now the Countess is on fire sexually, fast becoming one of the most interesting and complete psychological characters in all opera. Despite her participation in the farcical and erotic aspects of the plot, she nevertheless never loses her original depth of feeling, but increases her musical and psychological range. We hear her truly agitated and frightened when she believes that the Count will expose her having lied about Cherubino; she becomes properly angry with her husband; and, as stated, she becomes unconsciously erotically involved with her maid and teenage godson. Nor is she above the gratification of revenge: we hear her lusciously plotting the Count's downfall through his humiliating exposition. So she is not so pure, righteous and inhibited after all.

Then we reach the climactic moment: the Count realises he has been hopelessly outwitted and exposed. He kneels and asks for his wife's forgiveness. How easy it would have been for this moment to be an anti-climax! Yet, when we leave the opera house, we don't only remember all the delightful complexity of the scheming and farcical elements of the plot, nor do we primarily delight in the Count's humiliation, his just deserts. We remember this radiant moment. And, indeed, the Count is not quite degraded, precisely because of the particular quality of the Countess's forgiveness.

Why and how does this moment work at such a deep level? Part of the answer must lie in the simplicity of the music. Mozart eschews grandiosity. A lesser composer might have chosen to illustrate this grand moment with grand music. By contrast, Mozart gives us a lesson in "less means more". But also, the Countess by this point in the drama has developed into a much fuller, more humane personality than her original rather ideal, somewhat saintly character. Consequently, she does not sing "down" from a superior, superego position, even though the Count is kneeling before her. Despite the fact that the Count has acted out repeatedly from his narcissistic immaturity, the Countess's development has begun to make her aware – even if only incipiently, even if only pre-consciously – of her own sexuality, particularly her internal impulsive, erotic promptings, including even responding to elements of what Freud would have called her polymorphously perverse infantile erotism. She has now become more fully human, and she now relates to her husband on a more equal plane, rather than from a morally superior, victim position.

Implicitly, the Countess has dipped her toe into the slippery waters of erotic triangularity within marriage. In the opera, she initially appears only in the dreaded excluded third position, forced to witness her husband coupling with various other females, as well as combining symbolically with males and the powerful patriarchal social order to disempower her. But she then begins to pair up with Susanna on various different levels, including erotically, with Cherubino, and also with the couple Susanna–Figaro. In all these configurations the Count occupies the third, excluded position, initially unconsciously, but finally – to his horror and shame – consciously. She may not herself feel as though she is ever betraying her husband, but she has quite overtly felt pleasure and gratification in coupling up with others against him. I believe it to be her fully human participation in these dramas, almost all of them sexual, which lead to her being able to respond to her husband's much more serious betrayal not with revenge but with real forgiveness. By real, I mean to differentiate the forgiveness that is perhaps mainly coloured by internal revenge which may then be denied – forgiveness in the paranoid-schizoid position – from forgiveness in which the forgiver implicitly acknowledges the frailty of their own loving and moral nature (as in the earlier quotation from Blass; also see Grier, 2006). I believe this is also why the Count – at least as I hear the music – is not triumphantly denigrated. The Countess's music conveys affection and love, and there seems to be a moment in which this affection and love is felt, appreciated and reciprocated by the Count. He appears taken by surprise by the quite different quality of forgiveness he is offered. Instead of a Commendatore-like paranoid-schizoid command to submit and repent, he is lifted to a different psychic sphere, and invited to join the Countess in a depressive position where he can acknowledge the damage his betrayal has wrought on the oedipal parental couple, and where there is the possibility of forgiveness and reparation.

My final point is that this moment of forgiveness is, for all its operatic fame, just that, a moment. This strikes us as truthful, and moves us deeply. Such a moment of forgiveness in the context of the many betrayals – great and small – between sexual partners, can only happen spontaneously. What Mozart shows us is not a forced, ceremonial, ritualised, or otherwise symbolically underlined moment of forgiveness. It is just a moment, marked by emotional truthfulness. We do not know what will happen next. It is difficult to imagine, given the Count's character, that he will remain faithful. And, given the developments of the Countess's character so far, perhaps we can't be so sure of her either. But, paradoxically, it is the modest and momentary dimensions of this giving and receiving of forgiveness which convey its depth, sincerity and, even, its transcendence – becoming nothing less than, in the words of Joseph Kerman (1988) "a revelation".

Conclusion

These wonderful operas can be approached from many different angles. I have explored just one. But the axis of betrayal and, particularly, forgiveness, in its conscious and unconscious forms, seems to me to have been a preoccupation of Mozart's. If we can allow that the characters in these operas represent types of real people, we can perhaps also allow ourselves to speculate about them as if they were real persons. How is a person like the Countess able to forgive as sincerely as the music tells us she evidently does? Perhaps as a girl going through her oedipal dramas, she had been fortunate enough to have sympathetic parents. This may have helped her to forgive the Count's betrayal without mocking him. In contrast, we could speculate that Don Giovanni as an oedipal boy was perhaps ignored, enduring humiliation and hatred of his parents' sexual coupling, leading him in time to become a professional coupler himself, doling out lavish helpings of humiliation to others in a paranoid-schizoid universe where reparation and meaningful forgiveness do not exist. We could speculate that, as an oedipal boy, Don

Alhambra – the cynical *eminence grise* directing the betrayals of *Così fan tutte* – may have been perversely mocked, prompting his own cynical denigration on what he maintained to be the illusion of true love, again in a world either of no forgiveness or, at best, possibly a cynical form of forgiveness arising from sarcasm about the human condition. In our three operas, we can watch the characters move in and out of these oedipal positions, the paranoid-schizoid and the depressive.

Just as sexual attraction is elemental, so, it would seem, are experiences of betrayal and the anti-life forces of hatred aimed at breaking up the sexual couple. Sometimes there follows an impulse towards reparation, including forgiveness. Mozart's operatic music brings these fundamental drives – their conflicts, their vicissitudes, their dissonances but also their harmonies – to life with extraordinary colour, intensity and depth.

Note

This chapter was published in the *Couple and Family Psychoanalysis*, 10(1): 2, 8–42, 2020.

References

Akhtar, S. (2002). Forgiveness: Origins, Dynamics, Psychopathology, and Technical Relevance. *Psychoanal Q.*, 71(2):175–212.

Bion, W. R. (1965). *Transformations*. London: Heinemann.

Birksted-Breen, D. (1996). Phallus, Penis and Mental Space. *Int. J. Psycho-Anal.*, 77:649–657.

Bishop, B. (2006). "The Visage of Offence": A Psychoanalytical View of Forgiveness and Repentance in Shakespeare's Plays. *Brit. J. Psychother.*, 23(1): 27–36.

Blass, R. (2019). *On the Essential Goodness of Psychic Reality and the Desire to Know It: Acknowledging an Implicit Ethical Perspective in Freudian and Kleinian Theory and Practice*. Unpublished.

Cavell, M. (2003). Freedom and Forgiveness. *Int. J. Psycho-Anal.*, 84(3): 515–531.

Freud, S. (1913). *Totem and Taboo: Some Points of Agreement between the Mental Lives of Savages and Neurotics* (1913 [1912–1913]). *S.E., Volume XIII (1913–1914): Totem and Taboo and Other Works*. London: Hogarth.

Grier, F. (Ed.) (2005a). *Oedipus and the Couple*. London: Karnac.

Grier, F. (2005b). No Sex Couples, Catastrophic Change, and the Primal Scene. In: F. Grier (Ed.), *Oedipus and the Couple*. London: Karnac.

Grier, F. (2006). Ideals, Betrayal, Guilt and Forgiveness in Couple Psychotherapy. *Brit. J. Psychother.*, 23(1): 37–48.

Kerman, J. (1988). Mozart. In: *Opera as Drama*. Oakland, CA: University of California Press.

Lansky M. R. (2001). Hidden Shame, Working Through, and the Problem of Forgiveness in *The Tempest*. *J. Amer. Psychoanal. Assn.* 49: 1004–1033.

Lansky, M. R. (2009). Forgiveness as the Working Through of Splitting. *Psychoanal. Inq.*, 29(5): 374–385.

Rusbridger, R. (2008). The Internal World of Don Giovanni. *Int. J. Psycho-Anal.*, 89 (1):181–194.

Schafer R (2005). Cordelia, Lear, and Forgiveness. *J. Amer. Psychoanal. Assn.*, 53: 389–409.

Smith, H.F. (2008). Leaps of Faith: Is Forgiveness a Useful Concept? *Int. J. Psycho-Anal.*, 89(5): 919–936.

Steiner, J. (1999). The Struggle for Dominance in the Oedipus Situation. *Canadian J. Psychoanal.*, 7(2): 161–177.

Chapter 9

Forgiveness work in society, institutions and large groups

Gerhard Wilke

Introduction

In analytic large group work, there are always moments in a session when the presence of historical friends and enemies triggers some kind of process of us and them splitting to confirm the asymmetrical relationship between perpetrators and victims, insiders and outsiders, and age cohorts. The rest of the group unconsciously delegates all the good and bad to these two sub-groups and slips into the witness or bystander role. Simultaneously, there is a more benign exchange pattern at work in large group work. The conductor or a member of the silent majority can point out that the group pays too much attention to the perpetrator and victim sub-group and ignores the role of the sub-group of the non-speakers, who slip unconsciously into the role of the bystander. The triangulation of these three types of sub-groups creates a threshold or in-between situation in the large group when feelings of reconciliation aimed at overcoming inner hurt and suffering by connecting past, present and future in a new way can replace the desire for revenge and *Wiedergutmachung* (reparation and compensation). In such transitional situations, some members of the large group can forgive themselves and others by remembering a connected history without splitting.

In such moments in a large group, forgiveness can be accomplished between two people, within a small sub-group, and between sub-groups, acting on behalf of entire societies. Moments of reconciliation and forgiveness emerge best in crisis or threshold moments, either during a group session or in society with the help of contact rituals like diplomatic exchange, peace negotiation and politically constructed events, like the South African Truth and Reconciliation Commission. Large Group work is in my understanding suited to surface exchanges where the human qualities of accepting what has happened and can't be undone is linked to verbal remembrance and reconciliation. In such moments, forgiveness can lead to cooperation and mutually obligating exchanges, provided the dialogue is linked to some mourning work. Human beings in groups have an inner capacity to seek revenge but also, like other primates, an inner need to make up after a fight

DOI: 10.4324/9781003364313-9

in the service of group cohesion. In turn, group cohesion facilitates the ability within the group to tolerate difference and subdivision – or role clarity and differentiation to put it positively. The internal reference frame in the individual within a group is of course their internalised experience of forgiving each other within the family and the wider kinship network. People with ancestral memories of confronting hidden enmities and letting go of the past in order to move on by forgiving each other, can become the "location point" within a large group to name such issues on behalf of everyone else and change the energy flow from a regressive to a more mature flow.

Crossing enemy lines into exchange between human groups

My experience as a large group conductor associated with the training of group analysts leads me to conclude that forgiveness needs a place in our theory and an allowance of time in our work. Group analysis and psychoanalysis have unconsciously delegated forgiveness work to the theologians. Perhaps as a defence against the full realisation that our profession is not as modern as it pretends to be and has more in common with pre-modern healers and medicine men than with bio-medical scientists. The other reason could be that psychotherapeutic trainings tend to be infantilising in nature and the teachers have a need to rationalise the demanding standards, rather than acknowledge a need in themselves to forgive their own teachers and ask their students for a degree of reconciliation and understanding. The real secret is perhaps that most of us who chose our brand of analytical training have inherited unresolved issues connected with guilt, shame and societal and familial secrets – hence we unconsciously became analysts in the hope that we could find a way of understanding our siblings and parents as well as the communities of origin. In my case, the dynamic between a war child and a post-war sibling and the presence of a grandfather and father traumatised by war. But also, the presence of a strong and reliable grandmother and tolerant and accepting mother. Knowledge of these social facts and internal objects, has given me the strength to work with trans-generational issues and with victim–perpetrator issues in large groups.

The emergence of forgiveness in a large group session requires the presence of a safe person with authority, a secure setting and a space for uncensored expression. The conductor of a large analytic group can help create an atmosphere of enough mutual trust, where it is safe for group members to cross the threshold from a space filled with trans-generational anxiety, shame and guilt into a potential space that fosters connections rather than us and them splitting. Only in a secure relationship matrix can the desire to name taboo subjects, the need to open sub-group boundaries and to let go of old hurt and the desire to turn a new page emerge. The ethnographer Marcel Mauss (1970) wrote that any social order is divided and needs to deal with social integration by containing potentially or actually hostile sub-groups within its community boundaries. In relation to outsider groups rituals of "gift exchange" help open cultural boundaries. My assumption is that neighbourly relationships, the connectedness of the social order within a community and the contact between potential or former enemies within a large group session rests on such "gift exchanges" – like the offering and taking of each other's time, the willingness to let go of absolute notions of right and wrong and the wish for contact and reconciliation.

Each social order rests on relationships, mutual trust and indebtedness, in the context of cultural codes of justice, fairness and what is taboo to say and do. Implicit in the socially unconscious order of belonging and loyalty to each other is also a potential capacity for reconciliation and forgiveness. This capacity is covered under a blanket of silence between sub-groups whose peaceful connections have been ruptured by war, persecution and trauma. In peaceful times, subsequent to war, reconciliation and forgiveness repeatedly surface as a central theme in crisis or transitional situations – be it in a family, a community, a whole society or between nations. In a post-traumatic context, a group-analytic large group can become a safe space for a rite of passage from a time of war and hate, oppression and persecution, to a time of first contact and of careful or eruptive truth-telling. The social exchanges and connections that emerge within a large group session, are comparable to the psycho-social triangle on which Greek drama is based: perpetrator/hero and victim/anti-hero, in front of a chorus in the form of a merged or fragmented mass. Tragedy, be it ancient or Shakespearean, is usually set betwixt times when the world seems out of joint. As Simon Critchley (2019) writes in *Tragedy, the Greeks and Us*: "the past is not past, the future folds back upon itself, and the present is shot through with fluxion of past and future that destabilize it" (p. 14).

Tragedy as well as large analytic groups deal with betwixt and between social and psychological situations, where the conceptual order of things we keep in our minds, gets disturbed so that we can see and hear what is made socially unconscious in everyday life. It is the experience of joint disturbance and insecurity that can help members of a large group to reconnect with mutuality by opening the boundary between absolute loyalty to us and complete rejection of them and connecting on a level of a joint humanity. This process requires that one or a few members name what is taboo to say by breaking the conspiracy of silence and releasing long-repressed feelings of helplessness and impotence as well as grandiosity and omnipotence. When this happens in a large group the process bears comparison to a Shakespearean drama like King Lear.

Folly, lust, hatred and forgiveness

"No one escapes whipping ..." ruminates King Lear when he has emerged from his mad rage and looks back over his life's journey from the position of outcast father, at the edge of civilisation, to his position as King and absolute ruler (Shakespeare, 1974). Only when his rage has blown itself out, does he recover his link with the natural world and his sense of connection with some of his fellow humans. He converses with "Poor Tom", who pretends to be mad in order to preserve his sanity. He takes lessons from his court fool, who is the truth-seer in the drama. He connects with his most trusted former advisor who pretends to be somebody else in order to remain true to himself, to his master and to what he regards as a just social order and its moral code. Gloucester contains his own sense of hurt and rejection and forgives the King for his folly because he is secure in his inner sense of what a good and just social order is. This sense of securely knowing who you are enables him to be at ease with his role of trusted advisor. Accepting death as part of life seems an important pre-requisite for the capacity to forgive in a societal context as portrayed in this tragedy. Equally, important is the ability of social actors to "play-act" in order to contain and regulate the level of shame between the protagonists.

In the exchanges with his fellow humans on the wild heath, stripped of all courtly pretensions of power and office, Lear begins to see afresh, how the world is and relinquishes the idea of how he wishes his world and its social actors to be. He is suddenly able to look the truth of his own folly as a father in the face and begins to show remorse for having disinherited the one true daughter and thereby pushing his kingdom into war and self-destruction. He grasps that he was not worthy of his younger daughter rather than her being unworthy of him and his inheritance. He can see that he had put his selfish needs above the requirements of succession in kingship, where death decides when the next generation is to take over. Even more "offensive" to the feudal social order was his neglect of the fatherly duty to disinherit two daughters so that the chosen one can take over the realm, based on the rights of the firstborn or the right of the most suited. In a sense, Lear tried to avoid becoming guilty of being unfair within an unequal social order because he did not trust two of his daughters to forgive him, after he had done what was necessary in order to secure his inheritance and pass it on to one of his offspring. In some sense, Lear did not put his trust in the power of reconciliation to heal the wounds of injustice and relative deprivation, which is integral to securing peace and "good-enough forgiveness" in any sibling birth order and between generations in all societies with seemingly fixed status differences.

Only in the betwixt and between state of madness and as a dependant parent rather than omnipotent King, filled with gratitude to the daughter who takes on the task of caring for him without ifs and buts, is Lear able to forgive his own folly and can then be reconciled with his wronged child. She, in turn, forgives him. In contrast to his other daughters, who are unforgiving in their response to his old age and his misdemeanours. His avoidance of dealing with the inherent injustice of succession leads to Lear's expulsion from the body politic. He becomes an outcast. What he feared, has come to pass. Only through the capacity for gratitude and concern for his youngest daughter is King Lear re-admitted to the social order, and only then can he forgive and is prepared to face his death. He encounters the theme of forgiveness and reconciliation in the transition from life to death and during his passage of re-entry from wild nature to the established social order. Previously he was the figurehead of the royal state, with the help of his rejected daughter and her forgiveness he becomes an honoured ancestor. In this sense, the capacity for forgiveness in the individual and any large social group, opens up in a threshold situation, where the symbolic order is disturbed enough to make way for new patterns of connecting. It is the fool who knows this and says that ambivalence is the precondition for forgiveness and a return to a semblance of a social and moral order.

The unspoken trauma in King Lear is perhaps that he has lost his wife and his daughters their mother. Lear, instead of providing a safe holding environment for his children and involving them in sorting out his will and succession plan in a fatherly way, makes them compete against each other in order to ward off his fear of death. He fails in his duty of care, feels unconsciously ashamed and defends against it by feeding his narcissistic needs. The social and psychological processes in the play can therefore be conceptualised as an incomplete mourning process for the mother, combined with the failure of the father to become a dependable and good-enough caregiving object to his bereft children. As long as these two traumatising processes remain socially unconscious, the collective capacity for reconciliation and forgiveness is blocked and defended against by "perverted forms of attention seeking" and "repeated scenes of abuse". Lear's expulsion of his best-loved daughter and the abuse of him by the two daughters who succeeded him as figurehead of the realm are symptoms of a traumatised society. Revenge and violence are the ruling emotions in such a social context, not reconciliation and forgiveness.

Frank Kermode (2001) suggests that *King Lear* is a play about the Last Judgement on earth, not in heaven. A play about a godless universe and beyond Christian forgiveness. The play shows how humans themselves can reduce their social universe to an apocalypse just by letting their inner, potential inhumanity reign without restraint and by banning mutual trust and forgiveness from social intercourse. It can only be recovered beyond the boundaries of a world gone mad and without custom and law, in the wilderness of uncivilised nature and with the social help of fellow sufferers. Lear destroys the social forgiveness involved in dividing the inheritance after death in a succession. In serving his narcissistic needs rather than the kingdom he turns a considered and calculated hand-over of power into a traumatising social process. Perhaps a re-enactment of the disastrous loss of his wife, which left his children bereft of maternal care and him feeling impotent, alone and helpless. It is these unbearable feelings that he projects into his kingdom and the succession ritual. Therefore, the kingdom becomes a plaything of envious, treacherous and dishonest connections between people on the make and is ruled by greed and the lust for absolute power – at any price. Forgiveness and gratitude have no place in a life-or-death scenario. The act and gesture of forgiveness is a betwixt and between social interchange between I–you–us–them in a favourable social context. This place and time can only be found in the wilderness, where the sheer force of nature reminds the sufferers of their need for each other, for cooperation, empathy and reconciliation. Perhaps more importantly, the acceptance of mutual dependence among humans is in the play connected with the acceptance of unpalatable truths about humans and their society. Suffering is inherent in each life cycle and in human society. It results from the human tendency of those that see themselves as in the right to inflict evil on the rest, under the indifferent eye of a god.

Old-fashioned Freudians thought that the play was about the repressed incestuous desires of Lear for his youngest daughter, perhaps dealing in this abstracted way with the founding father's relationship with his daughter Anna. For me, these analysts have a point if one takes incest to mean that too much closeness and distance perverts a social order profoundly. King Lear is, however, also a play about being loved and hated too much and the kind of social chaos that follows in the wake of such excess. In a sense, the play is an attack on the idealised family and the explosive power of trans-generational dynamics and the delegation of working through processes to the second generation. The emotional forces unleashed overwhelms everyone and makes them collude in the dramatisation of tragedy and destruction. In turn, this leads to a loss of everyone's social bonds and hence any capacity for forgiveness, gratitude and reconciliation. Love and mutual obligation to each other are only restored at the end of the play, but those who commit to it, have to die. As analytical thinkers we know that life without death, pain, shame, humiliation and guilt is not possible. This being so, forgiveness must in a sense be central to the mastery of life's developmental stages, especially at the threshold of adolescence, old age and full maturity. If any of us are pressed down by guilt, shame and humiliation, we seek to alleviate the situation through rage and revenge against the perpetrators, through repetition compulsion and self-denigration. Or, if we have good-enough inner objects through repentance, reconciliation and forgiveness. The individual in a secular society can cover the guilt and shame of hurting others with a blanket of silence or work on loss, remembering and forgiveness when the inner mechanisms of denial and forgetting break down. Usually, such a social bridging process requires the help of an intermediary like a priest, a therapist, grandparents or a public working through ritual. In King Lear, it is the foreigner, the King of France, who becomes the "transforming" object, the "in-between-being", able to reconnect past, present and future.

Gestures of societal reconciliation and forgiveness

The transition from white to black rule in post-Apartheid South Africa is an example of how an innovative approach to working through a trauma, of retelling the story of the past and the work of truth-seeking through remembrance, reconciliation and perhaps forgiveness, can connect divided individuals, sub-groups and a whole society. Nelson Mandela as the designated leader of the new era understood that he had to let go of his hurt and sense of humiliation and degradation as well as the hate of the prison guards and the apartheid system, when he walked into freedom. If he had not done so, he once said, he would have remained imprisoned in the relationship with his guards and would have needed to go on living on their terms. This did not mean that he let go of the injustice and the abuse perpetrated against him and so many of his people, but it meant that he treated every South African – victim, perpetrator and bystander – as a human being and as a citizen with rights and obligations. He modelled in his first step into freedom that he wanted to take power with a "forgiving mindset" in the sense of thinking ahead and acting above his painful, hurtful, denigrating situation in prison.

Nelson Mandela was subsequently open to Bishop Tutu's idea of a "Truth and Reconciliation Commission". The Bishop thought that it was necessary for victims to tell their stories and confront their torturers and oppressors, out in the open, in front of witnesses. He also thought that the victims needed to hear the personal stories of the agents of the Apartheid state. Being a deeply devout man, he wanted to translate the core message of Christianity of "forgive your enemies" into practical politics in a traumatised society. He wanted to encourage his people literally to turn the other cheek in order to find peace in the eyes of god and give a reborn nation a chance of civil peace. He understood another element that is indispensable for people to forgive each other in social and public situations, to attach to and believe in something greater than the individual or the immediate belonging sub-group. Desmond Tutu (2014) thought that without forgiveness, without remorse and a public act of collective truth-seeking through remembering South Africa would descend into civil strife.

Unique about this process was the "exchange" deal on offer in the public proceedings: No persecution for perpetrators who publicly admitted their crimes against humanity and showed "felt" remorse in front of their victims. Tutu was also convinced that forgiveness and reconciliation required that the perpetrators broke their silence and talked in public about their role in the apartheid system and how they ended up doing what they did. The ironic twist of this story is that Tutu's "communal forgiveness work" used the Christian inheritance brought by the colonising missionaries into his native country. He seems to have wanted to forgive his own persecutors by confronting the last generation of the colonial oppressors with the African tradition of "Ubuntu" – "I am the way I am, because you are the way you are". On this basis, we can remember and not forget, but we can also forgive because both you and me, them and us have to recognise and affirm our shared humanity when we interact face to face. Tutu believed that this philosophy could facilitate a "restorative" justice and prevent "retributive" violence and division.

Hannah Arendt (2007) was sceptical in her writings about reconciliation and forgiveness between the victims and perpetrators of totalitarian rule. She did not think that the traumatising experiences of the Holocaust, for example, could be overcome or forgiven. Instead, the suffering needed to be remembered and worked with in order to find a form of exchange between oppressors and oppressed in a shared social context. Its primary purpose being to prevent collective forgetting and a repetition of the abuse and genocide. To this end, politicians, intellectuals and citizens need to create forums for tolerating each other's presence through joint and collective memorial rituals. In her view learning to live with each other again, was a first step and a kind of insurance policy against the repetition of a genocide. Instead of forgiveness, learning to live side by side was a good-enough achievement for Arendt.

Vera Kattermann (2007) studied the Truth and Reconciliation Commission and its relevance for the working through of the sense of collective guilt associated with the Holocaust in West Germany. She concluded that it is not clear whether reconciliation or forgiveness between former tortures, prison guards and police and their survivors can really be reached through a state-sponsored public truth and reconciliation process alone. The working through of collective perpetrator remorse, survivor guilt and the shame of the oppressor and oppressed needs, in her estimation, several generations. She concluded that a traumatising past would have to be "metabolised" by the whole body of the affected society, in each individual family that suffered and some of its "delegated" offspring over time. The collective work of reconciliation and forgiveness is in Kattermann's view connected with the collective capacity to remember and forget the trauma. How it is worked through, and who has the valency to take it on, is too complex and unpredictable a process to be classified systematically. Reconciliation and forgiveness will take many private and public forms like memorial days, novels, films, documentaries or a TV series like *Holocaust*. This series, which personified, the destruction of a Jewish family in the Third Reich, touched a nerve in Germany and opened multiple events and projects, dedicated to *Wiedergutmachung* (the work of reparation and repentance). The public process of truth and reconciliation can therefore not be fully comprehended or planned, but only understood retrospectively. What is clear is that working through, reconciliation and forgiveness processes are interwoven with processes of holding a society and its social structure together as well as lending its members a sense of identity, history and belonging.

Forgiveness, reparation and mourning in post-totalitarian societies

My own experience of working with post-war German guilt and shame in large groups confirms the findings of Maurice Halbwachs (1985) that remembering, forgetting and connecting appears to be an individual task but is in reality a social process. Remembrance of collective traumas, as well as the core foundation myths of a belonging group or nation, are evoked in threshold situations like funerals, and periods of social crisis like the building of the Berlin Wall and the Student Revolt in Germany. In large analytic groups such an "as-if" crisis situation is offered in a time-limited and contained space. Collective remembering, reconciliation across sub-group boundaries and the surfacing of collective social secrets and trans-generational transference phenomena need a "liminal" time and safe ritualised social interactions.

Large groups offer a betwixt and between space for testing the shared and sub-divided symbolic social order, a shared or divided sense of history and the place each member and sub-group adopts within this framework. In contrast to a set societal ritual like Remembrance Day, the large group offers a "threshold" space in which the "symbolic order" (the way we act, think, feel and order experience) within and between participants and the emergent sub-groups can be voiced and adapted. Social anthropologists believe that humans are not just social but also "classifying" beings. Therefore, all communities classify their world and the natural, social and cosmological order with the help of symbols representing the sacred and profane, the pure and impure, the core values and beliefs of what makes us unique and them different. In large groups the us and them distinction is a key dynamic as each large group negotiates three "threshold" phases: the separation and dislocation phase where the expected modes of social exchange are frustrated and alienated; a phase that transports the group members into the betwixt and between state, and, an attachment phase where people find their voice, their memory and recover the ability for exchange, dialogue, mutual acceptance and reconciliation. In such a phase forgiveness can be surfaced on the level of the self, between generations, between siblings and between divided sub-groups. It is important not to think of these three ritual phases in a large group as a logical sequence but more like an energy flow in a running stream of free associations.

Over a number of sessions, a large group will create a relationship matrix that contains us and them divisions, establishes psycho-social defences and deals with symptoms of trans-generational trauma rooted in events like the Holocaust, colonialism, Nazism, civilian bombings, war and abuse. Through verbal exchanges across the boundaries of its constituent sub-groups, a large group finds ways of seeing and sense-making, in relation to what integrates a community and what makes it split and fragment. Central in this process is what kind of collective memories, traumas, taboos and myths are triggered, enacted, named or made socially unconscious. By conveying trust in the large group and by accepting whatever is spoken and enacted, a group's convener can help it find its own way of overcoming the "dis-ease" between the speaker, the listener, the silent bystander(s) and the often moralistic and judgemental chorus.

Large group work seems therefore well suited to create a temporary space in which enough acceptance and forgiveness can emerge between sub-groups who historically are in a victim–perpetrator or historic enemy relationship. Indeed, large analytic groups can be seen as the best setting for "metabolising" and working through collective trauma and breaking the habit of the ethnic, religious or national belonging groups to repeat a cycle of denial, hatred and mutual destruction. This is perhaps so because the large group is experienced as "equivalent enough" to the way in which the "unspoken and taken for granted" processes of social interaction in a society and in everyday life work. In society, as in a large analytic group, social exchange is not just determined by individuals but also the interaction of sub-groups and their way of relating to the group as a whole. At the very core of such "social" – not just psychological – interactions are the tendency to idealise "us" and denigrate "them". The group and the conductor of a large group lets the potentially destructive interaction dynamic surface, where we are better than them because they are not like us. Only after this phase of mutual estrangement and differentiation, as well as denigration and idealisation can a cross-boundary relationship matrix become an object of identification. In this situation, the sub-groups can lower their defences and discover that there is a "third position" beyond good and bad, their common humanity. Only when this social wall has been opened does reconciliation, as a precursor to forgiveness, have a chance!

Show your wounds, Joseph Beuys urged. This dictum is implicit in his artistic work, which repeatedly dealt with his war experience. In a large group "encapsulated" trauma wounds can be opened, enacted and verbalised. The key is that a member of the large group breaks the ice and others join this person in forming a sub-group that can share a similar fate and story, not censored by the social taboos of the insider–outsider dynamic in enclosed belonging groups. This can happen because the large group puts each member under enormous pressure to retain the capacity to think and not to regress to a state of mindlessness. According to Pat de Mare et al. (1991), a large group opens the boundaries between superego–ego–id in the individual and between I–you–us–them in the fragile relationship matrix of the various sub-groups that encounter each other in a large group session. When a number of sub-groups have emerged in a session, de Mare has argued, the large group can become a highly sensitive reflection forum and turns itself into a laboratory for practising the chief virtue of a democratic society – the capacity of tolerating and fostering different voices and cultures within its social and psychological boundary.

At a workshop entitled "Psychotherapeutic Work in Post-Totalitarian Societies," three sub-groups met: East Germans, Russians and Ukrainians. I worked with a small group during the early phase of the conflict between Russia and West and East Ukraine. The military conflict was perceived by the participants from West Ukraine, who identified with the Hapsburg and Viennese culture, as a war between Ukraine and Russia. The East Ukrainians and the Russian group members saw the conflict as a protest by the East-Ukrainian Allies of the Russians against a colonial take-over from the West, especially NATO. The first two days of the group sessions were dominated by mutual accusations and recriminations, leaving the Germans in the position of the witness, a significant role reversal as German members were used to embodying the position of perpetrators in international groups. Myself, as a German conductor, responded initially to this unfamiliar experience by withdrawing into an empathic silence and thinking that without the invasion of these two countries by our fathers, this encounter would be very different. Will this group be as accepting of me when they remember this historical fact?

On the second evening, a German member of the group said that his wife needed him at home and that he would not come back on the last day. The next morning, the conductor left his chair in the circle and said that the group had started. Immediately, a retired East German psychiatrist got up and removed the chair and closed the gap in the circle. Whereupon the conductor put the chair back into the circle. The psychiatrist then said that in East Germany the collective came before the individual and that a member of the collective, who left, was "excluded from the circle of solidarity". In reply, the conductor said: "through his presence for two days, the absent member is in the mind of the group and its individual members. His absence makes him now more present than he was while he sat in his chair, bearing witness to the mutual accusations of the Russian and Ukrainian group members. His empty chair gives the group a chance to reflect on the theme of absence and presence, but perhaps also the theme of loss and remembrance".

This intervention was followed by a long silence. Suddenly, many members from both sides of the conflict shared stories of arrests, disappearances, transportations, executions, deaths and public humiliations affecting parts of their extended family during the Stalin years and until the collapse of the system. Underneath the divided memories of recent times – since the collapse of the Soviet Union – a deeper level of collective memory emerged, which broke the spell of the us and them interactions, where one side was the enemy to the other. The symbolic significance of the empty chair suddenly meant absent, lost and un-mourned family members. The empty presence had opened up a potential space in the group for mutual understanding, for connecting and differentiating the fate of individuals and collectives, in the time of totalitarian rule. When the violent and intrusive nature of the system in the lives of all families could be named, it was possible to share feelings of "failed dependency" (Hopper, 2003), "incomplete mourning" (Mitscherlich & Mitscherlich, 1967), "survivor guilt" and "trans-generational" symptoms of shame and guilt (Wardi, 1992). What became clear was that trauma is a neurological, psychological and social process, which generates similar patterns of affliction and working through processes in its bearers. It became possible to share and accept the perception that trauma is what it is and does not distinguish between those on the right and the wrong side of history.

It was in this group phase that reconciliation emerged as a unifying theme for the whole group. The East Germans who were descended from Nazis felt a sense of grievance on behalf of their parents against the Communist regime because their descent and "guilt by association" disqualified them from life chances. The German children of Communists whose parents were locked up by the Nazis in concentration camps shared their pain of either having broken fathers or, due to their descent, privileged and resented parents. The symptoms they suffered from, were not radically different. All the East Germans were presented as oppressed by the Soviet system and felt "colonised" by the West Germans after the unification of the country. They felt doubly discriminated against and victimised but discovered that their regime had, in a sense, been less terrorising and murderous than the Soviet Union in its effect on the Ukrainian and Russian families. In periods of great historical change like the collapse of the Soviet regime and the fall of the Berlin Wall it is normal that power relations can reverse and the accepted version of the shared collective past and future, which lends individuals and sub-groups an identity, needs to be adjusted. The group process on the third day of the workshop dramatised this process. The villains and victims of the first two days in the workshop suddenly shared a joint collective history and the repressed pain inflicted on their families by a totalitarian system. It was at this moment in the group that some group members found the strength in themselves to forgive each other for having cast each other in the role of oppressor or hated foreigner in the first two days in the group.

Human beings are the subjective shapers of historical processes and they are, at the same time, the object of the social system and its history. The healing power of reconciliation is released in group sessions when the rage and lust for revenge against the current enemy and the need to demonstrate loyalty to the belonging group is let go of and the capacity to share what everyone has in common is recovered. After such a moment the group can become a containing space in which exchanges across the us and them divide helps people to securely attach to the idea of a common humanity. This was the precondition for working through the Ukrainian, Russian and East German sub-group social defences of omnipotence and impotence in order to move on from being a victim or perpetrator of fate, to taking a separate as well as joint destiny into their own hands and becoming potent in the present, being momentarily free of the prison of the past. It was in this context that individuals could let go of resentment and the urge to demand moral justice and retribution. They jointly created a potential space for forgiveness, in which individual members of the group could say sorry on behalf of their parents and grandparents. Large group work is comparable to a theatrical tragedy in the sense that it explores what we, what they and what all of us jointly are? It opens a glimpse into the unknown future by letting us sense who we might become in relation to ourselves and each other. Large group work lends a voice to what suffers in us and evokes some of us to confront the memory of it. In addition, it creates social scenes between the participants that dramatise how we are identified, albeit unconsciously, with the trans-generational calamities that haunt us, our families, our nations.

Trauma, reconciliation and forgiveness in German psychoanalysis

Mourning in a large group means that the individual who shows the loss, can become the focal point for a sub-group and perhaps trigger a sense of recognition, acceptance and relief at the level of a shared collective and bottled-up experience. Past, present and future can become connected in the here and now and transition the group members into an adjusted symbolic social order. George Devereux (1984) claimed that such transitions always have a ritualistic structure, which can link individual, group and society. It is the mechanism of trans-generational transference that is crucial to expose how socially unconscious material gets enacted through "chosen" or "volunteering" individuals, who embody both encapsulated fragments of the collective trauma and a kernel of hope for the future in the whole group.

For several years I conducted three large groups once a year, at the German Institute of Psychoanalysis. It soon became apparent that the unique pattern of communication in this group was that someone spoke, another person answered and then there was a silence, before the pattern repeated itself with a changed theme. It was as if only a dyadic exchange, an exchange of one idea and one reply, surrounded by silence and disconnection, was unconsciously allowed. Initially, I thought that this had to do with the fact that most members of the institute preferred working as classical analysts and were resisting any attachment to what they expected to be a deeply regressed group. When I eventually shared my observations with the group and asked them what they made of this pattern themselves, an old group member revealed that she thought this pattern of communication had to do with the history of the institute: "I trained at this institute during the war and at that time it was not safe to speak with more than one person. People who broke this safety code endangered their own lives and that of others. If they said the wrong thing to a colleague, who also was an advocate of Nazi ideology, they could be put away. So, perhaps that is still how we relate in the institute and the large group brings this out in the open".

In response, the conductor said: this group seems akin to Bion's (1961) basic assumption defence of pairing. Two people can speak, and the rest of the group merges as a silent mass, defending against the lifting of the group secret or "chosen trauma" (Volkan, 2002). The group had recreated, as it were, the traumatising scene that has been made socially unconscious and become taboo for collective remembrance. The younger generation felt to me in the transference as if it was waiting for someone in their parent generation to lift the lid of silence and reveal what they carried inside and why. The relief to both generations was immediately palpable and a different, less fearful energy flow took hold of the group when the unspeakable history of the institute became the focus of the dialogue. Very quickly a trans-generational form of storytelling emerged in the group. The first and second generation told the third generation the following story.

When the Nazis had seized power and driven the mainly Jewish psycho-analysts from the country, most institutes of psychoanalysis were closed down. Hermann Göring, who thought of himself as modern and progressive decided to find some native practitioners who were willing to collaborate with the Nazi psychiatrists and ensure that three psychoanalytic institutes in Germany were kept going. These organisations are still known nationally and internationally as the Göring institutes. The group we were sitting in, shared this fate and kept it always in mind and felt polluted, ashamed and guilty by association. Therefore, it made sense that the oldest group member volunteered to be the truth-seer. She had a valence for this role because she had actually lived under the Nazis. What she said was rooted in her own fear of being in existential danger "there and then" as well as "here and now". She alone carried the open inner wound and felt shut up and helpless in the terror system. She still lived on the terms of the past in the present. She embodied the damaged self-ideal of the institution on behalf of everyone else. In contrast, the others present carried the transferred guilt and shame of the second generation on behalf of their parents and within this group for their training analysts in the institute, including the truth-seer.

During the next large group day, a year later, the truth-seer took the initiative, on behalf of everyone else. In a reversal of the trans-generational transference, she spoke movingly about the fact that the previous sessions had helped her to forgive herself for having been a collaborator with tea-chers, who had made their career at the expense of their own Jewish training analysts. In the interval between the large group events, she had become aware that she was young and was driven to finish her own training, because in a time of war she needed to earn a living. She now saw that in such a context the majority got sucked into a survival drama and political processes, much larger, much more terrifying and destructive than anyone could have dreamt of before. To resist them in hindsight seemed grandiose and false to her. Nevertheless, she felt at the time that something was morally wrong. "The need to survive", she added, "made us turn a blind eye to what was going on. I locked my decent person inside me up and so did everyone around me". What the last large group day had recovered in her was the memory of how "uncomfortable" and "false" she felt after qualifying, when she was taught to repeat to her own students that psychoanalysis was "Jewish psychology" and inferior to "Aryan psychotherapy". "It is these teaching sessions and my collaboration, which haunt me in my dreams sometimes". When sitting up rather than lying down as a trainee or patient defined the difference between "worthy" and "unworthy" professional practice and the right to "stay alive", she added wistfully. The re-enactment of the social interaction patterns during World War II helped her to realise that the current generation is still condemned to collude with the silence surrounding the "true history" of the institute. The majority of the founder generation had been Jewish, who were "systematically" expelled by their students, who became the collaborators with the "Nazi institute".

The children of the perpetrator and colluding generation found a more empathic view of their parents' fate during the Third Reich in this large group. The second and third generation were able, in response to the reconciliatory words of the older person, to take up a more forgiving position towards their "analytic parents" because they realised that they too got caught up or even volunteered for events that were beyond their imagination. As someone said: "Who am I to imagine now that I would have resisted and been braver than anyone else managed to be?" What has moved me most in these sessions is that it is very unforgiving and all too easy to blame the known collaborators with the Nazis for not resisting. If the group is a mirror, we can see in this large group that the silent majority delegates the evil deed of speaking to the collaborators and seeks shelter under a blanket of silence, where they can stay apparently, but not really, innocent. Why should it have been otherwise after 1933? If I am honest with myself and consider my own character, I might also have watched and collaborated in silence, if I had lived then. I would not have had the courage to put my life on the line. I would have rationalised my behaviour by saying that I wanted to help the group do its work – paying indirect homage to the "ruling Führer-principle".

In response to this powerful contribution, I thought to myself that forgiveness work needs to be at the core of productive large group work – at least for my own generation of post-war Germans who carried their parents' shame and delegated guilt inside for so long. Christopher Bollas's (1991) ideas on fate and destiny came to my mind and I said to the group: "Changing the story we tell others and ourselves, especially in front of empathic witnesses, opens up new options in life. In this large group, a liminal space for change has opened up. The boundaries between individuals, generational sub-groups and the whole group have become translucent. Some members of this group can suddenly stand in each other's shoes and begin to see the human being underneath the mask of the social role. Individuals and conflicted sub-groups within this large group have let go of their sense of hurt, their inner rage and victimisation. Remembering the past and breaking the silence surrounding its secrets has helped us work towards generational reconciliation and a degree of mutual forgiveness".

It is part of the working through of the effects of World War II and any totalitarian system that we, as a profession, are subsequently delegated the task, by the rest of society, to make sense of the traumas of persecution, genocide, bombing, displacement and war through our work. This is very tangible in Germany where the trauma of persecution, murder and emigration left the psychoanalytic community bereft of its founding father Freud and a large proportion of the first and second generation of training analysts. Post-war analysis could not simply get on with re-establishing itself. The burden of history affected the relationship of every analytic trainee since 1945 and his or her training analyst, their institution and its connection or disconnection with the international psychoanalytic movement.

Incomplete forgiveness work in the psychoanalytic community

Since the re-establishment of psychoanalysis after World War II, German training institutions have been split into the DPG (German Psychoanalytic Society) and the DPV (German Psychoanalytic Association). The DPG is to this day haunted by its descent from the Nazi institutes of psychotherapy. The DPV was founded after the first international post-war gathering in 1947 by colleagues from the USA, the UK and Israel as representing a fresh start and "break with the past". The international association recognised the "clean" and refused entry to the "unclean" German analysts, depending on their descent. This split into good and bad analysts met the need within Germany to personify "representative" and embodied guilty scapegoats and, by implication, lend a fresh start, without the burden of collective guilt, to the rest – who could then deny that they too had been sucked into the Nazi system. The division of post-war psychoanalysis also mirrored the dynamic of denial in post-war perpetrator families, where the children were told that it was "our neighbours, not us who did all the bad things". On a political level, the International Psychoanalytic Association (IPA) simply re-enacted the less-than-perfect de-Nazification process of the Allied Powers. They too divided Germans into active and guilty Nazis and the rest.

The theme of forgiveness is relevant here because the "unclean" German analysts are to this day not able to attend IPA Congresses – either at home or worldwide. They feel unforgiven and cursed by the Old Testament thinking that the sins of the fathers shall be visited upon the sons into the third and fourth generation. The DPG analysts await the reign of the spirit of the New Testament, which is to forgive thy neighbour and turn the other cheek. What the unrecognised German institutes and their third and fourth-generation descendants craved for in the decades since 1950 was the legitimation of their training, as it evolved after 1945. Understandably, they wanted to be freed from the stigma of having had the wrong analytic parentage. The split between the "clean" and "polluted" institutes produced an us and them split, between those who feel forgiven and could identify with the victims of the Nazis, and those who still feel guilty by association and identify themselves with the perpetrators. This spilt had the unintended consequence that the unclean institutes were unconsciously delegated the task of working through the sins of everyone's analytic parents. This group of analysts bore the mark of Cain without the protection of the analytic gods, who had fled Germany or been killed by their own ancestors.

In the German context, the personified split into pure and impure analysts, created enough pressure to research the past in order to understand the chosen trauma of collaborating with the Nazis. This search to know what really happened evoked an interesting split in the DPG institutes that I worked in as a large group conductor – those who wanted to know and remember versus those who wanted to get on with life and forget. Those who did want to know visited archives and studied the records of their training institute and through the work of remembering owned their history con- sciously and recognised their capacity to forgive and to be grateful. All col- lective remembering processes become meaningful, if they are intertwined with a process of collective forgetting. In other words, the searchers for the truth needed those who wanted to forget, lest the searchers forget to live in the present. In several DGP institutes, the two sub-groups could be held within one community with the help of large group reflection sessions. The large analytic group is in my view, a setting in which boundaries between split organisational sub-groups can be held enough to discover their mutual need for each other. When this has been achieved, potential spaces for reconciliation and forgiveness, but also for accepting that some things are not forgivable, but can be lived with, open up.

Conclusion

It has become clear that forgiveness is a social as well as individual process that can emerge and be accomplished in transitional or threshold situations. In this betwixt and between space individuals can begin to forgive themselves and each other and so can hostile sub-groups, like in a Greek drama, where enemies are held by the gaze of the chorus long enough to cross a threshold from hate and revenge back to mutual dependence. Large analytic groups and crisis situations in society evoke a liminal situation in which socially unconscious patterns of remembering and forgetting are voiced through col- lectively delegated truth seers. When this has happened another story and attendant feelings of reconciliation and forgiveness have a chance to be heard and internalised. Transitions are always a chance to rename things, to make social boundaries "translucent" (Foulkes, 1948) and for victims as well as perpetrators to become human beings with a unique history, rather than an object for us and them projections.

References

Arendt, H. (2007). *Über das Böse*. München: Piper.

Bion, W. R. (1961). *Experiences in Groups, and Other Papers*. London: Tavistock.

Bollas, C. (1991). *Forces of Destiny. Psychoanalysis and Human Idiom*. London: Free Association Books.

de Mare, P. (1991). *Koinonia: From Hate, Through Dialogue, to Culture in the Large Group*. London: Karnac.

Critchley, S. (2019). *Tragedy, the Greeks and Us*. London: Profile Books (p. 14).

Devereux, G. (1984). *Ethno-psychoanalyse*. Frankfurt: Suhrkamp.

Foulkes, S. H. (1948). *Introduction to Group-Analytic Psychotherapy*. Heinemann.

Freud, S. (2001), in Kermode, *Shakespeare's Language*. London: Penguin (pp. 183–200).

Halbwachs, M. (1985). *Das Gedächtnis und seine sozialen Bedingungen*. Frankfurt: Suhrkamp Wissenschaft.

Hopper, E. (2003). *Traumatic Experience in the Unconscious Life of Groups*. London: Jessica Kingsley.

Kattermann, V. (2007). *Kollektive Vergangenheitsbearbeitung in Südafrika*. Gießen: Psychosozial Verlag.

Kermode, F. (2001). *Shakespeare's Language*. London: Penguin.

Mauss, M. (1970). *The Gift*. London: Cohen & West.

Mitscherlich, A. & Mitscherlich, M. (1967). *Die Unfähigkeit zu trauern*. Grundlagen kollektiven Verhaltens. Munich: Piper.

Shakespeare, W. (1974). Hunter, G.K. (ed.) *King Lear*. Harmondsworth: Penguin.

Tutu, D. (2014). *Das Buch des Vergebens*. Vier Schritte zu mehr Menschlichkeit. Berlin: Allegria.

Volkan. V. (2002). *The Third Reich in the Unconscious*. New York: Brunner-Routledge.

Wardi, D. (1992). *Memorial Candles, Children of the Holocaust*. London: Tavistock.

Chapter 10

Forgiveness in the recognition of actuality

Karl Figlio

Introduction

Forgiveness is difficult to pin down because it is so commonly used for appeasing all types of disrupted equanimity between people, whether by debt, assault or dishonour. Perhaps as a result, there is a tendency to speak of obstructions to forgiving – a state of unforgivingness, which one might relinquish, commonly expressed as 'letting go'. With this formulation goes a moral direction, in which both unforgivingness and letting go are narcissistic resistances.

There is an elaborate philosophical literature on the forms of 'letting go', which compares it with a family of forbearances, such as excusing, pardoning, condoning, reconciling and showing mercy. This literature sticks with consciousness and an attendant implied agency, as if one could forgive as an act, perhaps by saying 'I forgive' (see Hughes and Warmke, 2017 for a detailed overview). But while letting go might seem adequate for conscious acts, including speech acts, it precludes the language of the unconscious, internal world. The conscious world is causal, based on metaphors of doing something in the external world, such as releasing the grip on a rope; the unconscious, internal world is ambivalent, embracing simultaneous, conflicted beliefs and relationships based on identifications rather than entailment.

The psychoanalytic literature on forgiveness finds an expanding complexity of defences, principally a narcissistic gratification in holding on to a grievance. In a comprehensive critique of the psychoanalysis of forgiveness, Smith (2008) argues that forgiveness encompasses a range of already recognized defences and functions. Forgiveness, therefore, means nothing more than the outcome of good analytic work. For Lansky (2009), good analytic work is also at the core, but the analysis of forgiveness requires the working through of an offence in the form of unconscious shame fantasies. These fantasies embody a retributive attitude towards someone to whom 'actual injury or a severe narcissistic wound' has been attributed, and they are split off from mainstream consciousness. Working through involves a 'resolution

DOI: 10.4324/9781003364313-10

of splitting manifested in antecedent retributive states of mind – resentment, grudge, blame, envy, vengefulness, spite, greed, hatred, and bitterness' (p. 383). Siassi, whose detailed clinical account of forgiveness (Siassi, 2007) Smith used for his critique, thinks of forgiveness as 'the healthy narcissistic need ... to create a new balance for the enrichment of the psyche ... [in] the internalization of ... a love object ... that validates the patient's lovability' (Siassi, 2009, p. 643). Similarly, Weintrobe (2004, p. 86) speaks of 'lively narcissism' and 'lively entitlement'. It embodies an introjective, reality-orientated relationship to the external world.

In this chapter, I will focus on overcoming the obstacles to forgiveness. In my view, the injury that provokes unforgivingness is a violation, which is an assault on psychic integrity. That is why the reaction is narcissistic. I would add that the violation is by forced introjection along with demonstrable injury. Embedded in the ego, it torments the psyche beneath the pain of physical assault. But instead of seeing narcissism simply as the principal obstruction to forgiveness, I think it can also, allied to defiance, facilitate forgiveness. To make this distinction we need to distinguish two forms of narcissism: a libidinal narcissism that allies with defiance and a destructive narcissism that drives grievance. Britton (2008) sees them as two forms of narcissistic ego defences against an ego-destructive parental superego: 'The formation of narcissistic object relationship can be motivated by the wish to preserve the capacity for love by making the love-object seem like the self [libidinal narcissism]; or it can be aimed at annihilating the separate object [destructive narcissism]' (p. 27). In my view, the defiance of libidinal narcissism secures the ego through libidinal ties that also seek recognition of the actuality, with a recovery of reality, sanity and integrity. The grievance and vengeance of destructive narcissism (Rosenfeld, 1971) seek narcissistic restoration by reversing the projective identification, returning the violation into the perpetrator.

Forgiveness should be considered together with reparation because they share a relationship between ego and object, in recognizing the actuality of an offence. I think this process underlies what philosophers call the 'change of heart' that promotes forgiveness. Although the plea for actuality is obscured by the stridency of grievance, it nonetheless needs to be recognized. Both forgiveness and reparation involve a relationship between a 'getting-better' ego and a 'getting-better' object. Forgiveness is a capacity of the ego, secured as an agent by being in touch with actuality. Reparation is a more mature capacity of an ego, secured as an agent by being in touch, in addition, with its destructiveness and concern for the object. It might seem counter-intuitive to suggest reparative concern for the very object that violated the ego, and in extreme cases, such as torture or the Holocaust, scepticism is fully warranted. But in the more ordinary situation, one can speak of injury to the persecuting object by narcissistically driven grievance.

We might say that, as agency is essential to the formation of the ego, the capacity for forgiveness is the precursor of the capacity for reparation.

Forgiveness is an unconscious response of the ego to the getting better of the bad object when, driven by the ego's defiance, the object recognizes the actuality of persecution. It is neither a historical record nor an internal reality alone, but a discovery in the analysis of a violation. Reparation is an unconscious process of making better the good aspects of the object, damaged by the ego's grievance. Forgiveness is a waystation to reparation.

Contradictions in forgiveness: agency and process

Forgiveness typically refers to reconciliation in conscious, external reality, while in psychoanalysis it is unconscious. Similarly, reparation refers to the internal world of reconciliation between the ego and an internal object. We commonly say, 'I do (not) forgive him/her', or, 'Forgive me', but we don't say, 'I do (not) repair him/her'. We repair cars and radio sets, but we do not repair damaged internal objects or their external representatives.[1] Instead, we refer to reparation. 'I forgive' is an action, not a statement that represents an interior state. It is what the philosopher, J. L. Austin (1962) called 'performative': it does what the sentence says.

The agency in forgiving is clear in its etymology. Forgive originally meant 'to give'. It took on the additional sense of 'to give over', an expression that remains current today. To give over means to relent from a strongly held position: to let go of a recrimination, a grievance, a thirst for revenge. It is to settle a debt, to balance an account, whether financial or of honour. Reparation, by contrast, is not a settling of accounts, but recognition of the value of the object in itself and for the ego.

The difference between forgiveness and reparation highlights a dissonance in the idea of forgiveness, which has been worked out for reparation but not for forgiveness. Just as a theory of reparation depended upon separating manic reparation, an omnipotent agency, from reparation (Segal, 1981), so too, a theory of forgiveness will depend on a separation of agency from a healing relationship between ego and object. Otherwise, the victim who 'chooses' to forgive would be indulging in a manic triumph, secretly holding the very grudge that forgiveness aimed to overcome.[2] Like reparation, forgiveness can neither be carried out as a plan nor accomplished. It can only be discovered to have been underway. This quality only makes sense with the dimension of an internal world, and marks a unique, psychoanalytic contribution (largely absent, for example, in philosophical discussions of forgiveness).

I aim to show that the destructive narcissistic obstructions (and pathways) to forgiveness are sequestered by splitting of the ego as disavowal (Freud, 1940[1938]; for a conceptual analysis of splitting, see Blass, 2015). While a strident, narcissistically aggrieved ego degrades the object, a defiant ego seeks recognition of the actuality of its violation. Splitting not only defends the ego, but also allows forgiveness to advance, less obstructed by narcissistic humiliation of ego and object.

Actuality and the forgiven object of reparation

Following on from the above, a violating object can become an object of reparation if it is forgiven. Reparation expresses an accountability of the ego, but not in a juridical sense. It is rather a capacity of an ego that can give an account of itself (Ricoeur, 2005), including an acceptance of responsibility in psychic reality. It is an aspect of the depressive position, a moment in psychic reality in which an internal good object is experienced as damaged by the ego and in which guilt arouses an urge to make it better (see Klein, 1935; Klein, 1940; Hinshelwood, 1991, pp. 138–155). And because the object remains blemished and can never again be as it was, so the reparative process remains incomplete, but in relationship with an object in reality rather than phantasy.

With reparation, the ego hopes for and recognizes its own esteem in the esteem and value of the object. The ego may be urged to repair damage in the external world, but the 'force' that impels reparation is guilt and identification with a better internal object, better as the object of reparation. This good object supports the ego's good capacity for reparation. It is a happening, not an action, in the internal dimension of guilt, conscience, identification and the superego (Klein, 1935, p. 265; Figlio, 2017, pp. 185–206).

Freud recognized two forms of reparative movement. The first is a returning or compensating for something taken. The second is making better an injury or damage. While a theft creates a debt that can be repaid and the account settled, an injury creates an indebtedness, an obligation, a responsibility. Freud spanned these two movements, running from reimbursement to mitigation, in five expressions, often translated as reparation: *Ausgleichen* (settling an account); *Entschädigung* (compensation); *Wiederherstellung* (re-establishing the original state); *Wiedergutmachung* (making good again); *Reparation* (making better as an internal, remorseful urge).

The shift from compensation to remorse and loving the damaged object requires a new vocabulary, in which introjective identification replaces paying off an injured party. The more the ego is composed of identifications (Freud, 1923, pp. 28–34), the more reparative its orientation becomes, and the more getting better becomes a process of unending, continuous development through the transformation of largely hostile object relations into largely loving object relations.

Forgiveness and reparation are complementary. Forgiveness begins by refusing an intrusive projective identification, as the ego moves towards establishing the actuality of psychic injury by the object. Reparation is a making better, based on introjective identification, in which the ego and the damaged object of its reparative urge get better together by identification – better in reality rather than the unreality of idealization and phantasy. Forgiveness holds to the actuality of an offence, which undergirds a process of overcoming a grievance at an attack on the ego. Reparation bolsters trust between a better ego and a better object. While there is a movement from forgiveness to reparation, they depend on each other.

Henri Rey reports a vivid observation of surmounting a grievance in a process that becomes a reparative process of making better.

> A female patient had the following experience. After the birth of a Down's Syndrome child, she had adopted a little Chinese boy. She also had other children. The little Chinese boy adored his adoptive mother, who well returned this love. When still very young, he said to his mother, 'I wish I could go into you and come out like the other children, then I will really be your little boy'. That story is disturbingly touching. The fact that objects and situations are projected into mother for transformations that the infant or child cannot achieve by themselves is a well-known process, but it must be linked with reparation …
>
> (Rey, 1994, p. 221)

What a beautiful example of a boy's wish to make his damaged mother (evident in her Down's Syndrome child) better, while she, in getting better, makes him better in his rebirth. They share a mutual loving, introjective, reparative relationship. In addition, the boy's wish speaks to an actuality for him and his mother: he is aggrieved at his deficient status, as well as reparative towards his mother's damaged state. In his reparative urge and his reliance on his good mother, he is also forgiving her as he relinquishes his grievance against her while sticking to the actuality that he is not her child in the way her other children are her children.

This relationship between forgiveness and reparation is also clear, albeit implicit, in Ostendorf (2012). Her patient, Mrs A, was snared in a persistent grievance against colleagues who felt pressurized and taken by surprise by her as someone who was not a team player. She found this criticism 'outrageous, an expression of resentment against her experience of being enriching and constructive' (p. 39; my translation).

Ostendorf finds that Mrs A struggled helplessly against a damaged internal parental object: a composite of a damaged mother, desperately needing her daughter, but withheld from her by father; and a father who excluded her, replacing the mother–daughter relationship with a gap that could nullify her. Any gap 'meant for Mrs A, not just an interruption, but an expulsion, precipitating an abortion, and with that, her rage became unbearable' (p. 49). In addition, this embedded object, allied to a persecuting superego, could infect her with the guilt of the parental couple. This embedded guilt, added to her own guilt, was also unbearable.

Mrs A sought to unburden herself by projective identification into repositories for hate, envy and aggression. She filled sessions with her belief that she was surrounded by idiotic colleagues at work, and she demeaned Ostendorf's interpretations as 'either harmless, of no use or attacking' (pp. 54–55).

Mrs A could not tolerate the guilt that would drive reparation proper, which left her stuck in a paranoid-schizoid cycle of manic reparation: repetitive, fruitless, treacherous and counterfeit. Her ego, unable to bear guilt, was lodged in her treacherous 'repair-analyst' (pp. 42, 44), whom she pressed to acknowledge the deceit and the attack on her. She could then spiral off into manic transcendence over her degraded object, pushing her analyst to retreat from her line of feeling and interpretation (p. 46). Ostendorf finally separated herself from this attribution and that signalled her capacity for mediating a transformation to reparation proper.

In my view, Mrs A's damaged internal parental object was forced into her by projective identification, and her grievance-ridden demeaning of her object-world aimed to reverse that projective identification, seeking a recognition. She then defiantly held on to her actuality. What supports this understanding is Ostendorf's perception that Mrs A, not only attacked, but *addressed* the object. An address seeks a response from an object that recognizes itself as a recipient of a message. The address, the response and the historical evidence together constitute an actuality.

> [Mrs A] had introjected [a projective identification into her, of] a flawed mother and a father who, in her experience, wanted to seize the mother for himself, and thereby forcibly excluded her. That produced an inner developmental foundation, on which she was overrun with depressive feelings. Hate, envy and aggression are elements that possibly can be sufficiently integrated with good containment; frustrated, however, they persist as foreign bodies, which press for discharge and *seek an addressee*.
> (Ostendorf, 2012, pp. 55–56; my translation and emphasis)

An address is different from a narcissistic, aggrieved, and vengeful attack on the object. For all the gratification of grievance, in reducing the analyst to feeling harmless to useless, Mrs A defiantly tried to hold to an actuality that she put to the object. The former is driven by destructive narcissism, the latter by libidinal narcissism and defiance.[3]

A sense of a continuous ego in relation to reality, which could extend into the future, rests upon the confirmation of an actuality, sought from an addressee. This is the beginning of forgiveness. The forgiven object, no longer only the repository of projected hate, envy and aggression, becomes less threatening, more an object damaged by grievance. Guilt becomes tolerable and reparation can follow. 'Only when the damaging feelings [which have been pressing outwards] are integrated by the ego and recognized as one's own responsibility, can reparative strivings begin and can the pathological process of projection and projective identification thereby stop' (p. 56).

In a vivid moment, Ostendorf had just sought to articulate for Mrs A her feeling disturbed at her analyst taking up with her what she would rather be rid of, which she experienced as a fatal allergy. Mrs A reacted with indifference ('Ach, ist ja egal'), then complained that Ostendorf did not understand how awful she felt, that she was being attacked and badly treated (by colleagues). Ostendorf interpreted Mrs A's putting her in the position of her colleagues and added that Mrs A feared the Ostendorf could not keep Mrs A's different feelings separate and help her. After a long silence, Mrs A replied with a lightly ironic undertone, 'Today is a lousy day and you are not exactly helpful ... Naja, nor am I; can certainly be different' (p. 52).

Her irony retains her superior position, but along with it she allows that she is also responsible for the state they are in. She introduces the possibility of releasing Ostendorf from her position as 'repair-analyst', guilty and useless at reparation, and with it comes the possibility of embracing her own guilt and reparative wish. In my view, Mrs A inches towards a reparative attitude, *but only if her actuality of the injustice she suffers at the hands of colleagues, but ultimately of her parents, is recognized, evidenced in internal and external reality.* In her double message, she separates defiance from grievance.

I take what Amati Sas (1992, p. 330) called the 'identificatory project' of the ego (attributed to Aulagnier, 1975) to be an extreme example of defiance in the service of actuality. In her work on the trauma of torture, Amati (Sas) (1987; 1992) concludes that torturers find the area of identity most vulnerable to degradation. That is where they concentrate their attack. She uses Bléger's (1967) concept of 'ambiguity' to specify a dissolution of identity, with the degradation of the ego to a primordial state composed of undifferentiated, pre-ego and pre-object fragments. For Bléger, ambiguity is prior to the paranoid-schizoid phase, which is an organized defence. Normal ego functioning depends on projecting ambiguous components into depositaries, in which they can be assimilated. 'Real' objects are not only objects of perception, but competent depositaries of ambiguity. The torturer aims to eliminate these depositaries, forcing ambiguity into the victim, which enforces a symbiosis between torturer and victim.

> Since shame arises in these survivor-patients as a signal of the emergence from alienation, it might be deduced that shame is a sign of something incorruptible in the ego [, which might be] the need to maintain the identificatory project ... at the moment when he recovers the sense of being able to choose his own behaviour and surrenders to the evidence ... of having alienated himself to another ...
>
> (Amati Sas, 1992, p. 335)

In shame, the victim's ego suffers simultaneously the offender's persecution and projective identification and the victim-ego's own internal degradation by the superego. The primal self-awareness of shame provides an objectification of an ego otherwise lost in undifferentiation, allowing the ego to recover itself through an emancipation from the persecuting object and its ego-destructive superego (Britton, 2020, pp. 75–84). From the angle of forgiveness and narcissism, grievance-fuelled destructive narcissism reverses the forced introjection of the perpetration and subjects the offender to the same degradation in psychic reality as suffered by the victim. In addition, libidinal narcissism preserves the ego as self-esteem (Britton, 2008). Together, they aim to retrieve and promote the ego's 'identificatory project'. But this ego-protective aspect of narcissism only makes sense along with defiance in its hold on actuality.

The conflict between defiance and grievance: Miss Ross

I was led to thinking of defiance as the route to forgiveness by a short story – "The Son" – by Freud's literary double, Arthur Schnitzler (1892; Figlio, 2007). A man has killed his mother, but before she died, she begged her doctor to plead in court for her son's innocence. She had tried, unsuccessfully, to suffocate him at birth, and her repentant, life-long devotion and love began the next morning, as did his defiance. In what seems to be inducing him by projective identification to take up her cause, her doctor comes to think that there can be a foundational, internal assault, embedding a murderous mother inside the son's mind.

Reflecting on whether he might go to the law, and what he might say to the court, the doctor muses.

> Do we retain confused memories from the first hours of our existence, which we can no longer make clear and yet which do not vanish without trace? ... Is perhaps a ray of sun that falls through the window the earliest source of a peaceful disposition? – and if a mother's first glance embraces us with infinite love, does it not gleam unforgettably back in the sweet blue eyes of the child? – If, however, this first glance is a glance of ambivalence and hatred, does it not burn with destructive force into the soul of that child, which absorbs thousands of impressions long before they can be deciphered? ... [N]one of you ... can know what of the good and the bad that he bears he owes to the first breath of air, the first ray of sun, the first glance of the mother ...
>
> (Schnitzler, 1892, p. 2039; my translation)

When I met Miss Ross, her situation had become dire. Although she was a respected professional, she was living in a caravan at the edge of a farmer's field, with no water, gas or electricity. Her plight followed the repossession of a house she and her partner had bought. They won a court case, but she derived no satisfaction from the victory, and the compensation money seemed to vanish.

They moved into proper housing but continued to live shambolically. Her partner seemed mainly to be drunk and to gamble and did nothing to improve their situation. I only gradually learned of her alcoholism. Gradually it emerged that her partner kept her chequebook and cash card and would withdraw money and forge cheques. But although Miss Ross was cheated into living in squalor and destitution, she was always there for her partner and others.

A bitter grievance at her impoverishment, compared to her friends, was a regular feature of our sessions. At the root, however, the target was her parents, particularly father. She reviled them for the narrow-minded, deficient home life of her youth. She wished they were dead – she could have their money, to which she felt entitled – but also yearned for them and was clearly distressed at their leaving her in desperate circumstances.

An experience as a teenager vividly portrays her sense of disenfranchisement from life. She had left home and was living in the home of a friend, where she was treated as a member of the family even when her friend moved away. But when her friend was due to return, Miss Ross no longer felt welcome: even more, she felt humiliated when, at a dinner gathering, her friend's mother said to the guests, about her, 'she wouldn't know about that (the "that" remained unspecified)'. This incident stood out to me as a crystallized nugget of injury.

There were other experiences similarly lodged in her mind. When she was 3, she was sent to a fever hospital with suspected scarlet fever. Fixed in her mind was the image of the ambulance coming for her, of her absolute terror, of her relying on father to protect her, of him slumped in a chair, facing away and not even turning around when she cried for help. She also believed she had a dim awareness of her earliest days in an incubator.

She had a vague memory of her early years with mother alone. Father's return from the war, probably when she was about 3, stood out in her memory as an intruding event. She also blamed him for her being sent to boarding school after she failed the 11+, inaugurating a period of intense loneliness. She would comfort herself by breaking into the tuck shop at night to eat chocolate alone. She became fat and pimply, and felt ugly. Her reproach was not much lightened by knowing her parents sacrificed to keep her in school.

Her bitterness did not wholly obscure evidence of a loving father: happy memories of him from her childhood, photos of him carrying a smiling child on his shoulders, visits to her in her boarding school, his looking through the window of her room in the isolation ward of the fever hospital. She also knew that the cannons that he had manned during the war had ruined his hearing and shaken him psychologically.

She was an only child but reported memories (?) suggesting that she felt deprived of her self- evident place as the loved and legitimate daughter. She recalled a cousin who had begun to visit her parents regularly, as if he were their long-lost child who had returned. She had a fantasy that she was the child of an 'auntie', who had had a child before her, whom her auntie had aborted. The father of the aborted child was an abusive man, but *her* ('real') father with this auntie was a kind man. In this 'memory', she was adopted by her current 'parents' after her ('real') father had died. From early in her life, therefore, she lived with a belief that there was a child of a bad father, followed by a child (herself) of a good father. But when the good collapsed, with his death, she was handed over to her current 'bad' parents. Her experience of her friend's (good) family as good next to her own (bad) family, along with her 'illegitimate' presence in this good family, repeated this divided life.

I formed the view that these different 'parents' in external reality were, in psychic reality, condensed into 'good' and 'bad'. On the one hand, she was advantaged, next to her 'sibling', with the good parents, but then, because of her pride, they turned bad (in her 'adoption' by her current parents). On the other hand, as the surviving sibling, perhaps a twin, she felt she had deprived her parents of the child they wanted. In either case, the slightest sense of advantage provoked intense guilt. As a result, she could only have something if she felt it was compensation owed to her by her parents, themselves held to be guilty. Her very survival seemed to be that compensation.

Alcohol found its way into our work from the outset, though it was some time before I realized it. She began drinking when, as a young woman, teaching in another country, she fell in love and had a relationship with a married man, with whom she hoped for a future. But he abruptly ended the relationship to return to his wife in the UK. She felt totally abandoned and broke down and was admitted to hospital. She returned to England but not to home: she lived again in the family she idealized, only to move out when she sensed that she was not welcome.

I came to think that alcohol became her reliable friend. She lived divided between two selves, one alcoholic, the other sober. Her sober self was cultivated, articulate, well-read with a wide interest in the arts. She was also racked with remorse, regret and guilt, and felt helpless and hopeless. The alcoholic figure, by contrast, was riven with grievance and a demand that she should be recompensed for the life that had been taken from her. Like Ostendorf's Mrs A, she heaped contempt on ordinary people and their ordinary lives, including her own ordinary self, and felt surrounded by crooks and idiots. Sober, she was, in ordinary usage, forgiving; alcoholic, she was unforgiving. When sober, she had no desire to drink, but remained vulnerable to the slightest triggering incident. When triggered, her drinking seized the whole of her. In sessions, these two personalities were quite different in manner as well as interests.

The schism between her two selves was poignantly enacted with her dogs, which she acquired from animal sanctuaries. She was devoted to them as an ideal mother to her children. She spared no expense on them and relied on their responsiveness to her care and their forgiving nature. Any doubt from others about her 'parenting' enraged her. An occasional lapse into aggression towards her dogs raked her with self-rebuke. From the side of the aggressor, she felt unworthy of forgiveness.

Her sober/alcoholic schism did, however, offer an insight into forgiveness. In my understanding, Miss Ross felt cut to the quick in her earliest days, deprived of the identity of a loved daughter. Whether in regret for what she felt were her failures, or in a knowing, icy contempt for those who misused her, she sought an acknowledgement of the nature of the wound. As I have argued, forgiveness is obstructed by destructive narcissistic grandiosity, but libidinal narcissistic defences also support an imperative to resume a relationship between a coherent ego and object, based on a coherent reality internal and external. I am calling this imperative 'defiance' and I am calling the reality that defiance demands, an actuality.

Ronald Britton's (2020) model of the phallic relationship between the daughter and her father helps clarify the mixture of grievance and defiance in Miss Ross' actuality. In what he calls 'forever the father's daughter', the phallic position in the female takes two forms, which he calls Athene and Antigone. Athene was born, fully formed and armoured, from the head of Zeus, her father. Antigone sacrificed her own development to the service of her father, Oedipus. In the clinical presentation of an Athene daughter, the woman shares his phallic superiority. Losing it is absolute. The Antigone daughter sacrifices herself to protecting her father's idealized phallus and fears losing her position to a competitor, such as a sibling. In both cases, the relationship to father is, in phantasy, idealized and exclusive, and losing it to reality is a catastrophe.

Miss Ross rebuked her father for failing to protect her and to accept her as his wanted daughter. The perfect relationship between her and alcohol could be seen as her sharing father's phallus in a grandiose bond that transcended the parental relationship. From its heights, 'they' scorned the ordinary world. She could ground her belief in what she perceived, but her rebuke was also driven by phallic disillusionment. But she was also driven by grievance against the father to whom, by living forever unfulfilled, she had sacrificed her life. Her benign yearning for loving parents who recognized her suffering held defiantly to an actuality, while a destructive narcissistic grievance lurked inside, ready to burst into savage verbal assault. In moments of forgiveness, reparation could proceed.

I will précis two periods in our work.

Period I: the tension between grievance and forgiveness

In a session, she said she felt let down by everyone: no friends, no-one phoned, she drank a lot. Maybe it's time to give it up. She phoned a friend and cried. Her friend came around. She stayed with Miss Ross, fed her. Seeing a supply of food for Miss Ross' dogs, but none for herself, her friend stocked her up. She also said she would pay for Miss Ross' hormone implant. Miss Ross grew suspicious; would she forget; why is she doing this?

In her next session, she lay quietly for a few minutes, then spoke in a quiet voice. The suspiciousness was gone. Another friend had invited her to dinner, and she stayed the night. Miss Ross overheard her friend wandering around and talking to herself. It was part of her friend's telling her, bit by bit, about herself and her gruesome past. Miss Ross would listen; trust was gradually building. Her friend was warm and welcoming to her and her dogs, and stayed in her room with her. She now had two kinds of friend: suspect and trusted. The splitting between them separated forgiveness and reparation from grievance.

I said, 'I think you're talking about wandering about in your mind, letting your thoughts wander, so that, bit by bit, we get to know more about you, including gruesome things that have happened to you. We have also become aware that you often tell me things indirectly, in the form of someone else speaking. I think you avoid telling me directly because you fear you will become dependent, and it will all blow up (she often referred to her explosive moods as Chernobyl, the nuclear reactor)'.

She continued:

'I know my thoughts wander. I don't know what I think. I've been reading these books (which she found at the 'wandering' friend's house). They speak of an inner force that guides you and finds expression. I don't think that happened with me'.

I said, 'I think you move over to books that speak of an inner force that will guide you, because we were just learning more about you here, and you become anxious that you would become dependent and you could blow it all up'.

She said, 'my mood changed since yesterday. You can change my mood'.

I said, 'Maybe it's not that I do something, but that yesterday you let yourself listen to both of us'.

She went back to her friend's hospitality. 'She offered me a sherry [a tempting situation, given her alcohol dependence], and I worried to myself, "should I dare?"' A trace of her alcoholic self surfaced, as she seemed cunningly to suspect her trusted friend's motives. 'She serves high-quality red wine. It is just what she would do. I drank two glasses and no more. It was almost beyond belief to hear myself say, "no, thank you" to further drinks'.

'You attribute your ability to drink moderately to the quality of the wine. Maybe there is something in this; maybe you wanted to appreciate the quality of the wine ... and maybe you also wanted to appreciate her generosity ... But I think it's your valuing her that made the wine high quality for you, just as your valuing your session today makes me seem able to change your mood'.

She added that they spoke about nutrition and her wish to come off amphetamines as well as alcohol, without getting fat and ugly, as she did when she broke up with the woman she lived with in the caravan. A bit of alcoholic dissonance surfaced fleetingly at this moment. She went on to say she came off antidepressants when our work first started, which she never thought she could do, but her optimism was not secure.

She was quiet and receptive, but I also felt edgy: if I pressed in an unwelcome way, she could explode as she had several times the previous day. Indeed, two days later, she reported repeated moments of suppressing an eruption of fury. She said I was always wrong when I said friends would help, including her friend (who had recently been very helpful).

In this sequence, we see a Miss Ross who warmed to kind people who recognized her injury (noticing her unstocked larder; welcoming her dogs as well as her). With that foothold, she was also forgiving, in finding an inner force through books at her friend's house, despite feeling deprived by her parents. She was also reparative, in appreciating her friend with the good quality wine as a good object, associated with me at the beginning of our work.

But kind people were also unreliable and grievance against them lurked beneath the surface. I think her grievance took hold in her fury that, in my interpretation, I did not recognize the actuality of her mistrust. Had I done so, we might have discriminated between actuality, and the defiance in its service, and the grip of grievance.

Period II: splitting in the promotion of forgiveness

Despite their fraught relationship, in a reparative period, she and her father reconciled to a large degree, and sessions suffused with this reparative character were warm and thoughtful. She regularly travelled a great distance to visit him. They expressed their love for each other. He gave his entire estate over to her management. When he fell ill, she did her best to arrange treatment and care for him. After his death, she rebuked herself for not doing more to help him.

Unfortunately, shortly after her father died, I suddenly had to be away for a week. She experienced it as my desertion and it lodged in her mind, to be rekindled repeatedly long after the event. In the first session after I returned, she did not give way to grievance at my treachery. She said she knew something wasn't right – I wouldn't just leave her – but suspiciousness set in, surfacing in a circuitous route. She said she had left some expensive shampoo and money in the gym and, of course, no-one handed it in. She couldn't face dealing with father's probate documents. She had also withdrawn some money – questionably – from his account, 'but there's nothing they can do about it', she said with a muted triumphalism. She would have to sell her house, because her partner was moving out and the rent money would be gone (she had, however, been trying to get away from her partner, even considering selling her house to drive her partner out). And, of course, I wasn't around. Grievance erupted, as she also eclipsed my interpretations. But along the way, she also spoke of her regret at so much lost and wasted.

This disjointed account of her reaction to my absence seemed to enact her fragmented state of mind, sunk in unresolvable conflict. There is nonetheless a coherence. We can see her struggle between helplessness in the face of deprivation and loss (shampoo, money, father's probate documents, partner) and her triumphal claim to her assets (her house and her father's money). I accepted my disrupting our work but added that she seemed to carry a grievance against me; that she felt her life and anything good had been stolen, as I had stolen her sessions last week. But nothing seemed worthwhile, including my interpretations. She said she hadn't been drinking for a year but might start drinking when she was alone (in fact, she had started to drink). My line of interpretation aimed to show that she was unavailable as a way of showing me how she felt left by me the previous week; that she foreclosed on my interpretations because she felt foreclosed by them. I also reminded her of her regret.

Later, she 'reminded' me that the moment we agreed to work together she had begun drinking after a long period of abstinence. This was an important moment. Only now was it clear that the schism that divided her had been embedded in our work from the outset. I interpreted her turning to alcohol as a grand alliance in a perfect relationship, against the disappointing father/me. She had split into an abstinent, cultured woman, who trusted life (recall that she had also come off antidepressants when we began our work), and an alcoholic, aggrieved woman, who was surrounded by idiots and faithless spongers (a 'grievance object', I called them, which she had to have in order also to feel regret).

I had also begun to think that splitting off her vengeful fury also protected a forgiving attitude and reparative urge. She spoke of the shock of her father's death and her disappointment at my being away. She knew about her father's death, but my absence was last-minute. She trusted that I would never cancel sessions lightly, but that could not overcome her grievance, and she started drinking again when it happened. I commented on her associating father with me – both of us let her down. I think she felt I had recognized her actuality, which stirred forgiveness. She said that she had broken her glasses, indeed several pairs of glasses lately, and she wondered whether she didn't want to see something. I put her breaking her glasses with her breaking her sessions: she could 'see' her continual denigration of our work together with regret. With regret and emerging reparation, she spoke of wishing she had done more to protect her father. I said that, in associating father with me and devaluing our work, she was trying to take control of her helplessness by pushing it into me. In a reparative spirit, she said she felt that recently we had got to grips with something important.

Overall, I don't think I sufficiently acknowledged her struggle with grievance and her emerging insight, as I also failed to do in the previous vignette with respect to 'trusted' friends. She did not believe she could bear the remorse and guilt associated with her reparative wishes and felt helpless against falling back into grievance. I might have spoken of her diverting her grievance against father to me, where we could get hold of the imperative of grievance, which had limited her belief in her reparative caring for father. Better interpreted, her grievance might have given way to defiance in holding to the actuality of her father's and my treatment of her. Her defiance might then have allowed her, first, to forgive her father, then to face the regret and guilt of reparation.

The next session confirmed this line of thinking. She retreated from her emerging insight. She began with her utter disappointment with me, but no reference to her being shocked and helpless at her father's death. She said she had 'held it together' all the time she was caring for her father, then after his death, during his funeral and after. But then it all seemed pointless, and she couldn't hold it together. Yes, there had been some reconciliation, but not enough and too late. She remembered good times when she was young, but also bad times. She remembered having gone to Russia many years ago with a friend and her parents showing no interest in her trip when she returned, though they used to tell her that she never told them anything.

Along the way, she dismissed my interpretations. I commented that she might feel I took no interest in the way she had held it together. She replied that she did feel let down, but in a tone of voice suggesting my irredeemable inadequacy. What I did not see was her attempt to remind me of the actuality of her feeling that something that had excited her was of no interest to her parents: a moment of defiance gave in to grievance. But in terms of her splitting, I could now see her grievance against me in a new light. She had struggled from infancy to establish herself independent of parental imposition into her inner world. Alcoholism offered a secure position from which she could mock her helplessness in this struggle, a helplessness projected into the 'idiots' who surrounded her, including me.

During this period, forgiveness and reparation in her caring for her father were evident, and it all seemed thrown into jeopardy by his death. This jeopardy accentuated her splitting. She could remain forgiving and reparative towards her father because she had also retained superiority over me and our work. Her grievance against me and use of me as a repository for projective identification of her helpless, sober self, sustained her reconciliation with her father and her regretting not achieving more with him. But in splitting of the ego, her two characters did not know each other and appeared as two separate individuals.

Although her grievance against me, diverted from father, allowed her to experience regret, remorse and guilt at her caring for her father, she sought, under the cover of grievance, a recognition from me that I had disappointed her in not recognizing the repetition of early abandonment in moments of terror: the actuality of abandonment in my sudden unavailability. In that way, she was not just aggrieved, but defiant in dismissing my interpretations. That defiance, separate from grievance, was a pathway to forgiveness. Only then could there also be reparation. This key session brought all these processes together.

Conclusion

I have sought a clearer view of forgiveness, distinct from satisfying a grievance at one extreme and reparation at the other. Forgiveness pivots around a core relationship between offender and offended. In this relationship, the victim addresses the perpetrator in a defiant demand that an actuality be recognized. The demand of defiance should be distinguished from the grievance.[4] The former is an assertion of the ego; the latter is a narcissistic defence.

The actuality to be recognized is a violation: the victim has been offended at the core by an invasion that reaches back to the foundational organization of identity. It is neither an imagination nor an event that could be documented for a jury. Violation forces the victim into what Amati Sas, following Bléger, calls 'ambiguity', a state of disorganization beneath abandonment and loss. Miss Ross' actuality included her parents' treatment of her, but more deeply, a belief that could not be grounded in documented reality: that her existence had deprived her parents of their wish for a child, for which she suffered the insults to her integrity and value.

The humiliation of the ego by an offender also garners the authority of the superego. Degradation is held inside the ego both by the forced introjection by the perpetrator and the force of the superego, and defences against humiliation are, in Britton's (2008) analysis of narcissism, defences against an ego-destructive superego. Although, in her unforgiving state, Miss Ross railed against the traitors and idiots who surrounded her, she also felt herself to be persecuted and unforgiven. Her vindictive reproaches, often driven by shouting or by icy denigration, were attempts to relieve herself of accusations from within as well as violation from without.

In my analysis, forgiveness comprises two parts: 1) grievance harnessed to a destructive narcissistic defence to drive the implanting of a debased identity back into its object by a reverse projective identification narcissistic defence; 2) a defiant claim of an actuality, harnessed to libidinal narcissism, to restore the ego's sense of internal coherence and its bond with reality (ego assertion). Recovery of self-respect and respect for others and for reality requires emancipation of the ego both from offenders and from the superego.

Miss Ross held these two attitudes in two selves, one alcoholic, the other sober. The alcoholic met the world with suspicious, knowing contempt for its easily uncovered wish to humiliate her. With alcohol, she formed an idealized parental couple for a child spared any treacherous abandonment or dismemberment of her identity, as well remaining, idealized, 'forever the father's daughter'. In her destructive narcissistic security, her actual helplessness was projected and ridiculed, as she had felt. From within her alliance with alcohol, she also demonstrated to her parents their failure.

Although her destructive narcissism, harboured in her alcoholic self, provided a protective shell against humiliation by projecting it, her defiance could then secure a claim on an actuality, a foothold for her sober self, forgiving and open to remorseful, reparative moves. In turning her rage on me when I had to be away for a week, shortly after her father's death, she could also forgive her father and allow self-reproach and remorse at his dying, along with memories of their reconciliation.

I will end with an incident that surprised us with its intensity and revealed something of her actuality. On one of her many trips to the vet, her favourite dog took fright and fled. She was distraught at her inability to calm him. In this moment, her hypersensitivity to failure and her deep wish to make-better flashed into view. She divided herself into perfect parents, aggrieved at their child's ungratefulness, while, in identification with her dog, she was a betrayed child on the run, aggrieved in her destructive narcissism at their betrayal.

Inside this relationship of grievance was a relationship between loving parents and a frightened child. As a parent, she was not just unforgiven, but insecure in her libidinal narcissism *and* saddened as loving and reparative. As a child, she was not just betrayed, suspicious in her destructive narcissism and unforgiving, but insecure in her libidinal narcissism, remorseful at the cruelty of her grievance and frightened in her dependency. The scene revealed an *actuality*: a daughter opposed to the belief that she deprived her parents of a child, who sought – *defiantly* – her legitimate place in the family.

Notes

1 Rey (1994, pp. 207–228) gives psychoanalytic meaning to the distinction between repair and reparation in psychic reality. Repair is an omnipotent stance – a manic defence in the paranoid-schizoid position – against involvement with a damaged object (cf. manic reparation; Segal, 1981). The object is concrete, and repair is akin to an action in a relationship removed from reality. Reparation is an internal process of involvement with the object – a quality of the depressive position – aimed at making the object better. The object is symbolic in a relationship that holds to reality.

2 And in consciousness, forgiving can annul itself. If the victim of an offence completely gives over, nothing remains to forgive. If the victim 'chose' to neglect an unforgotten injury, forgiving loses meaning. In either case, the offender's slate would be cleared without forgiveness (Akhtar, 2002 discusses a range of such nullifications).

3 The idea of an actuality in projective identification is implicit in Bion's (1957) discovery of projective identification as a communication, not just the projection of a bad (self as a bad) object. This primal mode had been denied his patient when it would have laid the foundation for communication. I see it also as seeking recognition of an actuality. Bion's patient *addressed* his plight to him. Similarly, Ostendorf suggests that, by becoming aware of an expulsion into the object of a forced introjection by the object, the analyst as addressee-object can help secure the belief in, and character of, an actuality.

4 Disconnected from actuality, to forgive can be interpreted as self-aggrandizing, even transcendent. In an earlier, religious culture, it stirred unease at the idea of a human being acting as only God could act. '[W]iping away sin is another matter: it is this that God alone can do' (Konstan, 2010, p. 118). In today's secularism, the narcissism of such transcendence should not obscure the agony of an actuality, such as Simon Wiesenthal's anguish when a dying Nazi soldier clutched his hand and begged him, as a Jew, to listen to his involvement in a horrific atrocity and to forgive him. In a poignant moment, Wiesenthal waved a bluebottle away from the soldier, who, head bandaged, could not see it: '"Thanks", he nevertheless whispered. And for the first time I realized that I, a defenseless subhuman, had contrived to lighten the lot of an equally defenseless superhuman' (Wiesenthal, 1969, p. 37). Wiesenthal later visited the soldier's mother and did not tarnish her image of her good son.

References

Akhtar, S. (2002). 'Forgiveness: Origins, Dynamics, Psychopathology, and Technical Relevance'. *The Psychoanalytic Quarterly* 71: 175–212.

Amati, S. (1987). 'Thoughts on Torture'. *Free Associations* 8: 94–114.

Amati Sas, S. (1992). 'Ambiguity as a Route to Shame'. *International Journal of Psychoanalysis* 73: 329–341.

Aulagnier, P. (1975). *La violence de l'interpretation*. Paris: Presses Universitaire de France.

Austin, J. L. (1962). *How to do Things with Words: The William James Lectures at Harvard University in 1955*. Oxford: Oxford University Press.

Bion, W. (1957). 'On Arrogance'. In *Second Thoughts: Selected Papers on Psycho-Analysis*, 86–92. London: William Heinemann; Routledge.

Blass, R. B. (2015). 'Conceptualizing Splitting: On the Different Meanings of Splitting and their Implications for the Understanding of the Person and the Analytic Process'. *International Journal of Psychoanalysis* 96: 123–139.

Bléger, J. (1967). *Symbiosis and Ambiguity: A Psychoanalytical Study*, edited and translated by J. Churcher et al. London/NY: Routledge, 2013.

Britton, R. (2008). 'What Part Does Narcissism Play in Narcissistic Disorders?' In *Rosenfeld in Retrospect: Essays on His Clinical Influence*, edited by J. Steiner, 22–34. London: Routledge.

Britton, R. (2020). *Sex, Death and the Superego: Experiences in Psychoanalysis*, 2nd edn. London: Karnac.

Figlio, K. (2007). 'A New Naturalism: On the Origins of Psychoanalysis as a Social Theory of Subjectivity'. In *Culture and the Unconscious*, edited by C. Bainbridge et al., 24–40. London: Palgrave.

Figlio, K. (2017). *Remembering as Reparation: Psychoanalysis and Historical Memory*. London: Palgrave.

Freud, S. (1923). 'The Ego and the Id'. *SE*:9: 1–66.

Freud, S. (1940[1938]). 'Splitting of the Ego in the Process of Defence'. *SE* 23: 275–278.

Hinshelwood, R.D. (1991). *A Dictionary of Kleinian Thought*. London: Free Association Books.

Hughes, P.M. and Warmke, B. (2017). 'Forgiveness'. In *Stanford Encyclopedia of Philosophy* (2019). Stanford: Stanford University, https://plato.stanford.edu/archives/sum2017/entries/forgiveness/ (downloaded 6 December 2019).

Klein, M. (1935). 'A Contribution to the Psychogenesis of Manic-Depressive States'. In *The Writings of Melanie Klein*, vol. 1 (1975), edited by R. Money-Kyrle et al., 262–289. London: The Hogarth Press and the Institute of Psychoanalysis.

Klein, M. (1940). 'Mourning and its Relation to Manic-Depressive States'. In *The Writings of Melanie Klein*, vol. 1 (1975), edited by R. Money-Kyrle et al., 344–369. London: The Hogarth Press and the Institute of Psychoanalysis.

Konstan, D. (2010). *On Forgiveness: The Origins of a Moral Idea*. Cambridge: Cambridge University Press.

Lansky, M.R. (2009). 'Forgiveness as the Working Through of Splitting'. *Psychoanalytic Inquiry* 29: 374–385.

Ostendorf, U. (2012). 'Repair oder Reparation? Bewegungen zwischen trügerischer Hoffnung und realistischer Veränderung'. *Jahrbuch der Psychoanalyse* 65: 37–58.

Rey, H. (1994). *Universals of Psychoanalysis in the Treatment of Psychotic and Borderline States: Factors of Space, Time and Language*, edited by J. Magagna. London: Free Association Books.

Ricoeur, P. (2005). 'Memory, History and Forgiveness: A Dialogue Between Paul Ricoeur and Sorin Antohi'. *Janus Head* 8: 14–25.

Rosenfeld, H. (1971). 'A Clinical Approach to the Psychoanalytic Theory of the Life and Death Instincts: An Investigation Into the Aggressive Aspects of Narcissism'. *International Journal of Psychoanalysis* 52: 1144–1423.

Schnitzler, A. (1892). 'Der Sohn. Aus den Papieren eines Arztes'. In *Ausgewählte Werke* (2017). Chicago: OK Publishing (English translation by I. Bamforth, *British Journal of General Practice* 57: 1007–1009).

Segal, H. (1981). 'Manic Reparation'. In *The Work of Hannah Segal: A Kleinian Approach to Clinical Practice* (1986), 147–158. NY: Jason Aronson/London Free Association Books.

Siassi, S. (2007). 'Forgiveness, Acceptance and the Matter of Expectation'. *International Journal of Psychoanalysis* 88: 1423–1440.

Siassi, S. (2009). 'On: Leaps of Faith: Is Forgiveness a Useful Concept?' *International Journal of Psychoanalysis* 90: 642–645.

Smith, H.F. (2008). 'Leaps of Faith: Is Forgiveness a Useful Concept?' *International Journal of Psychoanalysis* 89: 919–936.

Weintrobe, S. (2004). 'Links Between Grievance, Complaint and Different Forms of Entitlement'. *International Journal of Psychoanalysis* 85: 83–96.

Wiesenthal, S. (1969). *The Sunflower: On the Possibilities and Limits of Forgiveness* (1998), edited, with a symposium, by H. B. Cargas and B. V. Fetterman. New York: Schocken Books.

Chapter 11

In the grip of unforgiveness

Some notes on forgiveness and orientation from a German background

Claudia Frank

The Holocaust as an unforgivable fact – introductory outline

When the editors asked for a contribution to a book based on thinking from clinical practice in the light of my "own religious, cultural, philosophical or literary background", I spontaneously replied that I would think about it with a "background of being a German with a long-standing conviction, like many of my generation, that the Holocaust could never be 'forgiven'". A moment later I involuntarily flinched at speaking of this as a "cultural" background – those crimes against humanity so much represent the antithesis to any "culture", rather an all-pervading un-ground! How could I? Wasn't it unforgivable to answer in such a thoughtless way? In retrospect, that mini-sequence seems symptomatic: when I spontaneously respond with what came to my mind, a fundamental objection is immediately present, suggesting that in this specific German context, the term "culture" seems so fundamentally out of place that the use of the term feels like an unforgivable encroachment. Taking it as a first association popping up I thought, will further thinking show whether it is of some worth or whether it has to be put aside. But before it had the chance to be unwrapped an ostensibly "knowing" agency already dismissed it (or at least threatened to do so). Quite a pressure was exerted on me to stay in the grip of unforgiveness and not to allow any thinking – a familiar revenant I had hoped to have been overcome.

It took quite some time to approach what the embargo was more precisely, although I think that rationality should be included it was not that level I tried to aim at. For the most time, I would have been unable to name what this embargo was – it just seemed "natural". For decades I always felt relieved abroad not to be immediately recognized as German. I did not question that at all; it seemed the only way to allow for a limited time the illusion of being together with the others, knowing that there was essentially no escape from our horrible history. We as Germans of later generations would always be equated with devastating destruction, the annihilation of the European Jews – all the legacy of terrible perpetration, which was so

DOI: 10.4324/9781003364313-11

unimaginable because it was unbearable. A category like forgiveness was totally absent then – and would have been dismissed as it would easily have been understood as denying in one form or another what had happened.

For many years a majority of Germans would not acknowledge the dimension of the Nazi crimes. This hitherto unquestioned (and unquestionable) state of mind I am referring to only became noticeable when that changed a few years ago. And I would like to explore in this chapter the nature of the mental state, of unpardonable means unthinkable, and what elements might finally have contributed to the change.

One way is taking it on an individual level as a manifestation of a clinical issue we encounter in analytic practice, with patients who feel eternally unforgiven by some part of themselves for unknown or unspecified crimes. They can feel haunted to a degree of intensity that they collapse into delusional or near-psychotic states.[1] They seek help because they feel unable to go on, and at the same time transmit, that they have not "deserved" any of it and resist tenaciously thinking about it. It becomes clear that they are in the grip of unrelenting unforgiveness with apparently no way to escape except identifying at times with that very position. The patients were – as I had been in relation to my ancestral guilt – unaware of the very nature of their psychosomatically lived unconscious phantasy. To highlight the intensity of their denial, I shall give clinical examples, later in the chapter.

Another dimension of this complex is its location in a specific historic situation.[2] I shall outline what I think helped to foster other perspectives than the one evoked by the monstrosity of the crimes. It is a special German context with long-standing characteristics after World War II, and will be for a long time, nevertheless, some of its dynamics might apply, to people in other countries guilty of genocide.

For grasping those phenomena which present themselves just as "givens" (unquestioned assumptions) the following two concepts are especially relevant: 1) normal and abnormal superego-figures or organizations; 2) orientation work and disorientation. The relevance of the first might be quite obvious, the second might be less known, but seem decisive. How can one imagine a shift towards a realm where the question of what can be forgiven and what actually is unforgivable can be considered?

I shall begin by outlining those two questions – followed by clinical examples from my analytic practice. First with vignettes from the analysis of a Mrs A when we had reached a place where for moments the grip of being unforgivable was released; this allowed us to explore its nature to some degree. Then I give a view of the years of hard orientation work with a Mrs B. She had a tenacious, pathological organization governed by unforgiveness. I will illustrate this with parallels to *The Bacchae*. Then, I will continue the enquiry I started by taking my "symptom" as an indicator of what has to be worked through to obtain adequate differentiation: what can be forgiven and what is unforgivable.

The "autonomous" attraction and suction of the abnormal superego

It was one of Klein's first child analyses, in analytic situations with 2¾-year-old Rita, which made her aware of the enormous importance of guilt and of the superego – both of which Klein thought of as Freud's decisive discoveries. There is no unitary conception of what we mean by superego. Without going deeper into that discussion, Kleinian analysts would differentiate between a normal superego, which develops as a split-off part of the ego, functioning as a constructive guiding agency (though it might be in an early form quite strict), and other sorts of superegos, which E. O'Shaughnessy described as "abnormal", destructive, superegos which destroy "the self, and its object relations" (1999, p. 861). From Freud's work onwards, there were various characterizations of its nature: Freud would speak of it as a "pure culture of the death instinct" (1923, p. 53); Klein wrote of terrifying figures, split off in the deeper layers of the unconscious (1958, p. 86); Bion then named it an ego-destructive superego. I think, there is a whole range of abnormal superegos, varying in the manner and degree of adversity; what is important is the way they impair the ego functions: of paying attention and of judging external of the internal reality of the person.

What I would like to stress is the automatic immediate effects it has as soon as it is evoked: its determining atmospheric effect without words, unquestioned, all-pervasive and taken in fully without nuance. It is a monstrous version of a superego with enormous attraction and power, and it attacks the sense of reality. It destroys the ego's capacity to think. It can only be followed, obeyed and not questioned by the subject. Bion put it that it was a sort of superego that was "the" moral pointer with absolute certainty to all the wrongs. It is an "assertion of moral superiority without any morality" (1962, p. 97). It strips or denudes everything of goodness and produces an empty superiority–inferiority structure: there is condemnation but no psychic work. Clinically, as O'Shaunhgnessy put it, there is "impoverishment and deterioration of relations, with an escalation of hatred and anxiety that results in psychotic panic or despair" (O'Shaughnessy, 1999, p. 861).

With such an omnipotent *unforgiving object* there is no perspective of change – temporarily its opposite *may be* conjured up, an idealized object that will immediately forgive everything. That pseudo-forgiveness makes some analysts wary of forgiveness, which so easily becomes shallow, flat, superficial, sentimental, which may be a necessary transitory state in development when despair impedes any movement. But it is important to know the difference between true and pseudo-forgiveness. During analysis, some patients might for quite a time insist resentfully, that it is "the" only solution. Claiming that if only their good intentions would be wholeheartedly acknowledged, by the analyst their belief in total, unconsidered, forgiveness would assuage them.

True forgiveness as a process with normal superego-figures

A normal superego might enable moments of true forgiveness as an implicit element of the depressive position. Thorough forgiveness requires a complex process which includes the recognition of the pain, suffering, anger and resentment felt by the injured party. It means struggling, moving to and fro, differentiating what can be forgiven and what might only be almost forgiven or not forgiven at all. It implies some hard work with oneself – and knowing that one can nevertheless at times regress into states in which unforgiveness prevails.[3] And here my second concept comes into play, when we ask how true forgiveness can get a chance in the presence of an abnormal super-ego. In the long run, it will be decisive to realize consciously those moments in which one has a choice to get hold of what it is that tempts one to turn towards an abnormal superego, dispensing horror and terror. This might be connected with excitement, fascination and glorification. It means mourning the loss of power where one has to acknowledge what makes it hard, and feel it is impossible to make any other choice. This requires orientation which I propose and will describe.

Orientation as a fundamental feature

Orientation is usually not explicitly recognized as a fundamental concept as a factor needed for the evolution of psychic growth. As far as I can see, it was Roger Money-Kyrle, philosopher and psychoanalyst, who first elaborated on the place orientation has in the human being's cognitive development. For the non-psychotic part of the personality to develop the body-ego needs to turn to its original home.

> The first base, from which all others would seem to be derived, is the first object to emerge from the new-born infant's sensory confusion, namely the breast or perhaps specifically the nipple. The first space-time divisions to develop are three-fold: a period of enjoyment (being fed), a period of remembrance (having been fed) and a period of expectation (going to be fed). For this can be inferred from the way so many patients orient themselves in exactly this three-fold manner to their daily session.
>
> (Money-Kyrle, 1978[1968], p. 424f.)

There are manifold possibilities to be gained from or to lose the base. Money-Kyrle names, among others: The baby can disappear into it by total projective identification, either out of envy or as an escape from a persecuting outer world; or he can get oriented to the wrong base, in the sense that it is not the one he/she needs; or he/she can become confused in his orientation because his/her base (the desired object) is confused with a part of his/her own body.

Money-Kyrle's notions of orientation and disorientation, which are basic to forming conception and misconception are useful in understanding successful and unsuccessful processes of symbolic transformation. In the further course of development, it will depend on what "home" in which direction in the internal world will be used for orientation in situations of conflicts or injury.

Edna O'Shaughnessy took up Money-Kyrle's idea. She stressed that orientation was a more important element in the psychic life than had been realized so far (2006, p. 156).

> The finding of an object that satisfies both its emotional needs as well as its need for nourishment will transform the baby's state from one of un-integration into some sort of connectedness or integration (fragile at first) oriented towards that object. A metaphor sometimes offered for the amazing change brought about in the infant by the object that gives psychological containment and feeding is the (in its way, also amazing) physical ordering of a scattering of iron filings by a magnet that aligns them in one direction … If the experience is "good enough" the baby will feel psychologically contained and internalize the experience. The pieces of his personality will then be held together internally with an orientation to the satisfying object. As we also know, the infant oscillates between such replete, connected states and states of persecution from hunger, discomfort, delays in attention and the like. All are bad objects that threaten him with disintegration, even annihilation, which he fights by getting his good object to come to his aid. An infant who is not active in this way in both gratification and distress, an infant who is persistently passive has, I believe, suffered, and continues to suffer, some huge adversity.
>
> (Ibid., p. 154)

We know from experience, that feeling understood can feel, as O'Shaughnessy describes, like finding a patterned direction, while previously having to deal with multidirectional persecuting fragments. It is very different from the compelling offer of "meaning" urged by an abnormal superego. Although the picture of the inspiring effect of the good object might sound similar, its implication is quite the opposite: when feeling understood perspectives open up. In contrast to submitting to an abnormal superego, with the narrowing of the path that must be followed.

As in Germany the term orientation has become a commonplace part of everyday language; I would like to point out that its origin goes back to a philosophical debate of 200 years ago to mark its primary conceptual value. I would like to paraphrase Kant to indicate why I think his ideas on "orienting oneself in thinking" are so essential and helpful for us in our practice.

Kant emphasized that however exalted the application of our concepts, and however far from sensibility we may have abstracted them, they will always be attached to image representations. The function of these images is to make concepts, which are not derived from actual experience, but are usable for experiential use.

The literal meaning of orienting is "turn to the East", i.e. towards the rising sun; "sol oriens", using the French, and originally the geographical term, "orienter". This as a metaphor captures what in the mental world what is at stake: an active turning towards the rise of the first good object, the "breast", which gives milk, light and warmth. Patients are looking for ways of thinking which help them to face their psychic reality in ways that allow thinking to continue. This moment of actively looking for help in the right direction seems crucial for some who for various different reasons are unable to do so. The psychotic part of their personality is attacking their approach to goodness more or less successfully, so that disorientation dominates. A lot of work might be needed to find the determining unconscious phantasies producing misorientation or disorientation in order to regain a wider range of possibilities.

In clinical practice, I think, it is important to have concepts which are rooted in sensibility, which can then develop via the figurative into concepts that are "serviceable for experiential use", that allow a link with the patient's sensorial experience. One model underlying this in Klein's notion of development, is of having to negotiate early oedipal situations with primitive anxieties of various kinds. As Britton put it: "Klein's view of development is like an Odyssey, with shipwreck always a possibility" (2018, p. 139). To live, the infant is absolutely dependent on good caring objects without which an orientation by the infant towards good later figures will not be established. While this is well known, the inquiry into conditions producing disorientation is less discussed and it seems especially relevant for the subject of forgiveness.

Psychoanalytic orientation work is a consequence of this approach for analytic practice

Without a minimum of active orientation towards a helpful good object, survival of the analysis will not be possible. Finding re-orientation towards a helpful object will be decisive for development.

To do this analysis of why, in the transference and counter-transference, patient and analyst are likely to succumb to disorientation is necessary. In the example of Mrs A, the disorientation towards a relentless hostile, agency-inclined identification with this object by acting from a strong, superior, powerful position to deny the feared dependency. The vicious circle of again feeling at the mercy of such a figure makes for suffering, but orientation towards a more understanding figure means being in a receptive position. John Steiner has pointed out that Freud said that the repudiation and devaluation of a feminine position is the ultimate bedrock of resistance to change. This can lead to fear of helpless receptivity in either the transference or counter-transference which can become an obstacle to progress (cf. 1999, p. 176).

Clinical examples of necessary re-orientation

Under the sway of a death sentence – and obsessive symptoms fed by murderous anger

The relief of being able to experience another perspective than the conviction that death is all one deserves is often especially moving in analyses with obsessional patients. The crucial challenge is to resist the instinctively adverse reaction to any sign of potential hope in the analysis.

Mrs A had been desperately waiting to be able to return to her sessions after she had had to cancel two weeks due to a high-fever illness, which had started during a one-week holiday break from her analysis. She was still shaken by her panic of dying and the dominant feeling that her death would be best for everybody, as then she no longer could harm others, e.g. her family. The idea of damaging her 3-year-old son was so intolerable! And she named recent everyday happenings when she was convinced another mother would have known to do "the right" thing, thus that her son would be more skilful on the playground, more courageous, more ...

I linked the unrelenting judgement on herself with her son to the way that she had felt let down by myself, that I had unscrupulously done away with her and had "let her die" (by taking the break).

Mrs A answered that she "did not think it that way" – but remembered then how "totally left" she had felt and in the further course of the session she reminded me that she was given away for two months before the birth of her sister (when she was 14 months old). She "knew" that fact for a long time, but had never asked about it and never imagined how she might have experienced that. Towards the end of the session, she expressed that she now felt like "being herself".

In the following months, this was what she expressed thanks for – that our work helped her to "be herself". She realized how so often she was in a state of "being beside herself", driven by a conviction that however matters were, they were "wrong", that she had "no space" to explore and think.

But again, she felt analysis "made her ill" – all those terrible scenarios she had of shooting me or being shot by somebody when driving to the sessions; of terrible crimes being done to her son; of ... Shouldn't she leave analysis to be better off?

To my ears, the "should" nevertheless left a little space: next to what felt like a conviction that usually resulted from feeling exposed to a figure that inflicted all her "wrongs". This time there seemed an idea about a possible other link. When I managed to describe what I thought had her made so angry with me, the space increased again. Then a horror would fill her mind that I would terminate analysis. After some time, she could name how essential it was that I did not seem to get too anxious. There was much more to be worked through but I shall leave it here and just add the way my patient described how she experienced those processes. The help she got in "understanding her mental functioning" felt like being loved and forgiven, enabling her to let things stand still for the time, with the idea that it will evolve ...[4]

The conviction that death is all that one deserves results, I suggest, from an orientation (or better: disorientation) towards an agency, which I characterized earlier as an abnormal superego. In the case of Mrs A, it seemed especially true, as Klein put it: "[it] can never be felt to forgive destructive impulses; in fact, it demands that they should not exist" (1963, p. 313). The relief the patient felt stemmed from a different orientation to another agency which became accessible, through the analysis, an agency which took into account the complexity of the given situation. Instead of "just knowing", it strove to perceive the various facts, assess their meaning and to reflect on them to try and find the relative truth.

The chance to develop and acquire adequate forms of true forgiveness is also influenced by the culture of the way crucial family figures deal with conflicts and injuries. This in itself is embedded in the broader culture of the society or that part of society which is the relevant context for that individual/family.

The way it is lived might well differ from what is claimed to be the case. Are there objects who help with processing and what's the quality of the process suggested or imposed? In the case of Mrs A, her mother demanded that she would instantly embrace and kiss the younger sister, whenever the sister had treated the patient badly. An "immediate reconciliation" had to take place and was declared to be the only "right way" to behave.[5] And there was father who would insist at times with a merciless fury that the cleaning must be done "more properly" and although she could not see any difference she had to do it. Painfully, she realized that she sometimes behaved similarly towards her son, when she was "beside herself", "knowing" she should stop it, without being able to do so. She gained access to the character of the internal figure she suffered from and would at times identify with. She described its "psychopathic character", could admit how there was a feeling of elevation when convinced to just know matters better than anybody else. The powerful triumph of "perfectibility" often seemed irresistible – but more and more she realized its "very high price", how it distanced her from people she longed to belong to.

"No right of existence": analysis as a long process of re-orientation

There is a long tradition of thinking about forgiveness and believing one is unforgivable that can be found in the Ancient Greek tragedies, for example, in Euripides' play *The Bacchae*. The citizens of Thebes who pride themselves on their rational and intellectual life are sceptical of the story of the birth of Dionysius. Zeus impregnated Semele at her insistence but his radiance burnt her to death, and her baby Dionysius was taken by Zeus into his own thigh from whence he was born. Dionysius was furious with not being recognized as a son of Zeus by Semele's sisters and drove them mad and removed them to a mountain. The young king of Thebes Pentheus, whose mother was one of the sisters (Ague) who refuses to believe Dionysius' claim to be an Olympian God. The Dionysian revenge is to deceive Ague that her son is a mountain lion and beheads him taking the lion's head in triumph to Thebes only to have it revealed it is the head of her son.

In our context Dionysius the unforgiving is fatal to those who disregard his divinity. Agaue begs for mercy, confesses to having slighted Dionysus, but Dionysus' judgement is that this insight simply comes too late. He is the insulted god and therefore in the right and nothing else counts!

There is in every one some variant of such a god-simulating self and in some people they seek to live out these phantasies. We get hints of what might have contributed to that in the case of Dionysus: he grew up without his mother. He personifies the superego described by Edna O'Shaugnessy as an internal tyrannical, ego-destructive superego and worship of such or reluctant compliance can be the disorientation I am referring to.

The analysis of Mrs B was especially instructive to learn about a pathological organization governed by unforgiving. Thirty years old, Mrs B suffered from frenzied anxiety about not being good enough: in her studies, in her work, in her family and, of course, in her analysis. If she were not to tell me the right things, I would not be able to help her. She had to tell me the truth. But what was "really" true in all she ruminated about? On one level she was aware that her fears were generally absurd. She was highly intelligent, had done extremely well at school and in her academic studies, and because of her social competency she had been put into difficult classes from school age on. But nothing could keep this permanent desperate anxiety at bay; for example, she believed she would be sacked at work for being inadequate, if she were not constantly available.

The outward appearance of the patient was that of a well-brought-up young woman from a good family. Her glasses and hairstyle seemed to be from a past century. She endeavoured to do everything right, not be unjust to anyone, not to offend anyone, to be fair-minded at all times to everybody. Of course, she was committed to sustainable projects, such as fair trade, organic farming, species-appropriate animal welfare, etc. For a few years she had been in a relationship and for the same period of time she had had severe pain symptoms, no organic cause could be diagnosed, which became so much worse over time that even opiates brought no relief and finally she was referred to analysis.

This account suggested that she was under the domination of a "god-like", inhumane and merciless superego. This approach helped to give her an idea, and thus hope that her situation could be evaluated differently from the voice which kept her in check. In the first few weeks, I spoke in different ways about how she felt exposed to a permanently critical if not condemnatory gaze, when she was haunted again and again by doubts and fears about not being acceptable to me. She emphasized that she did not "really" believe I was such a figure and got to grips with her anxieties in this regard, and consequently I felt markedly less frantic.

However, when I addressed aspects of herself she disapproved of, such as her jealousy, envious, sadistic impulses and phantasies, when they showed themselves in the transference, she politely but decidedly rejected this just as Pentheus had done with Dionysus. She conceded intellectually, but said she just did not have these feelings! I noted that we ended mostly in a sterile state, but it was so well "substantiated" that it seemed as if there was nothing more to say. She would be glad to have "normal" feelings as even as a child she had not felt a child. I had to struggle in the counter-transference whether I had confronted her too directly in particular instances, but also had to resist the temptation to resign when under the sway of her all-knowing superego-figure she did not let me find access to her. On rare occasions, some blunder gave me a chance to intervene more directly but as a rule even this had to be rejected vehemently.

After two years of four sessions a week, both sides emerged more distinctly. She had not turned up for her last session before a break and had not notified me. After this break, the patient came back in a terrible state. She had felt that reality had slipped away from her, but she was unable to stop this. She remembered how she had sat at her computer some years ago hearing children scream outside and felt excited by this. Since this memory had re-emerged she had felt panic when children were near her. It was clear to her that she had to tell me this even though she feared I might end analysis with her now that I knew about her monstrous tendencies. I took up her infantile parts, among them her outrage about the holiday break, which "let her forget" the last session, to let me experience what it felt like to be forgotten, and how exciting it felt to have the power to make me feel that, and how desperate she felt when reality seemed to slip away from her. She gradually regained the feeling of "being on solid ground once more" and even though the anxiety might get worse over the weekend breaks, she had trust in the sessions being able to sort herself out again.

This was only the prologue to an even more severe crisis after she managed an important step in her real life, to move in with her boyfriend. She was now obsessed by the frantic anxiety of being a lesbian, or a paedophile or … or … With some insight she compared it to being a hypochondriac, only with psychological rather than physical illnesses. It took me a while to realize that these moments of insight were opposed by a regime which proceeded in the following way: the more frightful, the truer! She tore our work apart as if in a frightful frenzy – like an Agaue she tore her/our "child" apart (and any development that might have been made). I witnessed a "form of narcissistic cannibalism" as Brenman called the enactment by the Bacchae. The patient threatened to retreat into actual madness. She aptly described this difficulty in the transference with a quote: a canary says that milk is his favourite food, but it's a shame that he did not like it! Gradually the meaning of the "fascination with evil" became clearer and how she felt demeaned by actually needing help and being dependent on others. It was better to fail grandiosely in madness than "to eat humble pie". At the same time, she found it terrible to be so condemnatory, but felt powerless against the irrefutable internal pressure she experienced.

There were many months in which I stuck to interpreting the aforementioned details in the transference, for a long time to no noticeable effect it, seemed. Of course, I consulted a colleague as I wondered what I might have overlooked. How else could I reach her? Was it an expression of my disorientation when I insisted that one problem was that feeling slightly relieved in the session she subsequently felt compelled to undo everything all over again? Mrs B would repeatedly question how I would know what was really inside her, how I could be so certain? Or was it an expression of my "real" disorientation when I wished for a "panacea" so as not to have to deal with my own relative helplessness as I was watching the cannibalistic re-enactment?

For weeks on end, the patient saw the solution in a permanent "general anaesthesia" – when you think of the Bacchae, this is immediately comprehensible. How can one face the dreadful truth of having torn apart what was created within a relationship? It was therefore a big step when she resolved after months not to see full anaesthesia as the aim, but the hope that with my help she would perceive the seductive, addictively sought parallel worlds more clearly as such and thus be able to drive them into the background. Subsequently, it was important to register more consciously when and from what she wanted to/had to flee as the situation seemed too unbearable, but might actually not be "quite so" unbearable any more.

For a long time, she continued to be dominated by the idea that "the world" with all its inadequacies and injustices was intolerable – and at the same time that was considered as unforgivable thus that she felt persecuted by the conviction that she had no right of existence. She would have to "earn" that right, but with the prevailing (dis)orientation could not help but fail … That was most tormenting and at the same time unsurpassably intense. It took years of working through – with all the "to and fro" – that a more stable orientation towards more ordinary, limited aims was experienced as a relief that enabled feeling grounded in life. This included a struggle to find forms to reconcile with the way she was.

Cultural background: German generations after the Holocaust

The becoming aware of the verdict of an abnormal superego

In the two clinical examples, for forgiveness to become an option at all it needed a process of getting aware of (1) the very nature of the prevailing atmospheric presence of an unforgiving pseudo-superego and (2) what made the orientation towards it apparently so compelling. The analyst putting into words what was hitherto only an atmospheric assumptive belief contributed in the long run to strengthen the ego functions thus that ego judgements could finally question the superego's claims.

When I now return to my initial reaction to the editors' request for contributing to this book, the inescapable dilemma I was immediately stuck with, there are striking differences in the essential structural parallels. My actual reaction resonated with the former similar but stronger dilemma. What I had thought of as just a characteristic of my personality was my relief at not being immediately recognized as German, which I came to realize was one I shared with others of my generation. Not so many years ago – when matters changed, when it no longer felt quite the same – there were remarks by others, often in passing, on a side note, which were a variation of what I had felt. And in a way it was hearing it from others that I became fully aware of it.

And, of course, there is an individual part in it nevertheless, but it now became clear that a dimension brought about by the specific historic background also shaped it. And of course, that peculiarity was only a distant offshoot of our unsolvable dilemma of how to be a German with that terrible legacy. Some might have had difficult experiences when recognized as German, but most did not nor was it as relevant as it was for those of us born shortly after the Second World War. It was more: I think now that there reigned an unspoken atmospheric conviction that we as Germans should have been denied the right to existence after the Holocaust. Everything "German" felt suspicious – and we had reasons for critically scrutinizing and naming untenable German positions, but at the same time it felt unacceptable to masochistically circle around ...

What did in the end help me to become aware of the nature of that special inability to think properly? It was a long silent process with many factors contributing to it, which cannot be elaborated on here. All the conscious effort to learn about the Nazi era and its aftermath, and – with the analytic training and thereafter – to get to know which concepts might help to grasp the unimaginable. For example, Rosenfeld's description conveyed something of it:

> When psychotic omnipotence overwhelms a whole nation, the drive of recovery [*Gesundungstrieb*], to acknowledge the whole extent of the madness, is very difficult. Maybe only now, more than fifty years later, is it possible to begin to study the deeper psychological elements which overwhelmed the German nation. I am afraid that a complete recovery from this dangerous illness will still take much longer and will need active support.
>
> (1985[1984], p. 80)

Many encounters with colleagues from abroad were part of it. Over time I succeeded to get a glimpse of how to imagine – and not only rationally see – the difference between personal and collective guilt, what it might mean, though it often met at borders in thinking about it. Roughly spoken, I saw that it is as a German citizen that I have to take responsibility for a "Never again!" and that this will need to be grounded in taking responsibility for my own abysses, which will differ from those of the nation. And personally being a German for me it helped to learn that people let me know that they appreciated today's Germany.

For getting finally a clearer grasp of that kind of "automatism", the basis was, I would say in retrospect, of having had the chance to have consultations and supervisions over many years with British training analysts, during which they got to know me and my work and, as in other contexts, also would question when I "knew" how shameful, for a German, matters were, which for them was not at all clear in the very specific constellation we were discussing. I got re-oriented for the specific case we discussed, but it also helped over time to get hold of that specific thought disorder. I finally realized when I was misguided by a figure claiming (without words, just transmitting the atmospheric conviction) that Germany was "the bad object of the world", in all respects, forever, independent of what concretely was at stake. I came to see the phenomenon of feeling relieved not to be immediately recognized as German abroad as the effect of an abnormal superego-figure, who "answered" the monstrous deeds of Nazi Germany by judging being German as unforgivable.

My first own analysis was still marked by verdicts of unforgiveness and thus could not help with what I struggled with in that respect. Too young to be a part of the generation of 1968 (with parents who had grown up during the Nazi era), with an instinctive aversion against violence and the wholesale accusations or criminal attributions to "the" establishment, "the" Americans, etc. Not joining in the protests nevertheless was then quickly misconstrued by me as a lack of courage, as cowardice. I felt a great uneasiness in the face of some self-stylization as a victim, whereby, of course, I also felt apparent reassurance, relief for moments when my surname was associated with Anne Frank, the Jewish girl whose notes had reached us as teenagers on various levels. On the other hand, it was difficult to bear to be connected with Hans Frank, the chief jurist of the German Reich, the Governor General of occupied Poland, where he had the four extermination camps, Belzec, Sobibor, Treblinka and Majdanek, built, and who was sentenced to death for war crimes and crimes against humanity as the "Slayer of Poland" in Nuremberg.

These two names – Anne Frank and Hans Frank – stand paradigmatically, as it were, for the murdered Jews on the one hand and for perfidious, inhuman actions ultimately including mass murder on the other. To understand and to fully grasp what correlations these extremes (if we let them, for the moment, suffice) have in the individual inner world, what unconscious object relational phantasies are expressed in condensed form in these (or other) figures in an individual history is the task of the individual analysis. This is a painful undertaking and at the same time an elucidation in the best sense of the word, necessary in order to interact responsibly. My point here is that the entanglement with the effects of the aforementioned abnormal superego hindered to a certain degree a real thoughtful exploration in some contexts. Only when I got that clearer, re-orientation became possible and with it a more thorough enquiry into those situations. But for all this to take place a context was needed, which at least I would like to give a rough outline of.

Conditions for reparative efforts having a chance and not being pushed totally aside by renewed paranoid attacks in post-war Germany

The fatal effect of Hitler on individuals and groups/a whole nation had been formulated by Klein in 1938 – basing it on her analyses of various patients:

> The phenomenon of whole nations submitting to dictators and being kept under by them seems to me much more interesting even than the psychology of dictators. We get to understand this better if we study the reactions of people who are not directly implied, but stirred in their feelings by happenings like the over-running of Austria.
>
> (p. 91)

And a bit later she explored in some of her patients, what hindered them to fight against Hitler. This brought her to formulate in 1940:

> If the feeling that external war is really going on inside – that an internal Hitler is fought inside by a Hitler-like subject – predominates, then despair results. It is impossible to fight this war, because in the internal situation catastrophe is bound to be the end of it … If there is a better balance between internal happenings and external happenings the war inside is not predominating, then one can trust with strength 1978 and determination against the external enemy.
>
> (Klein, 1940, in Frank, 2003, p. 98f)

When an orientation towards a constructive superego-figure is possible, which supports the ego in judging what is bad and threatening in reality, then, it is suggested, an adequate reaction becomes possible. After the war (1951), he made use of the distinction between the depressive and paranoid-schizoid position and the corresponding nature of the superego for his task in post-war Germany in 1946. He applied this in an attempt to predict those Germans after the Nazi time capable of rehabilitation to responsible jobs ("humanitarians" – in the depressive position) and those with a sadistic and authoritarian superego who had flourished best under the Nazi regime, based on obedience and persecution rather than personal responsibility ("authoritarians" – in the paranoid-schizoid functioning). In a postscript he stressed another observation from that time:

> ... a widespread sense of collective guilt of a genuinely depressive kind. It was quite apparent, behind a truculent defence which often easily collapsed, even in the most hardened authoritarians and fascists. Of course, it had been brought nearer to the surface by failure. But it was not created by failure and would have been stronger, though less conscious, in success.
>
> (p. 243)

And it seemed important to him that they can take part in constructive efforts of other liberal-democratic states thus that the paranoid solution will not win again. And certainly Germany, at least its Western part, got the chance to do so. For this, I think, it was decisive that the Western victorious powers opted for constitutional means – and waived hate, revenge and retribution. Starting with the Nuremberg Trial of the Major War Criminals in 1946 and the further Nuremberg Trials the restoration of rule of laws [*Rechtsstaatlichkeit*] and human rights was the primary aim. Thus a process over decades with legal procedures [*juristische Verfahren*] and historical clarifications [*Aufarbeitung*] in Western Germany and finally forms of acknowledgement in the re-united Germany could come into being and serve as an orientation (acknowledging the complexities of relations without diminishing, trivialization ...). It goes without saying that it was a long and hard struggle, with vehement denials, severe relapses, etc. – and that it has to continue. Integration in Europe was and is crucial for all this – an ever-so-valuable endeavour for peacekeeping, which seems threatened nowadays.[6] For the conscious recognition of the Holocaust as an unforgivable crime by a majority of Germans it took decades – but the fact as such was ever present and with it for a long time the impossibility of thinking of ways to take the responsibility for that intolerable monstrous and shameful fact.

And it was, I suppose, unavoidable that it took its time and was part of the process needed. Without undergoing that process, the pre-condition of perhaps being forgiven a bit would be lacking. Again as *pars pro toto* I would like to refer to the great writer Amos Oz. He let us know that – when he got to know as a 6-year-old boy – so many of his relatives were murdered, he decided to hate the Germans. He could never forgive them. His mother replied that the Jews could forgive the Germans "perhaps at some point a bit" – but only if the Germans would not forgive themselves.[7] And he movingly described his own process: While reading Siegfried Lenz's *Deutschstunde* he now asked himself what would have happened if he had been born on the side of the perpetrators. The confrontation with the National Socialist past that began in Germany in the 1960s and 1970s earned him respect at the time. "I was forced to question the agreements from my childhood. It became increasingly difficult for me to hate Germany and the Germans, all those whom we once called 'a people of murderers' in Jerusalem, in the great demonstrations" (p. 47).

The Holocaust remains unforgivable as a fact, the challenge is to find forms in cultural work, and to take responsibility as a society for it, which includes facing one's own seductiveness and corruptibility ... It took a long to differentiate a constructive superego, which gives a helpful orientation in doing so, from an abnormal superego which equated Germany in general "as the bad object of the world", identifying with that view and at the same time getting aware that it has to be examined in which respect that is really true and in which respect it is not the case.

Final remarks

The ineluctable/indispensable [*unhintergehbar*] foil of this contribution is marked by the fact of the legacy of Nazi Germany's devastating destruction. Unforgiveness is an inalienable [*unabdingbar*] dimension of the Holocaust, which seemed to end my efforts at the outset. And while I consider it to be an ego judgement that unforgivable crimes against humanity were committed, the monstrosity tends to evoke a kind of monstrous superego-figure. That will induce a kind of immediate annihilating unforgiveness which might resemble the other in a way that it seems indistinguishable. The work I felt to be crucial was to finally get hold of the differing qualities in order to allow perspectives of deepening explorations to take place.

As a psychoanalyst, my point of departure was Freud's formulation of "Heilen and Forschen" [cure and research][8] in my analytic practice. The psychoanalytic concepts which I find helpful in thinking about true and pseudo-forgiveness: the relevance of abnormal or pathological superego-figures and of orientation or disorientation. While – during the stage presented – a quick shift between a (dis)orientation towards an abnormal superego and an orientation towards a more normal superego took place in my first clinical example, in my second patient I try to exemplify how a pathological organization might express and defend a kind of unforgiveness, whose nature is known for long as illustrated, for example, in Euripides' *Bacchae*. His majesty the baby might resent any change in its status by retreating into a parallel world in which it continues to be recognized as a god-like creature. When it fails to impose it on reality, it suffers from feeling denied the right to existence. The analysis of Mrs B gives an idea about a long and painful re-orientation which had to involve the step of forgiving herself to have been dominated by an omnipotent, god-like part of herself – a challenge we all have to meet although in varying degrees.

Embedded in a (very rough) sketch of how psychoanalytic findings were applied in conceptualizing issues from Germany under Hitler by Klein, I suggest one thread in post-war Germany was – and is – the recognition of a disorientation towards a pathological superego with a subsequent process of re-orientation. As the guilt is so enormous the aspect of intertwingled abnormal superego effects could only be identified more clearly after decades of dealing [*Auseinandersetzung*] with that disastrous heritage. Re-orientation would not have become possible without all the constructive effort and help to re-establish democratic structures in a union with others and thus an idea of some – limited – repair.

Notes

1 The patients I have in mind were able to manage their daily life to a certain degree, but felt tormented that they would end in hopeless terror.
2 "In the individual's mental life someone else is invariably involved, as a model, as an object, as a helper, as an opponent; and so from the very first individual psychology … is at the same time social psychology as well" (Freud, 1921, p. 69). I do not want to go into the discussion in how far that statement has to be extended or modified to do justice to the way particular cultures shape the link to the individual, as the crucial point of mutual impacts is relevant here and as such unquestioned. Melanie Klein vividly developed this into a model of introjection and projection between the internal and external world.
3 See also Roy Schafer (2005, p. 406f) – that we do not transcend the issue of forgiveness …
4 Not only in this case Kristeva's conception of psychoanalytic interpretation as "a postmodern version of forgiveness" (2010, p. 191) makes immediate sense.
5 With obsessional patients I quite often met variations of such a pattern in their history – in one the order was, that before judging and reacting on someone's hurt, one had to put oneself in that person's shoes/situation. And although one thinks that as part of a process of forgiveness it seems a crucial element to be able to put oneself in someone else's situation, one can easily imagine that its character will crucially depend on the way this is accompanied – whether with time and sympathy also for anger and frustration etc., or with an attitude of intolerance to any divergence.
6 See, e.g. the recently published book by Aleida Assmann (2018) about "The European Vision. Four Lessons of the History".
7 Amos Oz saw it similarly in his last years: As long as the German people speak the German language, enjoy German landscapes, as long as they draw with full hands from the heritage of earlier German generations, from literature and philosophy, music, architecture and art, as long as the Germans regard themselves as heirs to the culture of their ancestors, as long as they should neither repress nor extinguish the crimes of their fathers and mothers from their heritage. As long as German schools convey German heritage to German children, they should do it without omission, teach about Goethe and Himmler, about Weimar and Buchenwald, Heine and Heydrich, Michael Kohlhaas and Horst Wessel, Immanuel Kant and Alfred Rosenberg. Germany bears responsibility towards its collective memory as well as towards the victims of National Socialism.
8 The translation in the *S.E.*, Vol XX, is "inseparable bond between cure and research" (p. 256)

References

Assmann, A. (2018). *Der europäische Traum. Vier Lehren aus der Geschichte.* München: C.H. Beck, 2018.

Bion, W. R. (1962). *Learning from Experience*. London: Karnac.

Britton, R. (2005). Emanzipation vom Über-Ich: eine klinische Studie über das Buch Hiob. *Jahrb. Psychoanal.*, 51: 9–28.

Britton, R. (2018). Trauma in Kleinian Psychoanalysis. In: J. Borossa *et al.* (Ed.): *The New Klein-Lacan Dialogues*. London: Routledge.

Frank, C. (2003). Zu Melanie Kleins zeitgenössischer Bezugnahme auf Hitler und den Zweiten Weltkrieg in ihren Behandlungen. *Psyche-Z Psychoanal* 57: 708–728.

Klein, M. (1958) *The Development of Mental Functioning in the Writings of Melanie Klein*, Vol. 3. Money Kyrle, R. (Ed.). London: Hogarth (1975).

Klein, M. (1963). *On The Sense of Loneliness*. In: *Envy and Gratitude and Other Works 1946–1963*. London: Hogarth, 300–313.

Kristeva, J. (2010). *Hatred and Forgiveness*. New York: Columbia University Press.

Money-Kyrle, R. (1978[1968]). Some Aspects of State and Character in Germany (1951). In: *The Collected Papers of Roger Money-Kyrle* (229–244). Clunie Press.

Money-Kyrle, R. (1968). Cognitive Development. In: *The Collected Papers of Roger Money-Kyrle* (416–433). Clunie Press.

O'Shaughnessy, E. (1999). Relating to the Superego. *Int. J. Psycho-Anal.*, 80(5): 861–870.

O'Shaughnessy, E. (2006). A conversation about early unintegration, disintegration and integration. *J. Child Psychother.*, 32(2): 153–157.

Rosenfeld, H. (1985[1984]). Narzißmus und Aggression – Klinische und theoretische Betrachtungen. In: Luft, H. & Maas, G. (Ed.): *Narzißmus und Aggression. Arbeitstagung der DPV 1984 in Wiesbaden* (65–81). Mainz: Wiesbaden, Deutsche Psychoanalytische Vereinigung.

Schafer, R. (2005). Cordelia, Lear, and Forgiveness. *J. Amer. Psychoanal. Assn.*, 53 (2): 389–409.

Steiner, J. (1999). The Struggle for Dominance in the Oedipus Situation. *Can. J. Psychoanal.*, 7(2): 161.

Chapter 12

The unforgiving self

Ronald Britton

Psychoanalytic practice has convinced me that being forgiving and feeling forgiven is natural and that its impediment by interpersonal circumstances, internal object relationships of the mind, or developmental difficulties causes significant emotional disorders. Normally it plays an undramatic part in the traffic of self and its relationships in daily life; it functions like clearing the road of impeding rocks on our journey to our loved and significant objects. There can be of course be avalanches, landslides, road accidents, and other much greater mishaps obstructing our way to our loved ones, but the natural expectation is that we will be wanting to find a way.

For most of us, there are times in our lives when severe disruptions necessitate more considerable efforts to forgive and more profoundly disturbing consequences if we feel unforgiven. The ability to negotiate these transactions varies between people; nevertheless, I believe that it is natural and even when not managed the feeling persists that it should be.

From practising analysis and looking at religion, mythology history, literature, and contemporary events, I have asked myself whether this always the case? Are there some events of a collective or individual kind that are felt to be unforgivable? The Holocaust, for example, or the Atlantic slave trade or some personal interactions that seem outrageous or crimes that seem unforgivable, for example, the "Moors Murders" of small children for sadistic pleasure. I think that it is when the offence is thought to be *unnatural* that the crime seems *unforgivable*: when we cannot imaginatively identify with the perpetrator.

The historical accounts and myths chronicle the idea that the boundaries of natural forgiveness are culturally determined, by kinship, by tribe, by nation-state, or religious affiliation. The routine killing of strangers or foreigners has been anthropologically described as if they were, for their culture, "natural" events whereas within the kinship they would be unforgivable. In modern times an effort has been made to enlarge these boundaries, at first to the nation-state. Now we ostensibly try to include inside the boundary all members of our human species, *Homo sapiens*. The Nuremberg Trials of the Nazi perpetrators after the Second World War introduced the concept of "crimes against humanity" together with genocide, thus broadening the

DOI: 10.4324/9781003364313-12

designation of "unnatural" offences and the associated sense of "unforgivable". Nowadays we speak of "human rights" as beyond any national boundaries. but we may have to wait some time before our professed, or rational beliefs, become "natural beliefs", in the sense that the philosopher David Hume (1758) used the term, meaning latent, unspoken, unquestioned, assumptive convictions, not arrived at through reason nor logic. It is these natural beliefs we want to find in an analysis, not the professed beliefs however rational or reasonable. It is in that sense that I mean "natural", as applied to forgiveness and what might impede it.

In psychoanalytical practice what I have found is that what feels unforgiven or unforgivable is very personal, arising within the personal and family relationships of individuals. If unforgiving objects are internalized and merged as part of the self, they interfere with intentions and achievements and are a constant source of personal dissatisfaction. In some, the origin of what is unforgiven is not consciously known, only its consequences, similarly being unforgiving of something, may not be conscious, but a sense of bitterness and unfairness remains as a general state of mind. A prevailing sense of grievance that may blight pleasure in life.

I will describe one such, the poet Rilke, who wrote the *Duino Elegies*, an extraordinary subjective, autobiographical poem, because he felt desperately that he could not love, though that he needed it but distrusted it profoundly. He sought to describe his condition allegorically, in his autobiographical novel, *The Notebooks of Malte Laurids Briggs* (published in 1910), which is a prelude to the *Elegies*. In this, he writes of the "Prodigal Son", as the legend of a man who did not want to be loved ... so he left home because love falsified him. To be more precise, a loving attachment of another lead him, Rilke, to falsify himself by feeling compelled to be what the other wanted to believe that he was. Therefore, he purged himself painfully of love until, "He didn't love anything, unless it could be said that he loved existing", he wrote of himself. (Britton, 1998, pp. 152–153).

This was his starting point and he was urged to have analysis by his former lover, his only trusted confidante, Lou Andreas Salome. He hesitated, then decided instead to begin writing the *Duino Elegies* as he feared he would not be able to write again. They were written as a quest, but it was a quest with a difference. It was a search for something already present but not yet discovered, like a journey of exploration to a country already lived in but not known. In this respect, it was like an analysis.

Rilke's father was an army officer who became a railway clerk, and his mother was a devoutly religious woman. The year before he was born his mother had lost a baby girl and she named him René Maria, dressed him in feminine clothes and in their games called him "meine kleines Fraulein" (little miss). His schooling must have abruptly changed things when he was sent to a harsh military academy by his father at about five years. He did not change his first name to Rainer until after meeting Lou Andreas-Salomé when he was 22 and she 36. In his letters to his mother, however, he continued to sign himself René. He and Lou Andreas-Salomé became lovers and they made two trips to her native country Russia in 1899 and 1900. She was crucial to Rilke's poetic development: she became a pupil of Freud and a psychoanalyst in the latter part of her life. Freud's description of her, as the great *"comprehending woman"* of intellectual men, began at an early age. First with her husband Paul Rée a well-known Jewish philosopher, and then in an affair with Nietzsche when she was 21. Though Rilke and she parted as lovers, and he married Clara Westhoff in 1901, Lou remained to the end of his life the one person whom he believed would always understand him. He died of Leukaemia in 1926.

To illustrate what he lacked I will compare his development with William Wordsworth, a man who found forgiveness natural and felt that natural goodness transcended bad experience. Wordsworth wrote his great autobiographical poem, *The Prelude*, about his mental development, as did Rilke in the *Duino Elegies*. Rilke did not find nature good nor forgiveness natural, unlike Wordsworth. Both authors give an imaginative account of infancy that is in stark contrast and in both cases extremely illuminating.

The *Duino Elegies*

There are ten of them that took over a decade to write. The *Elegies* are not published chronologically as they were written, and it is very important to know the actual time of their compositions as they are spontaneous effusions written after intense periods of *"Ausfuhlen"*, his own neologism meaning "feeling through", which resembles the psychoanalytic concept of "working through"; I will identify them by their published number but comment on them by their written place and time in the sequence. For example, number 5 was written after number 10 and was celebratory, whereas number 4 was in despair during a long period of seven years when he was unable to continue writing them.

The first group, numbered the first, second, third, and sixth *Elegies* were written in the winter of 1912/1913. The fourth was in bleak isolation in 1915. Seven years later, in 1922, the seventh, eighth, ninth, and tenth were written in a short space of time. The fifth is a celebration of the completion of the one numbered the tenth, the "grande finale", in "the mountains of primal grief" when it is all over. This was followed almost immediately and freely by the very rapid production of the "Sonnets of Orpheus", with their lively, flourishes of feeling, beginning with the lament for the death of a girl.

To grasp the full meaning of his transformation one has to return to 1915 during the silent seven years. He wrote a fiercely, bitter, unpublished poem on his mother written in hate, in October 1915.

He had begun the first of the *Elegies* in 1912/1913, speaking in gratitude to his mother for her protective love: screening from him the terrible outside world and denying his inner world of terror, and atrocity.

Rilke wrote in the third Elegy of this situation where the mother's presence was needed to keep inner terrors at bay:

> Over his new eyes you arched
> the friendly world and warded off the world that was alien.
> How much you hid from him then. The room that filled
> With suspicion at night: you made it harmless.
>
> (Rilke, 1987, p. 163)

There is silence in the *Elegies* after this until November 1915 but in 1914 he had written to Lou that he had always blamed others for what was his destructiveness but now he could no longer feel persecuted ... The replacement, I think was despair. The next step was even harder to find how he now, in 1915, felt about his mother. He had already written to Marie Bonaparte in 1913 that he could not love anyone and perhaps did not love his mother. Now in 1915 he returns to the picture of infancy in Elegy 3 but this time in hatred, not love.

In an unpublished poem, he re-represents the infantile situation as his mother not providing a screen but destroying his attempted solitary identity (Britton, 1998, p. 157).

"Ach whey, meine Mutter reisst mich ein", he begins. I translate "reisst" as "demolishes," as it is used in German usually for battering down buildings, possibly to replace them:

> Oh what grief, my Mother demolishes me
> Stone upon stone I had laid to be myself.
> And stood like a good little house in the large space of a day,
> all alone.
> Then comes the Mother, comes and demolishes me
> She demolishes me in that she comes and looks
> She does not see what I have built.
> She walks right through the walls of stone to me,
> Ach weh, meine Mutter reist mich ein.

He wrote this shortly before the fourth Elegy as he discovers his hatred of his mother, the unforgivable destroyer of his identity by her profoundly misunderstanding love. In the fourth Elegy, "the Angel and the Puppet" he eloquently describes on the one hand his unreal puppet self which he fills with what they expect him to be. The Angel is a spirit who is already what should be internalized from the ideal infant interaction with the mother but without the experience. It is like Bion's pre-conception that waits to be fulfilled in material realization, but the Angel is without experience or substance. As we learn later from the ninth and tenth Elegies the Angels also lack any knowledge or experience of grief.

I think of this as a poetic personification of Bion's pre-conceptions. The Angels are pre-conceptions unrealized in reality, spirit not flesh, the unconsummated imageless expectations of the ideal infantile first object relationship. What he finds his way to is the idea that his mother's first child, the dead girl, lived on in her mind and he eventually thinks she should find a place in his and one with which he can identify as the version of himself that never came into existence in the relationship he should have had with his mother.

From this point on he produces more thoughts of existence, "being" and "not being". He resolves his sense of himself and the other, the pre-conception that never materialized, in which he would have been the chosen. Wordsworth described that when desperate about his abilities or achievements he would always remind himself, "But I was the chosen one". Rilke in the sixth Elegy, which preceded the bitter fourth: could only say to himself: "Thousands seethed in your womb, wanting to be him", but mockingly presented himself as the hero, asserting, "I prevailed".

During the silence before resuming the *Elegies* in 1922, he finds a way to clear his thoughts when he realizes his mother's state of mind after her infant daughter's death. When he resumes, he forgives her and feels forgiven. In the finale, the Angels become the Laments who take him to the Mountains of Primal Grief at the foot of which is the fountain of joy filled by the mountains.

The *Sonnets to Orpheus* are begun immediately at the conclusion of the *Elegies* described as a memorial to a young woman dancer who died an untimely death. He completed them in less than a month full of joy. In these, as Orpheus, he visits Eurydice in the underworld but he revises the myth and leaves her there to be annually revisited in winter in celebration of anticipated spring, with the dead. The notion that Rilke is keeping alive the preconception though it will never be realized, of the ideal first relationship of infancy is beautifully expressed in one small poem in Book II, it is about a unicorn, the philosophy textbook paradigm of that which is "known" though it has never existed:

> Oh! this is the animal that is not.
> True, it never was. But since they loved it,
> They had room ready
> And in that space it scarcely
> needed to be. They did not feed it corn,
> but with the possibility of being.
> (Britton, 1998, p. 163)

This is in accord with his insistence that he must, "Be – *and* know what it is like Not to Be". "Sei – *und* Weissen zugleich des Nicht-Seins Bedingung". I think the conjunction "and" rather than "but" is very significant for him as he keeps alive the experience he never had, as in the poem of the unicorn, *and* can never have but can keep it alive as a possibility.

He also understood he can never be the physical realization of his mother's maternal expectation, as he is not the dead girl she lost. So he can never have the syntonic object relationship of infant–mother, the mutual expression of pre-conception fulfilled.

So he tells himself he must, "Sei – und Weissen zugleich des Nicht – Seins Bedingun" "Be – and know what it is like Not to Be". A vital part of his recovery of himself is his forgiveness of her and his newly acquired capacity to forgive, including himself for not loving his inner objects but only using his eyes to observe and master them.

Wordsworth and *The Prelude*

There is no greater contrast between what I have described of Rilke than the autobiographical description of his mental development by William Wordsworth. It was his good fortune to have within him a spirit of maternal love, what Melanie Klein called a "good object", that is "a good object relationship". The absolute contrast to Rilke's experience of a mother who did not see, recognize, or understand him from his infancy.

Though Wordsworth's mother died when he was 8 and he was orphaned by his father's death at 13 he was confident of his own identity and of being loved. He retained an expectation of being forgiven even when he thought he was doing something reprehensible. Despite many terrible losses, bad experiences, and his disillusionment and horror in the French Revolution, he retained a love of life and the world in general. His need to be forgiving and capacity to feel forgiven was sorely tested throughout his life including the span of time covered in *The Prelude*. If continuity is a quality of our good internal objects, it provides a sense of inner security. If we can acknowledge our object's independent existence in our good, dependent relationship we grasp that we rely on something that transcends our intentions or just deserts. We can expect to be forgiven. This is based on belief we have an internal *object relationship* with the attributes of the "good mother" of infancy: of her returning when feeling abandoned, unsummoned, and unmerited – of an object relationship that transcends, expectation, belief, and justice. In Wordsworth's words:

> The morning shines
> Nor heedeth man's perverseness, Spring returns-
> I saw the Spring return when I was dead
> To deeper hope!
>
> (Britton, 1998, p. 140)

This was the case for Wordsworth all his life, even though it was one with terrible losses, disappointments and misfortunes. In *The Prelude*, the autobiography of his mental life, he imagined his infancy was especially blessed, giving him a love of the "natural world" and the gift to express it. This passage in *The Prelude*, now usually referred to as "the infant babe", was written in 1799 in Book 2 of the first version of the poem for Coleridge, posthumously known as *The Prelude*.

Part 1 was written during a miserable time in Germany in the coldest European winter of the seventeenth century. He was commissioned by his enthusiastic friend Coleridge to write a great poetic thesis on "Man, Nature, and Society" that was needed to tell the world of their new post-French-Revolution philosophy. Coleridge, also in Germany, was happily studying in Gottingen; his new philosophy was largely born of his own love of Spinoza, Kant, and German metaphysics with Wordsworth's pantheism. Wordsworth did not really share his friend's faith in this project, nor his friend's idealization of him as the ultimate poet. His own deeper thinking was coming from within, stirred to life by his childhood recollections. He began in order to justify his part in the project by giving an account of his mental development in childhood, it was meant to be only the introduction.

The poem started as two books in 1799 and covers childhood up to leaving school. Six years later it was 13 books covering his life up to 35 years old. Meant to be only the introduction to the great work that never materialized it became one of the greatest epic poems written, yet it was only published under the name *The Prelude* given by his wife after his death in 1850. Prior to that, it lay in his study only as "the poem to Coleridge". Though it is written very powerfully, it is retrospective, he was 29 when he began it and 35 when he finished the 13 books. The reader should remember that the writer is settled back in England reflecting on his eventful past.

In 1799 it was in two books; they begin where he was born in the English Lake District and end when his boyhood ended at 17, leaving for Cambridge. By 1805 it had grown to 13 books including the first two books and went onwards to life in Cambridge and London. It includes a tour walking with his friend from Calais through France across the Alps into Italy. Then in 1790, France was, as he put it, "standing on the top of golden hours, and human nature seeming born again" (Wordsworth, 1979, p. 204). He wrote retrospectively, "Bliss was it in that Dawn to be alive / But to be young was very heaven".

Later after idealistic participation in the Revolution, he was to see the worst of it as he witnessed "the terror", in its climactic period:

Domestic carnage now filled all the year
With feast days: ...
... Head after head and never heads enough
For those who bade fall them fall.

(Ibid., p. 376)

The Prelude is retrospective and the man writing it has experienced joy and disillusion and terror in revolution and a serious love affair broken off by war. Wordsworth had to leave France and was unable to either return or communicate with his love Annette; she was pregnant when he left Orleans where she was in a family in the Vendee, the part of France most opposed to the Revolution. His older brother and uncles were very disapproving and did not give any financial help. Their daughter was baptized in December 1792 in the cathedral church of St. Croix as "Anne Caroline Wordsworth, daughter of William Wordsworth and of Marie Anne Vallon with Paul Vallon Godfather and Madame Dufour as Godmother with Andre Dufour legally representing the absent father" (Legouis, 1922, p. 25)

The Prelude does not mention any part of this but Wordsworth did write almost as an insert a fictional story of a young tragically separated couple *Julia and Vandracour* as a means of describing his experience in feeling if not in fact. He remained in contact and supported his daughter, when he visited them in Paris years later she had children of her own and always called him father. His English relatives apart from his sister and brother John continued to disapprove and his first biographer his nephew destroyed any letters or documents that might disclose Annette's existence after William's death. I agree with Emile Legouis who wrote from France in *William Wordsworth and Annette Vallon* (1922) that the famous "anonymous Lucy" poems relate to his love of Annette. He wrote them in 1799 the same year he began the first version of *The Prelude*.

In 1792, back in England, he was unable to return to France because of the war, and unexpectedly financially destitute, he broke down psychologically. His recovery was mainly enabled by his sister Dorothy living with him and accelerated by his new friendship with Coleridge.

Meanwhile, Europe had moved from failed Revolution into the Napoleonic wars. France remained completely inaccessible until briefly during the Treaty of Amiens in 1802, when with his sister he met Annette and their child Caroline in Calais. He went there to meet his daughter and to ask Annette for her blessing on the marriage he was planning with Mary Hutchinson in England. He was fortunate in Annette remained friendly though disappointed. His parentage of Caroline had been recognized by her family at her baptism when she was Christened with a "stand in" for William as father; similarly when she married years later there was a "stand in" for William Wordsworth as father. The relationship remained unknown outside his immediate family in England, amazingly even in academic circles until the 1920s. The only rumour, and that inaccurate, was from Coleridge of an affair in France and a son.

In 1804 William lost his beloved brother John, the sea captain whose ship sank in a storm; this broke up the special Grasmere circle, of which John was a member, that had formed around Wordsworth, Dorothy his sister, Mary Hutchinson who became his wife, her sister Sara, and Coleridge who left his family in the care of his brother-in-law Robert Southey in Keswick.

John's death was the first of many great griefs he was to suffer in his adult life – the deaths of two young children, the mental collapse of Dorothy (his sister) and the death of Dora his daughter, and amanuensis in his older life when he was almost blind. The eventual recovery, from all of them, of a belief in himself and the goodness of the natural world followed the pattern of the loss of his mother when he was 8 years old as described in the 1799 Prelude without naming her loss by name:

> For now a trouble came into my mind
> From obscure causes. I was left alone
> Seeking this visible world, nor knowing why
> The props of my affection were removed.
> *And yet the building stood, as if sustained*
> *By its own spirit.*
>   (Wordsworth, 1979, p. 22)

The building stood to the end of his life, unlike that of Rilke's little house, despite further losses and very bad experiences.

This capacity was linked not only to experience by Wordsworth but he also had a theory as to how and why, which he explores in *The Prelude* and relates to his belief in the foundation of strong, internal object relationships in infancy. The capacity to forgive and the ability to feel forgiven is parallel to this resilience I think for the same reason. The contrast between Coleridge and Wordsworth in this respect is dramatically illustrated when they quarrelled over one relatively small issue that led to their estrangement. Wordsworth's capacity to forgive and Coleridge's incapacity to forgive is clear and remained so. Coleridge was leaving the Wordsworth's house in Grasmere and going to a mutual friend's house where he was temporarily staying to avoid returning to his wife and family. Wordsworth had let the new host know of Coleridge's poor state of health (he was addicted to alcohol and opiates).

Coleridge took great offence and regarded this as a betrayal, and became quite paranoid about the Wordsworth household, and he remained unforgiving and critical for the rest of his life. This was in considerable contrast to Wordsworth who not only forgave Coleridge but remained unstinting in his praise in *The Prelude* up to the 1850 version. This was for Wordsworth a loss of friendship and collaboration, but for Coleridge it was a loss of his mental health, as his isolation, from family, friends increased together with his addiction, until he spent his life effectively as an informal inpatient living in his good doctor's family house in Highgate.

The loss of his mother for Wordsworth was repeated in his loss of Annette and the loss of his idealization of the French Revolution. This period of recovery of the belief in the natural goodness and love of landscape led Wordsworth into a period of great, psychologically, intuitive poetry climaxing in "Tintern Abbey" in 1798. It was a return visit to the Wye valley after five years. He was now 28 and between then and his earlier visit had been his time in France. He describes in the poem his five years earlier passionate, thoughtless self, compared to his 28-year-old self,

> … For I have learned
> To look on nature, not as in the hour
> Of thoughtless youth but hearing oftentimes
> The still, sad music of humanity
> (Wordsworth, 1994)

Accompanying the still sad music, however, is the feeling of a *presence* that is "interfused" with the setting sun, round oceans, blue skies, the mind of man and all objects of thought. Abundant recompense for the loss of bliss. His verse is often at its best when evoking a sense of loss. He has always struck me as the poet of the "depressive position", but I cannot remember which way round it was when I first had the thought. Did I think of "Tintern Abbey" when I heard of the depressive position or did I think of the depressive position when I re-read "Tintern Abbey". The truth is that since then I can never think of one without the other.

The writing of the two books of the 1799 *Prelude* was begun a year later. For some of the Wordsworth "cognoscenti", it is the most hallowed version as it is the "original". For a psychoanalyst, it is the most remarkable, as it anticipates a great deal of psychoanalysis more than a century later. It begins:

> I, a four years' child,
> A naked boy, among the silent pools
> Made one long bathing of a summer's day
> [And with a nod in Rousseau's direction continues],
> "A naked savage in the thunder shower".
> (Wordsworth, 1979, p. 1)

The first book continues with a toddler's life into his boyhood. It includes what he described as "spots of time", a theory that anticipated Freud's concept of "screen memories". All of these, described one after the other are redolent of the Oedipus complex. The last one, "waiting for the horses", concludes with the announcement of his father's death, during that school holiday. If we have a Freudian analytic description of boyhood in the first book we have a Kleinian version of infancy in the second.

The "Infant Babe" passage (ibid., pp. 78–80) is amazingly like a poetic account of infancy that corresponds to the theory of Melanie Klein in the twentieth century based on her analysis of young children.

It begins after a scathing commentary on the unsatisfactory intellectual efforts of the eighteenth century on the mental development of children (probably Bentham and James Mill) and little faith that the newer ideas of Hartley on "association of ideas", reveal origin. "Hard task to analyse a soul, in which each particular thought hath no beginning", he wrote. This gave him a licence to offer his own deeply held beliefs on childhood mental development as beginning in infancy. So he begins, with the beginning – the baby at the breast:

> For with my best conjectures I would trace
> The progress of our being.
> ... Blest be the babe
> Nursed in his mother's arms, the babe who sleeps
> Upon his mother's breast, who, when his soul
> Claims manifest kindred with an earthly soul,
> Doth gather passion from his mother's eye.
>
> (Ibid., p. 20)

What follows as I paraphrased it are the propositions of Wordsworth following this opening statement. It begins with the notion that there is an *inborn expectation* of an object relationship from birth and the blessed babe, fortune's favourite, meets it at the breast when it finds itself to be the object of his mother's love and understanding.

"Her feelings, like an awakening breeze" kindle his enthusiasm for the new world. The contrast with Rilke's comment, "no wakening breeze ever came from her to me" underlines how both poets attach the sense of "being at home" in the actual world to this primary relationship.

Wordsworth continues, her feelings kindle his enthusiasm for new experiences, perceptual and somatic, and an urge to integrate them, "otherwise loathe to coalesce".

Klein emphasizes the crucial importance of the integration of the part-object relations based on different experiences and perceptions, from part-objects to whole object. Wordsworth says the enthusiasm generated from the *breeze* of mother's feelings, *inspires* the infant "to combine parts of the same object, else detached and loathe to coalesce". He continues suggesting that this daily relationship founds in him an expectation of a loving world and becomes a love of Nature irradiated by this beloved presence (Britton, 1998, pp. 135/136).

He produces within this passage in 1799 a feature that has become an increasingly important concept in psychoanalysis: an *innate imageless expectation*, named by Bion a *pre-conception*. It is shaped, as in this instance, when meeting mother's breast in a happy conjunction a founding good object is internalized within the core of the self, the ego.

If as I described in Rilke's case the pre-conception is never realized it cannot become a substantial internalized object. Klein suggested that the non-appearance of a desirable good object leads to a split between an extremely bad one and an idealized one. But she adds, "I also found that idealization derives from the innate feeling that an extremely good breast exists, which leads to the longing for a good object and for the capacity to love it" (Klein, 1957, p. 192). The belief that it should exist, though never encountered, keeps alive the ideal of goodness which may be sought in political or religious belief. In Rilke's case, the idea of goodness and beauty is kept alive as "something or someone that was never met and never will, the unicorn as an unrealized pre-conception". This is a state of mind I have met in psychoanalytic practice: sometimes, less happily, it may give rise to the phantasy of having been cheated or robbed even of dynastic origin in psychosis, sometimes as claims of royal descent.

We know from child and adult analysis that there are bad things, monsters, ghosts, fearful enemies that have their unrealized existences perpetuated in the phantasies of the most fortunate of children and in the dreams of their parents. There must be pre-conceptions of predators as well as breasts but there seems to be a reluctance in psychoanalysts to accept that bad objects may not only be the outcome of failed or lost good objects. Bion describes the absent pre-conceived object as the source of the internal bad object, as does Fairbairn. Klein, however, does decide that there are monsters in the "deep unconscious" as did Freud but later it gets mixed up with the "death instinct". I personally think it is more helpful to assume that fearful predators have a pre-existing identity as pre-conceptions, and if not met as tigers or whatever can linger on as fearful ghosts in anticipation as counterparts to unrealized good objects.

There were in some of Wordsworth's "spots of time" in *The Prelude* shades of fearful but unmet figures, but they become adventures and escapes during happy days. Later he was to meet real terrors in the external world of the French Revolution, and he reluctantly realized that monstrosity and cruelty were part of mankind's natural inheritance. As we find from *The Prelude* this does not permanently threaten his great love of the "natural world" nor his belief in the "goodness of life", though his disillusionment in social idealism depressed him profoundly. Based on his considerable capacity to recover his faith in his good object Wordsworth found again his love of life and nature. Forgiveness for him was natural and goodness was expectable. He was able to forgive, to expect forgiveness, and to expect better. The exception to this belief is expressed in *The Prelude* of Robespierre and his associates whom he continued to see as unforgivable.

His ode "Intimations of Immortality" speaks of his non-eradicable belief in the goodness and beauty of nature and of natural man, even as he announces that he can no longer see the world in a "celestial light". This was written in his mid-30s at the same time that Coleridge wrote his poem "On Dejection" following his reaction to Sara Hutchinson's rejection of him as a lover.

Wordsworth had already covered this ground, of disappointment leading to disillusion, in "Tintern Abbey", when he was 28 before he started *The Prelude*. It is in both, the "Ode" and "Tintern Abbey", that a poetic description of what Melanie Klein called the depressive position can be seen. She would have placed it developmentally not in mid-life but in mid-infancy.

> Though nothing can bring back the hour
> Of splendour in the grass, of glory in the flower,
> We will grieve not, *rather find*
> *Strength in what remains behind*
>   (Wordsworth, 1994, p. 297)

The unforgiving self: the internal saboteur

From the relatively early days of psychoanalysis, there has been an awareness that in some patients there is some part of the patient against recovery, progress, achievement in life or analysis. It was referred to initially as the negative therapeutic reaction. As it was further explored it became clear that some part of the person was hostile to the self as a whole which Rosenfeld described as "destructive narcissism", Freud introduced the concept of a "superego" which could be hostile to life, which was described by Bion and O'Shaughnessy as a destructive superego, Fairbairn referred to it as a split-off part of the ego that was hostile to any attachment of an affectional kind to another object as the internal saboteur. As he describes it as an object relationship that includes a segregated part of the ego, it is a self-object hostile to the main part of the self. My experience of a number of analytic patients brought to my mind Fairbairn's concept of "the internal saboteur": in particular three patients who all used language in the same way in an effort to describe their experience of this most distressing symptom. They had a quite conscious awareness of a splitting in their mind and used the same grammar to express it. "I know it was not so but my mind said it must be". In all three this led to behaviour that was determined by "my mind" against the judgement of "I know" and against the best interests of the patient.

I will write of only what they had in common and how that relates to a state of being permanently unforgiven by an internal object for an offence in advance of it, whilst believing in their innocence. They were all convinced that they would be found guilty of some uncommitted offence by an authority like "the police". Two were women patients and one male, they came from different cultures and countries: two were Christian and one Jewish.

Anyone who lived through the Second World War would be familiar with the term "internal saboteur", and would find it particularly appropriate

(Fairbairn, 1952, p. 103). In his paper on "Endopsychic Structure," he develops a theory of internal object relations in a model of a divided ego with a central core self ("I") and two split-off parts of the ego attached to internal objects. One of these, the internal saboteur, was hostile to any other attachments of the self, particularly of a libidinal kind.

I suggest that the internal saboteur is a disowned part of the self that hates objects different, or other than the self, that it is attached to an object relationship with a rejecting object. It is a kinship of the self with a rejecting object, a kinship of hate, not love, with hatred of love.

The internal saboteur is an internal enemy that to a compliant part of the self has formed an alliance of sabotage that is referred to as "my mind".

I know it is not *but* my mind says this is going to happen. "My mind" claims to function as a conscience with a timeless attitude. Past, present and future are not sequential nor irreversible, as in the ego proper and the "I" finds itself treating predictions as events that are not remembered because they have not happened. The suffering patients are unforgiven permanently in advance for being who they are, not as creatures of the natural world of sequence and consequence, but of a world of the imagination of a parental object that treats fearful expectation as a present possibility and probable past event, as an internal object when it claims the status of the superego.

In the patients I referred to, this was a repeated experience of childhood, where a parental figure became constantly suspicious of the developing child, anticipating misdemeanours and unforgiving in advance. The unforgiven offence in such cases may be one with ancestral history in the parent, or parent of the parent's past, projected into the future and attributed to the patient.

Fairbairn made the point that the internal saboteur was not the superego because it did not provoke a sense of guilt but persecution. I described this situation as the internal saboteur masquerading as the superego because the patients did not really believe they were guilty but felt helpless that they were going to be accused and wrongly found guilty. They had at times a sense that they were playing a part in a drama written by someone else as in Luigi Pirandello's play *Six Characters in Search of an Author*.

The internal saboteur's power over the patient is the need for agreement of the child with the parental figure and the conflict that arose when it felt it vital to achieve an independent mind. Where the need for agreement could not be put aside it led to a splitting of the self, resulting in the establishment of the self-object, internal saboteur undermining the central core self. The craving of such people is to be forgiven: to be relieved of feeling unforgiven. This is not due to unconscious guilt-seeking atonement in such cases, it is the *prevailing sense of not being forgiven* by parental role figures for unspecified, not yet committed crimes. This situation is described in *Alice through the Looking Glass*, where the White Queen says living backwards is better because "one's memory works both ways, so you can remember things before they happen … punishment comes first, then the trial next Wednesday and the crime comes last of all".

> "Suppose he never commits the crime?" said Alice.
> "That would be all the better. Wouldn't it?" said the Queen.
> "but it wouldn't be better his being punished", said Alice.
> "You're wrong there", said the Queen. "Were you ever punished?"
> "Only for faults", said Alice
> "And you were all the better for it I know", said the Queen
> "Yes, but then I had done the things I was punished for", said Alice.
> But if you hadn't done them said the Queen that would have been better still".
>
> (Carroll, 2007, pp. 234–235)

This was the mirror world my patients had lived in under the rules of the "White Queen". First the punishment, then the trial, last of all the discovery ghat there was no crime. Fundamentally it is a world where there is no forgiveness, only punishment, show trials and triumphantly, says the Queen, "no crime": a world governed by prophylactic punishment that says there is no need for forgiveness, and all the prospective crimes are *unforgiven* in advance and punished. Lewis Carroll's nineteenth-century fantastical dream for Alice, seems amusing. We saw it brought into existence several times in the twentieth century as daylight nightmares, of prophylactic jurisprudence in Germany, Russia, China, Cambodia, and other places under similar regimes: not so amusing.

The need to feel forgiven is driven by the wish to re-establish a vital object relationship of love and *understanding*. I have suggested that there is *an inverse relationship between the need for agreement and an expectation of understanding* (Britton, 2021, p. 130). Where there is no expectation of understanding there is a demand for absolute agreement, which is only achievable by submission or tyranny. In Melanie Klein's terms this would be the paranoid-schizoid position and feeling forgiven in whole object terms would not be possible. If, however, the expectation of understanding is high the need for agreement is lower and a position of "*agreeing to differ*" is possible. This is characteristic of the depressive position and makes forgiveness achievable and believable. Agreeing to differ is easy to say and hard to do; it depends on mutual trust being valued beyond justice and is incalculable rather than measured; it is based on love, acceptance of kinship, empathy and forgiveness as a natural process, like healing: we all need forgiveness because we all wound and are wounded in our relationships, some time or other in the "natural world".

References

Britton, R. (1998). *Belief and Imagination*. London: Routledge.

Britton, R. (2021). *Sex, Death and the Superego.* London: Routledge.

Carroll, L. (2007). *Alice in Wonderland & Through the Looking Glass.* London: Vintage Random House.

Fairbairn, W. R. D. (1952). *Psycho-Analytic Studies of the Personality.* London: Routledge.

Hume, D. (1758). *An Enquiry Concerning Human Understanding.* Ed. P. Millican, Oxford University Press.

Klein, M. (1957) *Envy and Gratitude in The Writings of Melanie Klein*, Vol 3. Ed. R. Money-Kyrle. London: Hogarth, 1975.

Legouis, E. (1922). *William Wordsworth and Annette Vallon.* London & Toronto: J M Dent & Sons.

Rilke, R. M. (1987). *The Selected Poetry of Rainer Maria Rilke.* Ed. & trans S. Mitchell. London:Pan Books.

Wordsworth, W. (1994). *William Wordsworth.* Ed. S. Gill & Duncan Wu. Oxford Poetry Library, Oxford University Press.

Wordsworth, W. (1979). *The Prelude 1799, 1805, 1850.* Ed. J. Wordsworth, M. H. Abrams and S. Gill. New York: W. W. Norton & Co.

Index

abandonment 102, 161, 162
abnormal superego: becoming aware of 176–179; description of 168; re-orientation, effects of 177–179; true forgiveness and 169; *see also* superego
acoustic resonance, use of 30
actuality 148
Aeschylus *seeOresteia, The*
Agamemnon (Aeschylus) 55–56
"agreeing to differ" 198
Arendt, Hannah 136
Ajātashatru, story of 43–45, 49–50
Akhtar, S. 36
Amati, S. 153, 162
ambiguity theory 153, 162
ambivalence 12–13
anal mechanisms 94
anal triumph 119
ancestral guilt 166–167
Andreas-Salomé, Lou 185–186
anger 93–94
anxiety 24–26
Austin, J. L. 149
authentic guilt 27

Bacchae, The (Euripides) 173–174
bad faith 28–29
bad objects 25, 84–85, 101, 149, 170, 195 *see also* good object, Holocaust, objects
Balzac, H. 6
basic assumption defence of pairing 142
Being and Time (Heidegger) 29
betrayal: *Cosi fan tutte* 120–122, 126–127; *Don Giovanni* 117–120; of Jesus 78; *Marriage of Figaro, The* 122–126; Oedipus situation and 85–86; parents' sexual love and 115, 116; *Prelude, The* 192; sexual,

dynamics of 114–117; variations on 123; *Wings of the Dove, The* 98, 101–102
Beuys, Joseph 138
Bion, W. R. 12, 13, 38, 47, 142, 163n3; on abnormal superegos 168; on innate imageless expectation 194; pre-conceptions 188
Birksted-Breen, Dana 71
Blake, W.: "On Another's Sorrow" 5; "Infant Sorrow" 4–5; "The Smile" 15
Blass, Rachel 117
Bléger, J. 153
Bolla, Christopher 143
Bonaparte, Marie 187
Boswell, Jill 113n13
Brenman, E. 175
Brexit 75
Britton, Ronald 71, 85, 93, 157, 162
Brown, Christopher 78
Buddha 44–45, 49–50
Buddhist Sutras 43–45

capacity to forgive 13–16
Care, forgiveness and 29
caritas 66
castration threats 46–47, 85, 94, 115–116, 120
"change of heart" 148
Christianity 73
Coephora, The (Aeschylus) 55
Coleridge, S. T. 22, 191, 192, 195
collective guilt 136, 144, 178, 180 *see also* guilt
collective remembering 137
collective traumas 137
compassion: of analyst toward patients 47–48; as emotional process 47; forgiveness and 42–50; forgiveness as

For Product Safety Concerns and Information please contact our EU
representative GPSR@taylorandfrancis.com
Taylor & Francis Verlag GmbH, Kaufingerstraße 24, 80331 München, Germany

www.ingramcontent.com/pod-product-compliance
Lightning Source LLC
Chambersburg PA
CBHW070326270326
41926CB00017B/3774